D1831769

A GARO JUNGLE BOOK

Owing to the antiquity and rarity of this book, certain pages are regrettably absent, and readability is compromised due to the blurring of the original text. If you possess any insights regarding the availability of these missing sections, kindly inform us. Your assistance is crucial in ensuring the completion of this significant work for the benefit of future generations.

A GARO JUNGLE BOOK
OR
THE MISSION TO THE GAROS OF ASSAM

BY

REV. WILLIAM CAREY

GYAN

Published by

Gyan Publishing House
5, Ansari Road
Daryaganj, New Delhi-110002
Phone: 011-47034999, 9811692060
E-mail: books@gyanbooks.com

Distribution Network
gyanbooks.com
India, USA, Canada, UK, Australia

© Publisher

All rights reserved. No part of this work may be reproduced, stored, adapted, or transmitted in any form or by any means, electronic, mechanical, photocopying, micro-filming, recording or otherwise, or translated in any language, without the prior written permission of the copyright owner and the publisher.

ISBN: 978-93-6280-061-9 (HB)
First Published, 1919

2nd Impression 2024

Printed at: Gyan Press, Delhi.

The book is sold subject to the condition that it shall not, by way of trade or otherwise, be lent, resold, hired out, or otherwise circulated without the prior publisher's written consent.

A GARO JUNGLE BOOK
Author: REV. WILLIAM CAREY

Gauhati, Showing the Temple of Umananda

A GARO JUNGLE BOOK

OR

THE MISSION TO THE GAROS OF ASSAM

By

REV. WILLIAM CAREY

A Missionary in Bengal

Author of

"Travel and Adventure in Tibet," etc.

AND OTHERS

TO

The Devoted Missionaries

WHOSE ZEAL AND EARNEST ENDEAVOR HAVE MADE POSSIBLE THE STORY OF SUCH A TRANSFORMATION, THIS BOOK IS APPRECIATIVELY DEDICATED

I AM in the position of the boy who has been to the circus; I have seen the wonders with my own eyes. I have followed the missionary over a considerable portion of the earth's surface. I have heard more opinions about him than you could shake a stick at. . . I have talked with the missionary's converts. . . I have attended his churches, gone with him on itinerating tours out in Simon-pure heathendom; I have examined his schools, I have visited his home, I have seen him in conditions which take from every one of us the shine. . . All this I have done with eye open to the joints in the missionary armor. . . Yet either I have been taken in completely, or else the average missionary is a pretty good sort of fellow. . . When it comes to playing tennis, or talking the gibberish which passed for language, . . or tramping over the country, or climbing mountains, or "roughing it" generally the missionary is in the blue-ribbon class. *For a good time out-of-doors give me a missionary companion.*

—William T. Ellis, in "Those Missionaries."

CONTENTS

APPENDICES

LIST OF ILLUSTRATIONS

LIST OF ILLUSTRATIONS

A GARO JUNGLE BOOK

I

THE JUNGLE LAIR

ALL that most people know of Assam is that it produces tea. But it is a mine of interest, for it offers for our inspection, and opens to our sympathy, a larger number of curious types of men than can be found in any other corner of the earth. Irregular in shape and narrowing as it goes, this little strip of territory has three distinctly marked longitudinal divisions; a tangle of foot-hills tucked under the Eastern Himalayas; a rugged range running parallel below; and a long, open valley lying stretched between. Through the valley, a length of four hundred and fifty miles, flows the great Brahmaputra River.[1] On both sides of the valley, rising in a succession of groups and peaks, covered with thick jungle, the "Hills" attain a maximum height of ten thousand feet. The groups run together, yet are wonderfully diversified, and make a series of

[1] This valley of Assam, British India's northeastern frontier, like an arm of Christian civilization, reaches far up into the great heart of the continent of Asia; as a beacon to the virile peoples of those hills, canopied under clouds of barbaric darkness. Assam is not only India's back door into Burma and China, but the most natural pass through the Himalayan range into Tibet and northern Asia. Toward this roads are being rapidly constructed, over which are to move evangelization, civilization, and commerce for those great northern Mongolian races. Through this valley, the length of which now run daily railway trains and a score of steamers per week, will, I predict, run the track of the great railway of the continent from Bombay to Shanghai.—*M. C. M.*

human nests, each one of which is the home and hiding-place of some savage tribe.

How they came here, each to his own, we do not know. But certain broad lines of immigration can be clearly traced. Some, whose faces bear the stamp of the Mongol, wandered across the steppes of their northern home and dropped down in straggling companies over the edge of Tibet. Others of a different race, but with the same restless spirit, trekked upward from Burma and Siam, picking their way through the maze of mountains, till they tapped the valley, and little by little, spread themselves over its fat pastures and flanking heights. Of them all it may be said that "their language is their history," or as much of that history as we are ever likely to learn.

The Garos, speaking Tibeto-Burman, were the first of these rude tribes to come within our ken, and of all the dark-skinned races settled in that strange rookery, none are of fiercer fame or have a more romantic story. Nor could any wish for a wilder retreat. The central fastnesses of their hills were held to be more impenetrable, and the belts of "*terai*" (low, wet land) at their base more deadly, than those of any other region, whilst the people themselves were regarded as the most uncouth and barbarous of all the border tribes. For more than a hundred years after the surrounding country had been peaceably settled under the British rule, this patch of jungle-covered crags stood out obstinate and defiant, the secret lair and inaccessible fortress of ruthless and dreaded foes.

The Garo Hills occupy a commanding position at the entrance to Assam. They round off a remarkable range, which, like an arm thrust forward to guard the Burmese frontier, separates the Assam Valley from the plains of

Mymensing and Sylhet. They form, indeed, a rough fist laid on the edge of Eastern Bengal. The armlike range keeps off the river for a length of two hundred miles, and the fist is outlined by the river's magnificent bend as it swings around toward the sea. It will thus be seen that the Garo Hills stand singularly exposed, though strongly protected; exposed because they face the broad sweep of the plains and the main entrance to the valley; protected by the close curve of the river and the back-hills of the range. The position is that of a natural fortress with the great river as its moat.

The fortress of the hills, however, has played but a feeble part in the fortunes of the valley. It has repelled approach, if at all, rather by grim and silent menace than by any wide-flung challenge. Its aggressive acts have mostly been in self-defense. Only once, as far as we know, have the Garos descended to take sides in a contest for the mastery of Assam. This was in 1671, when they helped the Ahoms to expel some Mohammedan invaders. There is a legend that one Shanka, a king of Garo affinities, centuries before the Christian era, founded the city of Gaur, which for two thousand years remained the capital of Bengal. Gaur and Garo may, therefore, be more closely allied than by similarity of sound.

The valley may be described as an elongated, alluvial plain, wide-spread at its western end. Through this it offers a broad and easy access from Hindustan, but it is virtually a *cul-de-sac* when you get inside. Only aboriginals know the knotted paths at the eastern end. Its sides are the flanks and spurs of the mountains which extend here and there to the fever-smitten swamps. Its river, the noble and bountiful Brahmaputra, is credited with divine origin, and, for one day of the year, is as sacred as the Ganges into which it flows. Born on the lofty plateau above the Himalayas, fed by the melting of the snows, and by over fifty affluents from the lower hills, the great river winds through this sultry land-gulf, and, clearing the outstretched arm, heads straight for the sea. Seen from the hills in the cold season it is merely a faint streak on the horizon haze. But at a closer range it stands revealed as a mighty stream, swift and deep, cutting for itself innumerable channels in the soft bed, and casting up banks of wind-swept sand, presently to become sedge-grown "chur" (flats of river-built land). Here and there the confined current makes a rapid rush dangerous to navigate. Elsewhere, flowing placidly past high banks, it mirrors for a moment a temple or bungalow seen through the trees. Powerful steamers ply up and down in constant succession, which, with attendant flats, not to mention the thousands of heavy-laden country boats, bear the freight of a province to Calcutta and Chittagong, thence to be distributed to the markets of the world. But to gage the strength of the river we must see it in the "rains"! It then becomes a brimming flood of wild, yellow waters, which for three months or more spread themselves over field and jungle far toward the foot-hills. An immense amount of fertilizing silt is thus annually deposited. But the flood is sometimes a desolating, terrible thing. The thunder of the falling banks; the scum of floating wreckage; the subsidence of whole villages, leaving the tops of their houses visible; and the resistless force of the current, carrying all before it, give an impression of power let loose, which once seen can never be forgotten.

Such then is the Valley of Assam; "unequaled," as the name implies; a spacious, steamy, well-watered, mountain-locked land; luring to conquest; haunted by devotees; a fine field for proselyting priests; passing rich in

Photo by Major Playfair.

A Garo, Ancient and Modern

Reproduced from the original in Vol. I, "Asiatic Researches," 1789.

A Century Later.

natural resources, and maintaining a large commerce; but, nevertheless, a "Sleepy Hollow," with its wealth only half exploited, and its life lived apart from the world. Yet great dramas, both religious and military, have been acted on this simple stage. Hither came the hero Sri Krishna, in the mythological legend, one of the most popular of the Hindu gods; and here, on this heated plain, hemmed in and sometimes occupied by savage tribes, grew up and flourished that debased form of Hindu worship, the Tantrik, which revels in bloody and licentious symbol. Kamrup,[2] indeed, became the chosen seat of magic and mystery, unnameable ceremonies, and fearsome deeds of sacrifice. Its chief temple, even now thronged with worshipers, is dedicated to Kamakhya, the goddess of sexual desire.

The floor of the valley is strewn with ethnological deposits, relics of the "nations and tribes and tongues" which poured in from the East and from the West, had their day and ceased to be. Wild races choked each other in the long struggle for supremacy and power. Afghan adventurers, followed by the legions of Delhi, swept proudly up from Bengal, while Mongolian and Burmese hordes forced their way down, till both met in the shock of battle, and the lesser streams ran red with their blood. The mountains looked on, but offered no obstruction, and the combatants left them alone. During these incessant conflicts tribe after tribe fell back on the hills, drawing off from the fight to the safe shelter of the dark, untrodden jungle and the inaccessible recesses of mountain, crag, and gorge. The Garos doubtless thus drifted to their present homes. Shorn of primitive strength, shrunk to a mere cluster of barbarous clans,

[2] The old name of the country, and the present name of a large central district about Gauhati.

unable to do battle in the open, they fled to this wild retreat, a lair wherein to lie in wait, a hiding-place from whence to spring and pounce upon the prey.

As a den of wild beasts, and of still wilder men, the lair was long left alone. Within, the fiercest passions held sway, and gruesome superstitions, such as made the blood of the Bengalis run cold to think of, wrapped them in an atmosphere of ghostly fear.

II

THE GAROS ON FIRST ACQUAINTANCE

IN the cold season of 1788-1789 Mr. John Eliot, Commissioner of Dacca, was sent by Lord Cornwallis, then Governor General in Council, to the Garo frontier on a tour of inspection necessitated by the growing disturbances. Mr. Eliot went by budgerow to the foot of the hills, and thence with elephants and tents worked along the whole southern border, visiting the markets and passes. Here the Garos gathered around the white-faced stranger with pleasing frankness, fully conciliated by the bright scarlet cloth which the Government had provided for distribution among them. Eliot asked them innumerable questions; studied their appearance and habits; inspected their houses; joined in their jollities; watched their feasts and dances; witnessed a marriage and other ceremonies; examined their sacrificial altars, charms, and spells; sat down in a council of chiefs, and was even requested to become "a company's zemindar."

Returning to Dacca the Commissioner recorded his impressions in a valuable report to Government, dated August 6, 1789, and contributed an article, faced by a full-page portrait of "A Garo Man in His War Dress," to the third volume of "Asiatic Researches."

Let us look at the sketch of "A Garo Man" with which he embellished his account. The facial features are more Hindu than Garo, which shows that the Commissioner was meeting the people along the edge of the hills who, while retaining the habits of the hill people, are in a degree Hinduized, and of mixed specimens rather than the pure-blooded type. The Garos are generally stout, well shaped, hardy, with flat nose, and eyes oblique, which are very dark, mostly brown, but giving the impression of being black as jet and bright as beads. But the spring of the figure, the characteristic dress, and peculiar weapons are all very faithfully drawn.

Every man among the clans wears that strip of colored cloth, passed between the legs, the end of which, hanging loose, is "sometimes ornamented with brass buttons or bells" and sometimes with "rows of a white stone, half an inch long" (wampum beads). Very few, indeed, wear anything else, except on state occasions. When they came before the commissioner the chiefs were distinguished by a silk turban, a bag at the girdle for money and betel-nut, and a net for tobacco. That "blue cloth, covering a part of the back, and tied across at the breast," is an indispensable item in the accouterment of a "man in his war-dress." The highlanders always bind themselves in this way, *phana,* as it is called, when about to join in battle or do any desperate deed. The injunction to "gird up the loins," so appropriate to people whose limbs are impeded by flowing garments, would only mystify a Garo with that meager strip. But tell him to tie his *phana,* and he will know what you mean. The shield is the usual *sepi* made of bamboo or wood, and the sword cannot be mistaken. It is the genuine Garo *melam,* long and narrow, with a slight curve, double edge, and blunt point. It lacks, however, the usual hilt-guard or crosspiece, ornamented with black tufts of hair, as seen in the later photograph, and among the weapons. When in liquor the Garos are merry to the highest pitch; men, women, and children dancing until they can scarcely stand. A birth, a marriage, a death,

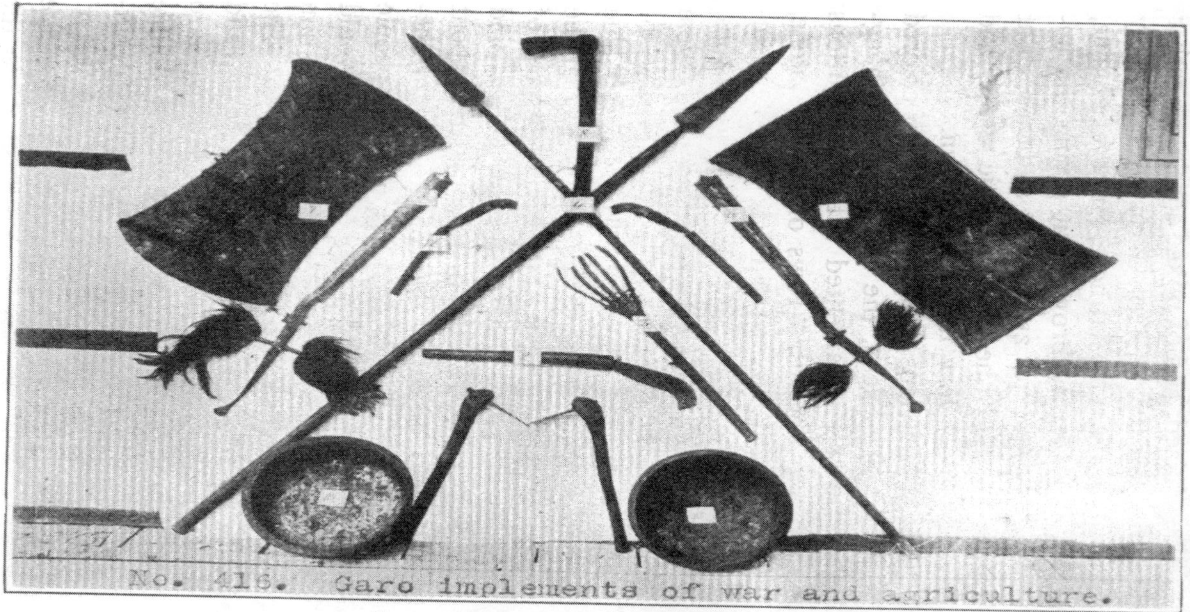

Garo Weapons and Implements

No. 1. Hoes.
No. 2, 12, 13, Ates, or Choppers.
No. 3. Bamboo Rake.
No. 4. Spears.
No. 5, 6. Swords.
No. 7, 9. Shields.
No. 8. Ax.
No. 10, 11. Gongs.

the opening of a market, the sitting of a council, the trial of a delinquent, almost any and every event serves as an occasion for feasting and an excuse for drink. The liquor, which is generally a weak home-brewed beer, of a milky color, made from rice or other grains, is even poured into the mouths of their babies as soon as they can swallow. Their festivities sometimes last for two or three days. Drunkenness is the tribal weakness, the almost universal habit. Wild as these savages are, their normal temper is not ferocious, nor are they morose. They are human and interesting withal, practising a domestic economy in advance of some modern ideas, grateful for kindness, and with this righteousness about them—fidelity to their spoken word. "They possess," says Dalton, "that pearl of great price, so rare among Eastern races, a love of truth."

Garo women cannot certainly be called prepossessing, though one may see many pleasing types. Even Dalton dubs them "the most unlovely of their sex." But he hastens to add, "I was struck with the pretty figures, the merry voices, and the good-humored countenances of the Garo girls." And that is a qualification that ought always to be made. Their dress is a reddish cloth striped with blue or white, about sixteen inches long, which is tied at the upper corners on the left side, leaving the thigh partly exposed. This dark apron of rough cloth is still the distinctive dress of all Garo women, the wealthy ones sometimes wearing in addition a white girdle of shells or wampum. Their necks are adorned with strings of wampum beads, thirty or forty times round, while in their ears they wear brass rings from three to six inches in diameter. The slit in the lobe of the ear increases with the weight of the rings, which is partly supported by a string passed over the head.

The great brass earrings are the joy and pride of the women's hearts. On my first visit to the hills I met an elderly woman who had forty-two in one ear, and forty in the other. Each was a thick circle of solid wire, three and a quarter inches in diameter, and all were passed through the lobe of the ear. She willingly stood to be photographed, with the rings on, but was hardly persuaded afterward to part with them at even a fancy price. Each ring had to be sprung loose separately, and those on one side were found to weigh two pounds and fourteen ounces. On my second visit I saw a woman with sixty-five rings in one ear, each two inches in diameter. She would not part with them for any consideration. The lobe of the ear had a hole in it five and a half inches long, and large enough for a child to put its fist through. The bottom of the loop was a ligament as thin as a slate pencil but tough as a leather bootlace. I could not weigh this bunch, because the owner would not permit them to be removed; but another set shown me, taken from a single ear, had sixteen rings, each five inches in diameter, and weighed four pounds and ten ounces. The record set, however, is one preserved in America, which has a total weight for both ears of just ten pounds! Yet undoubtedly some Garo duchess actually strutted the jungle and bent at her work in the fields with these auricular appendages! It should be added, however, that these rings are wholly discarded by the Christian women. And in most cases where their former use has deformed the ear, the women have these earloops cut away and the ear shaped as if such rings had never been worn. Moreover, they all instinctively increase their wardrobe.

The Garos of the north early won an evil reputation for murderous raids. It was even feared they would

Garo Jewelry

A Garo Mother and Child, with Modern Shawl Wrap

overrun Bengal. The policy of non-interference established by the Mogul rulers was adhered to for the most part for a hundred years, until it became intolerable that a savage tribe should thus menace the peaceful inhabitants of contiguous British districts.

In 1807, four times within a few days the Garos rushed from their hills, plundered two official headquarters, fired several hamlets, and left the headless corpses of twenty-seven men and women on the ground. A month later an armed band attacked a large village within two miles of a strong police force, inhumanly killed four women, and carried off a man whom they probably tortured later in the hills.

Raiders who succeeded in massacring their landholders on the plains, would, on their return, collect vast numbers of their relatives and neighbors round the reeking heads; and filling these with wine and food, would eat, drink, and dance, chanting songs of triumph. The heads were then buried, to be dug up later, cleansed of their putrid flesh and hung up as trophies in the houses of their slayers. The skulls of persons dying naturally were abominated. The sacrificing of kidnapped Bengali slaves at funerals was intended to demonstrate that the oppressed had power to avenge themselves on their oppressors. Their own dead they burned to powder lest a Garo skull be palmed off for a Bengali; and the cremation was a rare ceremony.

When two Garos quarreled, each would plant a tree and solemnly vow to eat the juice of its fruit mixed with the blood of his antagonist's head. If a generation passed before the revenge was possible, the feud became hereditary. When accomplished, the head was cut off and carried in procession with the fruit of the tree, the mixed juice portioned out, and some of it drunk by the victor. The tree was then felled, and the feud was at an end.

The Government reports of this period express the hope that further outrages may be prevented through the influence of friendly and commercial intercourse, and by inducing the chiefs of the Garo tribes to encourage among their subjects the pursuit of the arts of industry and peace.

The ascendency gained by the Garos and the terror with which they inspired the poor cultivators of the plains is seen in the following brief extract from one of Mr. David Scott's able reports:

> It is no uncommon practice with the Garos to enter the villages and make demands for pigs, goats, fowls, or any other article they take a fancy to, with which the ryots (peasants) are of course glad to comply, knowing that, if they do not, there is neither the fear of punishment nor any better motive to deter their visitors from murdering them on the spot. Such occurrences are seldom, if ever, reported to the police authorities. The people purchase the forbearance of the Garos by a donation of *mata-raksha* (blackmail), which means "preservation of the head."

So through the years strange tales are whispered abroad, such as make the flesh creep, tales of the impish wild men lurking in these hill fastnesses, and ever and anon coming forth to slay and steal. Rumors followed of more daring exploits, of annual incursions and raids on the unprotected plains, far afield, till that jungle lair at the gate of the valley, and so near the throne of Bengal, became an object of terror to the province, and everywhere the Garo's name was spoken with bated breath. Soldiers and merchants, whose business took them up the river, and strings of wayfarers and pilgrims, tired with dust and heat of the road, shuddered as they must needs bivouac almost under the shadow of the listening hills, and crept closer together as they thought of that demon-haunted darkness, and fed their fires through the long anxious night. If they slept, it was to turn uneasily in their dreams, haunted by the fear of a Garo's sword.

III

GLIMPSES OF THE HOME LIFE

GARO houses, called *changys,* are bamboo structures, from thirty to one hundred and fifty feet long, and from twenty to forty feet broad. Each house is built out from the cliff rearwards, and supported on piles. The fronts are flush with the ground, or raised a couple of feet above it, perhaps a line of them on the crest of a ridge, or a cluster crowning some conical hill. "The walls and the floor are of bamboos, cut open, and woven as mats." In many houses a veranda runs along the side, and there is always a platform or porch at the back end. Through a trap-door in the flooring all manner of filth is thrown down to the scavenging fowls and hogs below. The house porch is often used for pounding rice, the mortar being a hollowed stump of hard wood, the pestle a thick pole. Front verandas are often piled up with skulls of stags, bulls, boars, leopards, and other ghastly relics. Human skulls—the most prized of all—have happily now disappeared. When the British occupation took place, in 1873, Captain Williamson ordered them to be brought out and burned. What heaps there were, and how reluctantly yielded up; but what immemorial feuds those fires quenched for evermore! By some the porch is used for stalling the bulls. There are generally two, one on each side of the door, and very sleek and fit they look. The Garos do not breed them, but buy them at the markets. On public festivals the creatures are taken out and brought together to fight, being goaded if slow in attack, and the vanquished is then sacrificed and eaten.

The interior of a Garo house consists of one large apartment, or general living- and storeroom. A portion of this is screened off for the sleeping-room of the husband and wife. The cooking is done on a slab of earth in the middle of the floor; not much, however, is required. The Garos take their meat warmed through, but almost raw. Dogs, frogs, and snakes make an appetizing menu, and blood is a delicacy, while milk is abominated as an unclean secretion. There is a general air of filth about the whole place. The stench of fowls and pigs comes up through the springy floor of plaited bamboo; and there are other smells equally obnoxious to us, but dear to the nostrils of a Garo, which proceed from bits of dried snake or frog, or dried fish, and, above all, from a jar of greyish fluid call *chu,* the intoxicating beer made of rice. The rotten fish, of which they are inordinately fond, is believed by many to be the cause of that dread disease *kala-azar,* a sort of fever which blackens the body and kills like the plague.

Household utensils are of the simplest description. The people seem quite ignorant of the arts; their pottery is of the coarsest; their weapons, pipes, or ornaments all have to be bought at the markets. But their wants are few, and, at a pinch, can be supplied from the bamboo growing in the jungle. They eat with the fingers, and drink from dried gourds. A good house will have one or two rough metal or stone dishes, called *rongs,* some of which are heirlooms and greatly prized. They were once a species of currency, but are now used chiefly as ornaments and as gongs.

The influence of the women attracts notice. The wives of the chiefs have as much authority in debates as the chiefs, possibly a little more. All property belongs to and descends through the women, and the youngest daughter is the heiress of the house. Each clan is divided into "motherhoods," and a man has had sometimes to marry his mother-in-law in order that, through her, he may succeed to the estate. Some receive nothing, but have to look to the family of their wives for their support. Women of means are allowed to choose a temporary husband, and when tired of him, pay him off, and take another. But these customs vary in different parts of the hills. In some sections there are slave-wives, and a man marrying an old woman may become the husband and proprietor of all her daughters. A man may have more than one wife, with the consent of the first. Few, however, have more than one. Occasionally a man may get his wife by capture, but usually it is the woman who kidnaps him, that is to say, her male friends do it for her. One may still see such press-gangs bringing home their spoil. In the early days, the missionaries were inclined to rush to the rescue, thinking that violence was being committed, such is the noise made by the struggling youth! But they found that the reluctance and resistance were by no means as real as they sounded. It sometimes happens that a Garo girl will select the lad she wishes to marry, and failing other means to secure him, steal softly in through the dark and lie down by his side. If he dislikes the match, there is rarely any redress.

The villages are irregular straggles of houses in deep hollows of the hills, or on clinging spurs, surrounded by higher jungle-covered heights. In either case they are usually well hidden, and one can often hear the clamor or carousal coming up from the bottom of the gorge, without being able to perceive any way of getting down. The jungle, largely of the close bamboo kind, resembles

A Luskar

Photo by W. Mason.

The Nokpante at Bangshi

A Nokma

a forest of stout fishing-rods, green and furnished with leaves. The paths zigzag across the peaks or descend the craggy hillsides in most capricious ways, and in the old days were carefully planted with *panjis* or bamboo spikes, short, sharp, and dangerous. Sad was it for the shoeless feet that stepped upon them! Nowadays the only enemies are the wild beasts and demons.

Elephants sometimes approach the villages in search of grain, and to prevent this, long bamboos are stuck obliquely into the ground on either side of the path of entrance, their sharpened ends pointing outward like bayonets ready for a cavalry charge. With their heads thus pricked, the lumbering creatures slip away. Sometimes even a light rod stretched across the path a few inches above the ground will suffice to puzzle the beasts, and they make off, fearing to investigate further. Perhaps an intuitive sense of danger, based upon the experience of the herd, and sharpened by the fate of unwary individuals, has now become common property. Doubtless the tragedy is told or trumpeted of how some have tumbled into innocent-looking pitfalls, and others been transfixed by loaded spears, cunningly suspended from a tree, and brought down upon the wanderer who touched a hidden string with his foot. In spite of all this, the crops have to be watched at night, and, if elephants are heard, the alarm is given, the whole village turns out, and the night is made hideous with shouts and waving torches to scare away the intruders.

The village life circles about a large building, the *nokpante,* standing in an open place, its posts and beams fantastically carved. Here the *nokma* holds his court; bulls are baited; and the bachelors sleep.

The nokma, or head man of the village, holds the lion's share of the land, and gets others to do his coolie work. The position is one of honor, not of pay. He is comparatively rich, and the villagers obey him, though he has no legal authority. The *luskar*, on the other hand, is a Government officer who tries cases and collects taxes, getting ten per cent commission for his pay. He has power to impress labor for the making of roads and for keeping them in repair, and annually receives a present from Government of a jacket, turban, and shawl. He is a very important personage, second only to the biggest man, the *mauzadar*.

In their law-courts offenses were formerly punishable mostly with fines, the money being spent on feasting and drinking. Mr. Eliot proposed the abolition of pork. They would not hear of it for a moment. The village chief, he tells us, acted as magistrate and judge, except in cases of adultery, murder, and theft, which went before a council of chiefs, and were punished with instant death. According to other observers, lying was a capital crime, and adultery and murder do not figure on the list.

Near the village is the *jhum,* or cultivated clearing, on the side of a hill. It is constantly being changed. After a year or two, each clearing is abandoned and another made. In a very short time all traces of the former have disappeared. The process of "letting in the jungle" will be familiar to all readers of Kipling, and is a regular part of the Garos' agricultural plan. But the old site, which now again looks like a virgin forest, remains the property of the village, and is the cause of frequent disputes. A jhum is made by first cutting down the jungle, that is, the bamboos, canes, and brushwood. This is done in December, and the material allowed to lie till March, when the hot weather dries up and thins the forest. Then the clearing is fired. Representatives from every house take portions to cultivate for themselves. Each

Photo by W. Dring.

The Jhum

man picks up a small stone from his section, and weaves a bamboo basket about it. These being placed in a heap, sacrifices are offered, and a jangling prayer is chanted to the demons—"You bless others, so bless me." Then sowing begins. In some parts the soil is dug up a little; in others the seed is simply put in with bamboo sticks. Rice, Indian corn, pepper, pumpkins, and gourds are sown in March, cotton in April. These crops often grow together among the ashes of the trees and undergrowth, but they come to maturity at different times of the year. A jhum is a very repulsive sight, with its rotting or half-burnt stumps of trees standing gaunt against the sky, and the crop struggling with the weeds of the jungle. The cotton is a staple product of harsh, woolly fiber, much of which finds its way into Europe and Japan, being used with wool for the manufacture of felt and carpets. Some who read this may be resting their feet the while on cotton grown in a Garo jhum. The only implements of cultivation are a *dao,* or small bill-hook, an ax about the size of a broad chisel, and a stumpy little hoe fitted with so short a handle that the laborer is compelled to bend almost double while at work. Both sexes toil in the field, the women sowing and weeding, the men cutting down the jungle, making fences, and carrying the produce to market. Temporary huts are built on the jhum, and occupied while the crops are standing. Day and night watchers must be there to keep off birds and beasts. Some of these huts are forty or fifty feet off the ground in the branches of the trees, or hung by rattan ropes from their boughs. Rice is harvested in July, Indian corn and smaller produce from August to December, cotton from December to March. The rice is gathered by simply pulling off the ears; these are then stripped in the hand, and rubbed with the feet to thresh them. After harvest a big festival takes place, and much rice is wasted in drink.

Lac is cultivated, the insects feeding on pulse plants, grown for the purpose. The crude product is stick-lac, consisting of bits of twig with a hard lump of gummy substance round them, very dirty-looking and dark. You may see loose heaps of this lying on the floor in some houses. The gum, when washed, is seen to be of an orange color, and the dead bodies of the insects are embedded in it. The famous "Benares toys" and swings for children are coated with lac. It is not easily soluble and the children may suck it without danger. From it are obtained coloring matter, shellac, sealing-wax, etc.

Before the entrance of the houses of the wealthier sort you may see grotesquely carved stumps of wood stuck into the earth, rudely painted to represent deceased members of the family, and adorned with necklaces of beads, brass earrings, and bits of bright-colored cloth. The poor erect simple memorial poles, roughly notched, sometimes a whole sheaf of them, to indicate the number of deaths and as a propitiatory appeal to the spirits of the departed not to return and hurt them. When the family becomes Christian, these witnesses to ancestral worship and demon superstition are instinctively uprooted and thrown away.

IV

THE WILD MEN AT HOME

THE Garos number about one hundred and sixty-four thousand, and probably represent one of the earliest race movements of the Tibeto-Burman border. They recognize tribal differences and also have names for numerous clans, one of the largest of which, the Sangma, is said to have sprung from the union of a woman with a gazelle. But, in fact, the Garos have no reliable traditions, either of origin or arrival, which afford any clue as to how or whence they came. As a tribe they have now been under British rule for about forty years.

Near Tura, at some of the border markets, and along the government roads, there is a noticeable tendency to take the manners of the town; the women are learning to cover the breast, and the boys are ambitious to attend school. The villages of the interior, except where Christianity has come, are much as they used to be, barring the liberty to practise inhuman rites and perpetuate bloody feuds. Still wild at heart, at the sight of a stranger they bury themselves in the forest like startled deer. But on the whole, their spirit is manly, self-reliant, and pushing; a refreshing contrast to the temper which prevails among the people of the plains, where the use of opium enslaves, for the Garos are notably free of this deadly habit. Though short in stature, their bodies are lithe and muscular. Their speech is a forceful jingle, sounding at times like the sharp clink of metal on stone.

These wild men believe that the earth is a square, flat body suspended at the four corners by strings; the hooks attached to the strings sometimes giving way, cause earthquakes. Some hold that a squirrel is always trying to gnaw the strings. There is a legend that a slave-spirit was once appointed to check this, but he became tired of his task and looked away for a moment, and the squirrel seized its chance. As a punishment the dilatory spirit was struck blind, and now the squirrel has it all his own way. What wonder that earthquakes increase! It is feared that some day when two or three of the strings are gnawed through, the earth will turn upside down! Another view of seismic disturbances is that Mother Earth is rocking her child. One who has once seen a Garo woman carrying her hapless babe in the baglike bundle on her back, with its head uneasily flopping as she whisks about at her work or swings along on a journey through the hills, will appreciate the vigor of this apt hypothesis.

The sun and the moon were sisters, the latter the brighter, till the former from envy spattered her with mud, hence the darkened parts of the moon, the wonder of all children since time began.

Among the demons a great spirit had died, and buffaloes for sacrifices were being driven en masse to the slaughter, when the noise of drumming and wailing frightened them, and they stampeded across the sky, making the unsteady track we call the Milky Way.

The imagination of the Garos is contantly darkened and terrorized by the presence of evil spirits, malignant and powerful, whose sole occupation is to trap and hurt mankind. To appease them is the one hope of existence. Every field, foot-path, and fence has its bamboo shrine or clump of sticks, smeared with blood, and decorated with feathers, egg-shells, cotton, flowers, and cornstalks. In the center of every village is the great sacrificial fork, in which the heads of strong bulls are pinned, to be cut off with a single sweep of the Garo sword. No journey can be taken unless the fates are propitious, no war engaged in without a sacrifice, no land cleared for cultivation without impaling a monkey or a goat, no marriage solemnized, or birth celebrated, or sickness tended, no experience of the coming of death to take away its victim, without the shedding of blood. Certain mountains are feared as the special abode of departed spirits. The journey to a mountain called Chikmang, on the south side of the hills, is that "bourne from which no traveler returns."

Deep waters are similarly regarded with superstitious dread because of the demon at their bottom with a golden boat, and there is a prejudice against saving persons from drowning on this account.

They have, indeed, a dim, specterlike conception of one omnipotent Spirit, well disposed toward men, whom there is no need to propitiate, but who, nevertheless, does nothing to protect them from the spiteful machinations of the evil spirits of the air.

The Garo priests have little power, being usually forced into the service, and selected on account of having some physical defect, because of some general apprehension that, through ignorance or bungling, the wrath of some demon will sooner or later put them out of their way; and those who can best be spared should therefore undertake the risk.

All sorts of omens are marked. A rainbow in the east means prosperity; in the west, sorrow. On setting out for a journey it is bad to sneeze, to see meteors, to hear the bark of small deer in the jungle. Burning places and white ants' nests, being haunted, are avoided as much as possible. It is good to wear charms, and the Garos have strong faith in them. A tiger's claws hung round a woman's neck are a great preservation in childbirth, for they keep off giddiness. The skin of the snake is a cure for external pains when applied to the parts affected. Bracelets of grass and leaves, wolves' teeth, the hair of goats or dogs, python's claws (it is said to have two on which it rests when raising the head), and above all iron, of which all demons are afraid, protect the wearer. But blood is the great appeaser. There is virtue also in spittle. The Garos spit upon their bodies when passing affected spots. Dreams have a special significance. To dream of getting lac means that you will cut yourself and spill blood. A tiger-bite in dreamland bespeaks hot weather, and a drink of *chu* means rain. If you dream of a broken tooth, a death is foretokened; a double tooth signifies the death of a parent, a single one the death of a child—and beyond death there is only the great dark.

Is a child born? There must be a feast, and if it is a first-born, a sacrifice. If the father should be absent the child is likely to be a fool. His presence is greatly desired at the moment of birth both for the mother and babe. Its head is shaved and the name of some ancestor given it, but care must be taken not to court a quarrel. Two persons might claim the same name as an inalienable right. The name is considered to be in some way an essential part of the man. For instance, when a Garo is attacked by a tiger, and escapes, he changes his name so that the animal may not know him again. If he is killed, all his relatives change their names to escape the same disagreeable recognition!

Is there a sickness in the house? Some demon must have caused it. That is the first thought. The priest must find out which demon and offer an appropriate sacrifice. If a chicken is offered, he holds up the entrails to see if the demon has let the sick one go; if they fall apart, it is a sign that he has released him. Sometimes the priest squats on the floor and calls on the demon while he daubs the patient's body with the blood of the fowl. A few old country folk to whom powerful drugs are known, have a reputation for skill in doctoring, and one of these should be called. Charms are believed to be very efficacious. In strong fever what can be better than a bear's beard laid on the breast? And who does not know that shells worn around the throat cure and prevent a cold?

Should the patient die there is no sense of pollution, as among the Hindus, but drums are beaten, gongs sounded, and horns blown to summon the friends. Mr. Eliot says that

> after death the body is kept four days, and then burned on a pile of wood. The pyre is lighted by the nearest relative exactly at midnight. After this there is a feast; all dance, sing, and get drunk. If the dead man be a person of rank the pile is decorated with cloth and flowers, and a bullock is sacrificed. If he be a chief the head of a slave is burned with the corpse; and if a great chief, his people sally out to the hills and bring back the heads of Hindus whom they have treacherously slain. Cremation completed, the ashes are put in a hole, dug exactly where the fire was, roofed over and railed around. Every night, for about a month, a lamp is burned inside. The clothes of the dead are hung on poles at the four corners of the fence, and allowed to rot. The fenced graves are sometimes adorned with picturesque images of animals which are placed near-by.

A dog is sacrificed to be a guide to the departed on his long journey to Chikmang. If the dead be some great one, especially a woman, bullocks must be offered at the moment of the lighting of the pyre, one on the spot, and others by signal at surrounding hamlets. There can be no doubt that human sacrifice would still take place if allowed. One of the present missionaries not many years ago was asked to petition the Government for permission to sacrifice a girl. The morning after cremation the ashes of the deceased are gathered up and placed, with food and dishes for his use, under a tree to await a convenient day for the final funeral procession, feast, and booze. Should contagious disease threaten a village all turn out with clubs, shout, and beat the jungle, fence off all paths with brushwood, and offer a sacrifice to the demon.

The altar of sacrifice is a little mound of earth in a square enclosure. A pit is dug in front, and the animal is sacrificed over it. The manner of it is this: Grass is strewn on the ground; the bull bends to eat, and the priest raises his sword; then, as the animal lifts its head, the sword cleaves through the neck; at the same moment an assistant cuts the hamstrings from behind, and the beast falls lifeless where it stood. The blood is collected in a pan and placed with the head and a lighted lamp under a sort of canopy near the altar. All present bow themselves to the ground. A white cloth is then drawn over the arch, and all is left undisturbed for an hour that the demon may come and take what he desires. When the veil is lifted cooking begins for the feast.

The ceremony of oath-taking is very solemn. They lift their hands to heaven and bow down their heads to a stone, and looking stedfastly toward the hills, give their evidence. "When the first person swore before me," said an official,

> the awe and reverence with which the man swore forcibly struck me. My assistant could hardly write, so much was he affected. As an equivalent for "kissing the Book" some were observed to

put a tiger's bone between their teeth, others grasped their weapons, and a few took a handful of earth.

Worship consists of bloody and cruel sacrifices. Cocks, bullocks, slaves, and kidnapped captives are offered according to the gravity of the occasion, the greatest of which is death.

Is a man's sight bad? Well, the thing for him to do is to try to transfer the affliction to another. He should take a clod of earth in his basket, and go out professing to have chickens for sale. If any one stops to look, or to ask the price, he has only to shy the basket at him and run away. Then the trouble is transferred!

Marriage is by consent, the bride taking the initiative. She goes to fetch the bridegroom, and it is etiquette for him to hide and resist until victoriously carried off. A cock and a hen, furnished by the girl's people, must be sacrificed and eaten. But only the wedding pair can partake.

The priest takes hold of the cock and the hen by the wings, and holds them up to the company asking some questions, to which they reply, *Nama* (good). Some grain is then brought and thrown down before the fowls, and when they are employed in picking it, the priests strike them on the head with a stick, and the whole company, after observing them a few seconds call out as before, *Nama!* A knife is then brought, and the priest makes an incision, drawing out the entrails of the cock. The people shout, *Nama!* He performs the same operation on the hen, and again they shout, *Nama!* They look on this part of the ceremony as very ominous; for, should any blood be spilt by the first blow, or the entrails break, or any blood come out with them, it would be considered an unlucky marriage. Then there is a feast; all dance and get drunk. The dance is a rythmical slow movement of the feet, each person apart from the rest. Drums are beaten, and a noise is made with the mouth, but it cannot be called a tune.

V

AT THE FRONTIER MARKETS

THE fierce black clans had always been, at some point or other, breaking loose from the hills, and it was necessary to hold them in check. In the days of Moguls this was accomplished by selecting men of local influence, living near the foot of the hills, and permitting them to hold their lands, with large additional grants, rent free, on their undertaking "to prevent the incursions of the Garos" and to pay a nominal tribute to Delhi. These Chaudris, as they were called, had military rank conferred upon them as a further recognition of their protective service to the state. They were required to keep up very considerable establishments of armed men. Their tribute was merely a nominal present to the king of a few falcons and mynas (talking birds), some captured elephants, and a small quantity of sweet-smelling wood. Later a trifling revenue in cotton was substituted, and this was assigned to the maintenance of the Dacca Artillery Park.

The Chaudris, thus created powerful zemindars, administered their great estates at enormous personal profit, and practically independent of control. They established markets for the Garo cotton, by which their revenue was still further swelled, and kept the passes with an armed force, as much in their own interests as in fulfilment of their contract with the imperial power.

Mr. Eliot went half-way round the hills and gives a panoramic view of the life at these frontier *hats* (weekly markets). The submontane tract was divided into several estates, each of which had its separate string of markets. There seems to have been one at or not far distant from every opening or pass into the hills. In a few cases they were fairs rather than markets, held only once or twice a year, and after due notice had been given.

Through the neighboring district millions of ryots made their clothing, thread, and quilts from the cotton grown on the Garo hills, and Bengali merchants were as eager to buy as the Garos were to barter for their needs. The Chaudris levied duties from both parties and reaped a lucrative harvest.

Owing to the danger and difficulties of the journey, the Garos had to be humored and feasted, or they would not come down to the markets. As an encouragement "the farmers were obliged to give them *arrack* (native liquor) every time they came to their *hats!*" The head Garos were, at some markets, presented with turbans or cloths, and fêted and cajoled till they promised to return in a certain number of days with fresh supplies of cotton. But they never remained out of the hills beyond the second night. If their cotton was not disposed of within that time the daroga of the pass had to take it off their hands. At one of the principal markets no Garo would come down until hostages had been first sent into the hills, and it was always stipulated that they should be smiths who should bring their implements with them so that, if any trouble arose, the Garos might have means of sharpening their weapons and the Chaudris none.

A large part of the Garo's life is to this day taken up with traveling to market. It is often a journey of four or five days, across very difficult country. He dare not go alone. A dozen or more men and women travel together, in single file. The men carry the heavier loads. If there is a moderate load and a baby, the man takes the baby and the wife the load! Most things are borne on the back, in bamboo baskets, with a long strip of bark to place round the forehead in lieu of a handle. The baskets may contain cotton, lac, peppers, mats, rice, poultry, dried fish, kids, puppies, pigs, plantains or bananas, corn, melons, eggs, beads, earrings, swords, pottery, and of late cloth, clothes, sugar, and umbrellas; bulls for fighting and sacrifice are also still abundant at the markets. Some of these things are luxuries easily done without. It costs a wild Garo very little to live. He raises his food and the cotton from which his wife weaves their coarse bits of cloth; he uses no oil, for he goes to bed at dark and needs no light. For salt there is potash, and he has only to burn the leaves of an old plaintain tree to obtain it. His blanket is the bark of a tree, soaked in water, flattened out by being hammered on a board for hours with a stone, and then spread on the house roof to dry in the sun. It has a warm brown color like a jaeger cap; otherwise it is a rough wrapper, but it serves his turn. The Garos have never erred on the side of excessive clothing. Sixteen ounces of cloth to sixteen pounds of brass earrings, stone necklaces, and other ornaments, is about his idea of a just proportion. Probably all such primitive costumes will soon disappear, submerged by the wave of civilization and the currency of the rupee. The growing popularity of the processions to and from the markets in peaceful order will bring about the change. There are no hostile clans to bar the way. They run along merrily, one behind the other, shouting and laughing as they go, camping under the trees at night, or in some kinsman's village, and talking of the bargains they hope to make. But each one has his sword or spear ready, for at any moment some wild beast may spring to the attack. There is always a reluctance to take a place at the tail end of the line, the tiger's habit being to let the rest go by and pounce down upon the last. As a rule they defend themselves bravely, and even the women do heroic deeds. A man whose wife was trotting along in front of him one afternoon, was suddenly seized and held beneath the tiger's paws. The woman, hearing his screams, dropped her basket, and clutching the *dao* that was in it, rushed to the rescue. Coming to the tiger, she lashed so vigorously at his head and face that he retired roaring from the fray. The woman thus rescuing her husband, took him home and dressed his wounds. The man recovered and was pointed out to me as a familiar figure in the Tura market some years ago.

The bringing of the cotton is a very interesting sight. It is packed in long, tubular baskets of braided bamboo, four to eight feet high. The bearers carry these on their backs, bending slightly forward, the weight being partly supported by a band of bark passing over the forehead. The man is altogether lost in the vastness of his burden, and you behold hundreds of these elongated baskets, apparently furnished with legs, walking to market. The dazzling white of the cotton, which oozes out from every crevice, and froths over at the top, contrasts vividly with the dark skin of its human bearers. Women as well as men carry these heavy loads. I remember a woman who had just arrived at the market-ground. The weight made her body quiver as she stood facing the lens; but my companion, a fellow ignoramus from the plains, thought nothing of it, and declared that he could run away with the thing if only given half a chance. When this was interpreted to "Miss Savage" she took in the situation at once, set down her spire of snow, showed him how it should be lifted, and then with an amused smile invited him to display his powers. He was tall and muscular, but quite too unblushingly confident, and was put on his mettle by that provoking smile. The ground sloped a little from the basket. He sat down, carefully following instructions, adjusted the strap of bark to his forehead, and tried to rise! But his strength melted like the waxen wings of Icarus in the Cretan sun, the perspiration streamed from his face, and the basket refused to budge! When at last he was obliged to admit that the woman had the best of it, the crowd shouted with delight.

In early days with each large basket, weighing about one hundred and twenty pounds, a "bacha" or baby load, had to be brought as toll for the zemindar. This was carried in one hand and the Garo's sword in the other. Everything was priced according to its value in cotton. A maund of cotton (eighty-two pounds) would buy five pounds of rice, or one of tobacco; it would sometimes also buy a bull. For one of the "bacha" loads (twenty pounds) a fowl could be purchased, perhaps even a small puppy, or a sucking pig.

There were often perilous but amusing instances of rough and ready justice inflicted by these hillmen on those who endeavored to cheat them.

The shop merchants practice every art, stratagem, and roguery to impose upon the unsuspicious Garos, who are sure, when they detect them, besides chastising them, to take back their own cotton, and the grain they were about to barter for as a punishment for the intended fraud. After this they resume trade with another man, and seem to bear no enmity beyond the moment.

With this sketch of wrathful discovery and good-humored revenge should be placed a companion picture, painted by Colonel Dalton, in which the Bengali scores:

Photo by W. Mason.

Bringing the Cotton to Market

The Garos rush about with bundles weighing two pounds, and the small change with which to provide their wants. One of them has fixed his eyes on that fine chanticleer.[1] He wildly rushes up to the owner, into whose hands he thrusts a bundle of cotton, and seizes the bird; but the poulterer turns coldly away, as if he and his cock had only come as spectators, and were not inclined to do business at all. The poor Garo, as excited as a gambler, doubles his bid; at last a bargain is effected, the hillman joins his companions, exulting in the possession of his cock; and the Bengali methodically proceeds to weigh the cotton, and calculate how much he has made by the transaction!

The general situation at these frontier markets is, therefore, one of more or less excitement and expectancy, spiced with danger. The merchants move up from their homes or bazaars on the plains, the Garos come down from their wild hills, and both meet on the market-ground. There are knavish tricks on the one hand, and outbursts of rough horse-play on the other. Sometimes, and not infrequently, a savage onslaught is followed by sudden panic. Let us try to picture the scene. It is the eve of the day announced for the opening feast. A space has been cleared by the river near a spur of the hills. It is ringed round with trees, and shadowed by that sharp ridge showing black against the sunset glow. Booths have been erected, and the merchants are here. You can see the flames curling round their cooking pots, on the bank, or making a glowing interior of bulgy boats, with a shining reflection in the stream below. They have brought up bags of rice, boat-loads of dried fish, baskets of salt, trinkets and tobacco, to sell to the despised savages of the hills. They sit up late, smoking, and talking bravely of the prospects of the morrow. They are ready

[1] White cocks, or capons, are very highly prized by the wild Garos, chiefly on account of their feathers which are used for personal decoration.

on the instant to cast off and glide down-stream in case of alarm. They have interviewed the daroga, and bribed him to give them special protection should need occur, and to tell the truth, they wish the hazardous enterprise well over for another year. The morning clears. The booths are furnished with goods. Hindu sweet-venders and pastry-cooks squat behind their stalls. Mohammedan dealers in poultry and puppies hawk these about in their arms, or stand with them huddled at their feet. Fruit and vegetables, salt and tobacco, are temptingly displayed, while the warm sun shines over all, and the green foliage everywhere catches the gleam. Burkundazes swagger up and down, priming their matchlocks, and boasting of their prowess in the last fray.

And now come the Garos! Every one turns to look at them as they trip down the mountainside, or trot along the jungle path at the bottom, and at last swing out into the open, and drop their heavy loads. What a procession it is of black, weighted, nude-limbed, chattering creatures! How furtively they look at you as they crouch beneath their baskets, arms hanging free, and sword held firmly in the right hand ready to strike! The chiefs go first to that stout building under the trees where the daroga sits on a raised platform with his burkundazes on guard about him. Here each gets his turban or bit of scarlet cloth, and puts it on proudly among his circle of friends. Presently with the dinging of a gong the market begins, and every one is busy. You never saw a more noisy and clamorous crowd. The few interpreters have a distracting time, and business for the most part is done by looks and signs. The merchants and shopkeepers have a wholesome fear of these wild, jolly animals, as they watch them stroll about, peering at everything, handling their blood-curdling weapons, and chattering and laughing incessantly. But it is good cotton they have brought, white as snow, if not as soft as swan's-down, and very cheap. There are other things too; gums and rubber, aromatic herbs and lac, all of which will fetch fat prices in the bazaars of Bengal and Assam. It is worth a little risk to make such good bargains. Then comes the promised feast. There are caldrons of greasy pork, stuffed roast puppies, smoking mountains of coarse rice, and huge tubs of beer. But over this unsavory repast and subsequent drunken carousal let us draw the curtain.

VI

THE GOVERNMENT AS A MISSIONARY BOARD

PERHAPS in no other service in the world, from the days of the "Honorable John Company" to the present, have there been such constant and conspicuous examples of wide ability, steady devotion to duty, high-minded statesmanship, and tried administrative capacity as in the Indian Civil Service; but the increasing pressure of official routine now tends to cramp individual expression; the situations in which uncommon qualities of resourcefulness and tact are called out do not so frequently arise; and there seems to prevail a less intimate and more artificial relationship between the rulers and the ruled.

David Scott was a fine specimen of the freer creative type of the old school. His freshness, humor, and clear foresight, combined with unusual vigor and directness in carrying out his work, endeared him to all sorts and conditions of men. "A breezy, burly man, fearless and keen; a sagacious officer of extraordinary tact and ability; a Christian and a gentleman with the love of the people in his heart, he proved the greatest figure of his time on this turbulent stage." To him more than to any other belongs the honor of having laid the foundations of good government and redemptive influences among the tribes and clans of the northeast frontier of Bengal, of which in 1823 he became the civil commissioner and the agent of the governor-general. At the close of the Burmese war in 1826 he was entrusted with the administration of the whole Brahmaputra valley, recently ceded to the British but practically in a state of anarchy. He ruled and loved his people. He introduced the mulberry plant to increase the production of silk; brought workmen from Bengal to improve the mode of spinning; established an agricultural farm; introduced the potato and other vegetables; and labored to improve the breed of cattle. Prisoners in the jail were taught useful occupations; and Bhutias were brought over from the Himalayas to teach their methods of terracing the hills. He made many expeditions into the territory of savage and treacherous tribes, who not infrequently attempted to take his life. They lay in wait for him with poisoned arrows and spears; they shot at him through fissures in the rocks; they surrounded his little guard in the jungle and tried to cut him off. Once with a band of ten or twelve men he was surrounded by hundreds of Garos, who guarded the points of egress, and shut off every way of escape. Thus beset, he was compelled to build a stockade, and remained beleaguered for seven or eight days until a company of militiamen came to his relief. The idea spread abroad that he was invulnerable, and after failing in several attempts to kill him, the mountaineers felt he was beyond reach of their power and cunning and gave up in despair.

Garos were his favorite soldiers from the day when one of them attacked a troop single-handed and saved Scott's life. Had he been a British soldier the plucky Garo would have had the Victoria Cross. As it was, his nickname in the regiment was *Bilati Garo,* or " Foreign European Garo."

On these expeditions, being too heavy to climb the almost perpendicular heights, Scott frequently "harnessed a team of brawny mountaineers, who laughingly tugged him up by a trace fastened round his body."

Again he would twist the tail of his Arab steed and hang on to that till safely landed on the crest.

During the year 1816, when Scott was selected to deal with the trouble on the Garo frontier, a hundred and fifty villages had been burnt and an almost equal number of heads carried off as trophies into the hills. In a short time he had induced no fewer than a hundred and twenty of the independent chiefs to enter into terms with him. This splendid achievement was hardly accomplished when, in 1823, the wider field drew him away, and for many years the Garos were left alone. Scott had hoped to find his way into the heart of the hills. His plans were, however, neglected by his successors who were unable to face the dangers to which they would be exposed.

With David Scott it was not the exercise of personal influence, though he relied much on that. Still less was it the strength of armed men, although he made full use of them. It was something more subtle and more powerful than any of these. It was the spiritual force of the principles of Christianity, applied through the medium of the schools. In his view neither captain nor civilian was so necessary to this design as the missionary of the cross.

He was one of the pupils taught Bengali by Doctor Carey in the College of Fort William, Calcutta. Like many another young civilian who came under the same influence he acquired a reverence for his teacher and a faith in the missionary cause. As early as 1822 we find him corresponding with Serampore on the subject of a missionary to the Garos; and two years later the fifth report of the Serampore College mentions "three Garo youths sent by David Scott, Esq., the Commissioner of Kuch Bihar," who probably bore the entire expense of their maintenance. We know nothing further of them except that one named Wake was "particularly docile and studious."

Unable to secure a missionary from Serampore, Scott wrote to his agents in England, instructing them to select and to send out suitable men. Evidently at a loss to know how to deal with this strange request, they suggested the propriety of his applying to the bishop of Calcutta. Scott accordingly wrote to Mr. W. B. Bayley, Secretary to Government, asking permission to apply to the bishop, saying:

> I am satisfied that nothing permanently good can be obtained by other means, and that, if we do not interfere on behalf of the poor Garos, they will soon become Hindus or half Hindus. I would greatly prefer two or more Moravian missionaries who, along with religion would teach the useful arts. If the Government would insure them subsistence only, I would be willing to take on myself the expense.

Secretary Bayley sent a most encouraging letter in reply closing with the words, "I do not think the favorable opportunity for making this very interesting experiment should be lost." He also forwarded Mr. Scott's letter to the bishop with commendations of his own. Bishop Heber replied in a long and enthusiastic communication, containing a number of recommendations, dated Chauringee, November 29, 1825. Mr. Bayley forwarded this to Mr. Scott, who at once wrote to the bishop, commenting in a statesmanlike manner upon the many suggestions he had made. Unhappily the good bishop died before anything further could be done.

The next stage in the development of this extremely significant proposal was the submission of the whole matter for the consideration and orders of the right honorable the governor-general in council. The scene was the council-chamber in Fort William, October 12, 1826. A letter was read from Mr. Scott, dated June fifth, enclosing all the previous correspondence and memoranda on the subject. It was ordered that the secretary send a reply, which furnishes us with a pleasing picture of the august council entering fully and sympathetically into the project of a little school for the benefit of the wild mountaineers; and the interest is heightened when we remember that Lord Combermere, presiding, was a soldier and a commander-in-chief, to whom the Garos might well appear a mere pestilent nest of savages to be burned or bayoneted out of their retreat. The suggestions of the lamented Heber and of David Scott were adopted, and Mr. Valentine William Hurley, assistant apothecary at Chunar, was appointed schoolmaster of the Garo school. This school was to be established at Singimari, "or at some other convenient spot in the neighborhood, for the education of forty Garo boys upon the general principles recommended by the late bishop of Calcutta." Mr. Hurley joined his appointment in due course, but did not commend himself to Mr. Scott as quite fitted to conduct the enterprise.

On July 10, 1827, the commissioner wrote again to Government, suggesting the appointment of Mr. Fenwick, a Baptist missionary at Sylhet, as superintendent, and Mr. Hurley's retention for the service in the medical department. He proposed the clearing of an extensive space upon the summit of the mountain Rangira—about half-way between Tura and the plains westward, often called " Little Tura "—as the best site for the new colony. Scott's lengthy appeal, broadly based, practical, and strongly urged, did not come before the council until June 26, 1828, eleven months from the date of writing. Mr. Hurley in the meanwhile had thrown up his work in disgust, " too much depressed at the dismal prospect of residing among the savages, insulated, as it were, from all the comforts of European society." In communicating this fact to Government the commissioner wrote, "In an undertaking of this kind an ardent zeal in the cause of religion is of a *sine qua non,* and unless that is possessed in a sufficient degree to place a man above the inferior considerations of society, and many little comforts to which Europeans are accustomed, ultimate success can not be expected."

The governor-general in council accepted the resignation of Mr. Hurley and promised that the appointment of two missionaries and a well-educated native doctor for the schools would receive the early consideration of the Government. It was, however, considered desirable to secure the services of a missionary of the Church Establishment, willing and qualified to undertake the work, and on that rock the scheme, as originally conceived, was wrecked. Government withdrew from it, not because of its missionary character, but because of the difficulty of procuring a particular type of missionary. Yet the idea was not wholly abandoned—it was merely postponed. Failing a missionary, a schoolmaster was appointed in Mr. Hurley's place, a Mr. Fermie, a junior teacher of English and geography in the Hindu College at Calcutta.

Mr. Fermie accepted the appointment and in July proceeded to Goalpara to place himself under the order of Mr. Scott; he began his work at Singimari, and there died suddenly in November of fever occasioned by the unhealthful climate. Alas for the Garos! and alas for this abortive plan! Even the Commissioner was now almost in despair. He reported the loss. It was the last act in the drama. The Government scheme was dead. It was decided to carry on the school, however, under the direction of the Bengali master to a sufficient extent to provide competent interpreters and local officers for the duty of the Garo Hills and the Duars. The inspiring spirit of the Government missionary school, from the first to the last had been the personal sympathy, energy, and solicitude of David Scott. But his days were numbered. Broken in health, he lived only three years more and was already disheartened by the apparent hopelessness of the difficulties to be faced. When after an interval of forty years another mission to the Garos was established, it was under circumstances so new and unexpected, so free from human initiative and official control, that we stamp it in a peculiar manner as the act of God. It is a pleasure to add that, once established, it derived and has continued to enjoy help and encouragement from Government sympathy and support.

VII

THE OPENING OF THE LAIR

THE history of the Garos for these forty years following the Burmese War, 1824-1826, presents a sickening series of raids and retaliations, of bloodshed, misery, and muddle. The darkness was occasionally relieved by men who knew what ought to be done, and who urged Government to do it. Two courses were open: either non-interference, save when some murderous sally necessitated a punitive expedition; or complete annexation and control. The former was a half measure, attended with violence and irritation, without adequate advantages; the latter was the only path to permanent prosperity and peace. The former policy was the one persisted in till 1866. The Garos of the inner hills were left to themselves, and only on the outer edge was an uncertain control kept up and a sort of spasmodic order preserved.

> When now and again some more than ordinary ferocious raid had desolated whole villages and filled the little frontier marts with horror, a company of sepoys and police would struggle up into the hills, and after burning the first villages they could find, hurry down again, half of them ill with fever and the rest halt and maimed from stumbling over the pitfalls of an enemy they had never seen.

While the war was still in progress there was a serious outbreak in the south. About ten years later acute troubles began toward the north. The independent Garos tried to prevent Government from collecting tribute from the dependent villages, and thus rough waves from the interior seas of barbarism constantly broke over the barrier of semisettled villages. Little was done to check them; they gathered strength and sometimes came in like a flood.

Not until 1848, after one of the independent clans had withheld its tribute for years, committed a number of outrages, and defeated two or three parties of troops, was the Government moved to take effective measures. Even then the expedition brought to pass only temporary peace.

Nine years previously Captain Jenkins, who saw from the first the only true solution, had proposed a survey of the hills, and the appointment of a special officer to take entire charge of the tribe. But the governor-general in council, Sir C. T. Metcalfe, "did not think the Garo race of sufficient importance to call for the service of a special officer." Well would it have been for the Garos, and for the poor cultivators who became their victims, had the enlightened views of the Commissioner found favor with Government. The civilization of the tribe would have been moved forward thirty years and the lives of scores of unoffending villagers been spared.

Foiled in one way the Commissioner tried another. Following in the wake of David Scott, he set about establishing a Garo school. Proceeding with much tact, Captain Jenkins finally secured the support for a little school which was carried on for several years, but seemingly with small success, for it "attracted only lowlanders and people from the outer hills," drawing no lads from the interior. Yet it was destined to play a most important part in the civilization and redemption of the tribe. Of the first ten boys admitted eight ultimately became Christian workers; four of them ordained preachers, and the "illustrious hopes" of Bishop Heber began to be realized, as will be seen as our story proceeds.

In 1852 the Goalpara frontier was again harried by the hillmen, who raided seven times in three months and carried off more than forty heads. Lord Dalhousie thus expressed his mind:

> I have already said that I deprecate these extreme measures, while anything else remains untried. But as these savages will neither treat, submit, nor rest, it is due to our own subjects, whose lives and property are in jeopardy, that we should have recourse to punishment, which, though severe, is the only thing that they comprehend or feel. I consider that further military operations would be a waste of life uselessly. It is probable that the exclusion of the Garos from the plains will be effectual. It has been so when tried on the hill people on the opposite frontier to the northwest. I request therefore, that they may be rigidly excluded from the plains, and that the chiefs may be informed that the exclusion will be continued till satisfaction is made by the delivery of the murderers. They are at the same time to be informed that if they are found in the plains while thus in resistance to the Government, they will be seized and disposed of as the Government may think fit. I am aware that these measures will probably inflict injury on the innocent while punishing the guilty. I regret it, but individual interests must yield to the public interests, when there is, as in this case, no alternative.

The measure did to some extent prove successful. It was found that the trade in cotton had become so materially a source of profit to the Garos, that the closure of the *hats* was felt as severe punishment. They gave up some of the offenders and promised to arrest and deliver over the others. Captain Jenkins continued to urge the military occupation of the hills, but it was thought no European could survive their deadly climate. Indeed David Scott had written:

I know not of any healthy spot in the hills. The danger from sickness I must not disguise; it is very great. I have myself been twice on the point of death from fevers contracted in these hills, although I have never had even an ague-fit during a residence of twenty-five years in any other part of the country.

Still no hand strong and just enough to tame the central clans was laid for more than a moment upon them, and their wild barbarism shook itself free, unchallenged, and lay in ambush for further depredations.

In 1856 raids were numerous and atrocious, and for the next three years continued to harass the border. Numbers of heads were taken. In 1860 a really effective expedition was sent into the hills. It consisted of two columns which entered from the north and south sides respectively, punished almost all the offending villages, and obtained the fealty of a few friendly chiefs. The Commissioner again urged the appointment of an officer in charge, and the construction of two roads, one to go round the hills, and the other to cross them. The whole case was forwarded to England and the secretary of state replied:

It is very clear that we can not reclaim these wild inhabitants from their savage habits, or induce among them a higher state of civilization by the mere display of military strength. These objects can only be effected by peaceful means, and by gradually increasing our intercourse with them, and I have therefore read with regret the statement of Captain Jenkins that although the Garos have been almost a century under our jurisdiction, it is not on record that we have ever had a single officer who could converse with them in their own language. The unfavorable condition of things will not, I trust, be of long continuance.

Finally, after another murderous raid, early in 1866, "the lieutenant governor proposed to the Government of India the appointment of a special officer for the Garo

Hills." Now, at length, in April, 1866, the step that had been urged by those best acquainted with the field for more than a quarter of a century was taken, and a deputy commissioner was entrusted with the direct management of the turbulent tribe.

The newly appointed deputy commissioner, Lieutenant Williamson, lost no time in taking up his station.

> He possessed accomplishments that at once awoke the wonder, and ultimately the respect of the suspicious Garos. Unerring skill with the rifle, and a soundness of wind and limb that enabled him to beat the village leaders in a race up-hill, were a better introduction for him than even his armed police.

We soon find him sitting in a charmed circle of seventeen chiefs, fourteen of whom had never paid tribute to man. The late Sir Alexander MacKenzie, whose words always glow when eulogizing the work of brave men on outpost duty in frontier regions, adds:

> We doubt if the residents of town and favored stations, the frequenters of the band-stands and croquet, ever realize the position and life of the gallant young fellows, who, amid jungles and swamps and rugged hills are rough-hewing the savage peoples of the frontier to shapely members of the body politic. The solitude and self-sacrifice of such a life are but little understood. With no companions but his police guard, no recreation save that afforded by his gun; exposed to the deadly miasma of the valleys; a native doctor his only medical adviser; liable at any moment to treacherous attack; no aid or succor within many miles; his house a hut, his food uncertain; with no luxuries and few comforts, the hill track officer must have heart in his work, or he will utterly fail, and be of all men the most miserable. But if he sees his efforts prospering; if he sees savage communities abandoning their lawlessness and burying their feuds; if he finds them coming to him for advice, for redress of injury, and adjustment of dispute; if barbarous customs drop quietly out of use, new industries spring up, new

> wants arise; if he knows that a nation is awaking to new being in his hands, we can imagine no reward more rich, no satisfaction more pure than his. . . Such men make little show when visiting a lieutenant governor or secretary. A card with a well-known name is brought in, and there enters a shy-looking, weather-beaten young man, who can scarcely be brought to tell the facts of his last exploit, how he seized with his own hand a murdering chief in the center of his astonished clan, or stormed some well-nigh impregnable stockade filled with angry and excited braves.

Sir Alexander unstintedly commends " the admirable tact of Lieutenant Williamson " and rejoices over his " bloodless victories."

Thus the wild Garos began to be tamed. Infrequent but serious disturbances among the independent tribes led, however, to a strong expedition for the complete subjugation of the hills, during the cold season of 1872-1873. The force was divided into three columns, one entering from the north, by the Nibari Dwar, in the Goalpara district; a second from the Mymensing district on the south; while the third, or main column, under Deputy Commissioner Williamson, marched from Tura, the headquarters of the Garo Hills District. The expedition was singularly successful. All the independent villages submitted, and thus was filled up the blank which hitherto had disfigured the maps.

A Garo, now a portly and wealthy luskar, gave me a vivid account of the occurrence. His father was one of the independent chiefs. There had been an exciting meeting the night before. It was then determined to oppose the advance of the approaching troops. In these last strongholds of the savage clans no sound of firearms had yet been heard. The chiefs were ignorant of the manner of British troops, and the nature of their weapons. Rumors had reached them that the English

Ancient Map of Bengal

Dated 1854, August. This map shows the Garo hills as an unknown country inhabited b

had hollow spears that could spit fire from a great distance, and repeatedly, without leaving their hand, and the fire struck where it hit, and had great power to kill. It was ordered that each Garo brave in order to protect himself from so terrible a weapon, should cut down succulent plantain trunks, peel them, and bind large pieces of the cool inner coat in moist layers over his bamboo shield. This, it was hoped, would effectually quench the fiery darts of the enemy. When morning dawned, the warriors manned their stockade, two-edged swords, spears, and plantain-covered shields, all in readiness to await the attack. It was long in coming; the sun had climbed to its zenith when the invading column emerged from the leafy gorge into the sort of amphitheater with the village in front. The trees all around were thick with wild Garos crouching like monkeys, still and invisible among the leaves. Their quick eyes watched intently every movement of the troops, as with flashing weapons and determined faces they formed for the attack. The precision, the strength, the sense of mastery so manifest in every movement, powerfully impressed them. Dread of the mysterious fire-spears, now for the first time seen, and doubt as to the efficacy of the plantain shields, together with admiration for their foe at sight, led them with one impulse to drop from the trees, to go shouting, leaping, and throwing down their weapons, and welcome the invaders as friends. Thus by a trivial submission, the hillmen preserved their force, and almost without bloodshed the whole country was annexed.

The lair, when explored, turned out to be very different from expectations founded on weird accounts. Instead of barren rock and unprofitable wastes, a wealth of timber, coal, and cultivation was discovered. The surveyor, Lieutenant Woodthrope, found "most exquisite little pictures" and skilfully painted them on the pages of his report.

> Some of the most beautiful effects of color and light are seen then at sunrise or sunset from the top of some high point overlooking the low hills; and to those who can admire the smaller works of the Great Master's hand, the Semsang and its affluents, in combination of wood, rock, and waterfall, present pictures that will live forever in memory. Here the strong rapids carry the angler's bait spinning away down into the deep, green-purple pools, flecked here and there with sunlight, where, beneath the tall gray rocks made glorious with orange lichen and ferns, and crowned by graceful trees, lie the big fish that yield themselves ready victims to the tempter. . . On a fine morning the view from Tura is glorious. The tops of the low spurs of the hill of Rangira, lighted up by the rising sun, with many delicate tints, blended and harmonized by the soft foamy gray mists still filling the valley, seem like so many islands of dreamland. The Brahmaputra glitters golden in the morning haze; and beyond, the low country of Rungpore and Kuch Bihar is faintly visible, while above the obscurity of the distant plain, rising sharp and clear on the far-off horizon, the rosy peaks of the Snowy Range close in the scene.

Commingled with the wildness of savagery is the beauty of the natural surroundings. The story of the coming of the kingdom into these savage hills and wild human hearts is now to be told. It is a strange and thrilling story. It contains the secret of much of our administrative success, yet in origin and progress moves widely apart from administrative efforts—the unfettered work of the Spirit of God.

VIII

MAN-CUBS AT SCHOOL

LONG before the annexation, and some years before any officer was appointed to administer the hills, an unseen force had been at work, hallowing forever, by its presence and memory, one corner of the land; and being destined to spread widely, and with great acceptance, it has already changed the lives of thousands, and supplied the most precious element in the work of humanizing and uplifting this people. This spiritual force was born in the hearts of two Garo lads who were among the first to attend the Garo school established by Captain Jenkins, at Goalpara, in 1847.

It was not by accident but by true intuition that the Government adopted the plan of civilizing the Garos by means of missionaries. The end sought was not unworthy, but it was inadequate. The missionary idea, promulgated mainly as a service to the state, died and was never revived.

From David Scott's day, when punitive expeditions entered the hills, exacting vengeance for raids, they sometimes captured young, bright-eyed, clean-limbed, laughing lads, and brought them away as hostages for the good behavior of their clan. These boys, if they did not give their captors the slip, were taught to read and write, and afterward employed as interpreters at the courts, or drafted into the frontier police. But most of them were disappointments. Their slight introduction into the world of knowledge familiarized them more with the evil than with the good of civilized life. Many became mere hangers-on at the station, loafing about the local bazaar, drinking a deadlier liquor than their mountain *chu*, and acquiring other vices than those to which they were born. Their civilization was merely a veneer. The savage had been weaned from the jungle. He had learned to don a coat and to strut about the streets; but in instinct, in passion, and in palate he was a savage still.

There were exceptions of course, as will be seen. The first object of Captain Jenkins' school was "the education of a few respectable lads, who may hereafter be sent into the hills as the instructors of their brethren." But the school perished miserably like its predecessor, after years of fitful life, and was counted among the failures of the Government effort to educate the mountaineers. However, sixteen years later, two boys of that first group, who were destined to be the pioneers among their people, returned to inaugurate a new era and bring in the "better hope." These two returned, not because they were civilized, but because they were Christians, eager, not to echo their experience of the world, but to impart their knowledge of God.

Yet the school provided them with the equipment and opportunity for discovering the truth. It opened their eyes and awakened inquiry in their minds, and was part of the means by which they were taught of God. "It attracted only a few lowlanders and half-breeds," says the state historian, dismissing the matter in a sentence; and from one point of view he is entirely right. But to the eye of the missionary student, that school at Goalpara is of peculiar interest as the earliest training-ground of the first apostles of the Garo tribe.

These two, Omed and Ramke, whose home was in the northeast corner of the hills, were devotedly attached to each other, though in temperament very unlike. Omed was the natural leader, impetuous and forceful; Ramke was of a meditative and docile spirit. As the elder by six or eight years, and uncle of Ramke, Omed exercised a certain right of protection and guardianship. This was the more necessary as Ramke early lost his father, and was not a favorite with the man his mother subsequently married.

Their life as boys in the jungle was full of interest and excitement. They could recollect in old age the details of more than one bloody raid—the gruesome preparations, the treacherous band of braves stealthily setting forth from the village at dead of night, and the return with their dripping load of heads. Both were in deep dread of demons. But the younger felt a sharper fear than the elder as he thought of the unseen evil presences all about him. His boyish hands were forever busy smoothing little places of sacrifice and smearing them with the blood of tiny feathered creatures which he had trapped or speared; and, believing as he tells us, "that certain persons turn into tigers and kill and swallow men, if it was said that that man was such an one, I feared him very much."[1] Ramke was essentially religious and devout. After picnics of pure animal frolic, when he and others of these savage lads behaved as nearly like bear-whelps or monkeys as man-cubs can, the demons would dissolve into mist and be almost forgotten. They may even have laughed at them then; but the laugh would sound hollow at nightfall, and the fear would come back to grip them with a closer hug.

There were rare days of enjoyment when they were taken to the weekly market down on the plains. The

[1] Most of the facts concerning Ramke were gleaned from a manuscript autobiographical account, written in Bengali in 1866.—*William Carey.*

journey, the bustle, the bartering, the ceaseless chatter, the glimpses of a larger world than their own, the rumors afloat of a white people who had come to govern Assam, of the Sahib at Goalpara, and the still more powerful one at Gauhati—all this fired the imagination and swelled the pride of these jungle lads. Most of all were they impressed with the importance and influence of the Government interpreters, Garos like themselves, who could speak Bengali, and could write mysterious signs on paper which held fast the spoken word and gave it back syllable for syllable when required. Both were seized with an ambition to be able to read and write, and began by tracing the figures on a mile-stone, and copying them in the dust with a stick. Soon they tried such characters and symbols as they saw on bits of paper or bales of goods at the market. In particular they hung around the raja's cutchery where a friendly babu taught them the letters of the Bengali alphabet. Omed learned to speak a little both in Assamese and Bengali during those visits to the plains.

One day in 1847 news was circulated at the market that the Government wanted boys for a school at Goalpara, and would feed, clothe, and teach them, and, of course, turn them out great men. The word spread to the villages above, and soon Omed with his nephew Reban and two others, Ramsing and Jongrin, were en route to Goalpara. Ramke, to his great disappointment, could not join them. Only a week or two before he had fallen from a tree and broken his arm, twice at the shoulder and once at the wrist. The pain and loss of blood were very great; and when the other boys started for school he was still unable to move or bend his arm.

The day of the start from Watrepara, their home, was one of great excitement. The parents had many misgivings, but the lads were highly elated because of their great adventure. Omed was over twenty, the others twelve and thirteen. Merrily they went down the steep, leafy defile, swinging their black swords and blazing the jungle on either side, and having gained the open, trotted down the familiar road to the market. There a rest and a meal at midday under the shade of a tree, a chat with the friendly babu, and another start, their faces turned to the setting sun, and twenty long level miles before them. Hot of foot, for all hillfolk hate the level, they halted for the night, sleeping under a tree, and arrived at Goalpara early the following day.

They found the large institution filled with Hindu, Rabha, and Mohammedan boys, studying English, Bengali, and Persian. When Omed introduced himself and his squad, Pentu Sahib, the master, said: "You are too old, you had better go home; the others may stay." But the others chimed in, "If he can't stay, we won't," and that settled it; Omed being retained to look after the younger boys. They soon discovered that six Garos from another village had already been admitted. One of these, Gongaram, was ordained in after years. At sunset two bottles of liquor were divided among them, and they were encouraged to dance and sing as a cure for homesickness.

But the new element did not unite with the old. The Hindu boys scowled at the Garo savages, the parents of the politer race made a fuss, the deputy commissioner came over, and a separate set of buildings had to be put up, removed from the town, for the Garo pupils. Omed acted as interpreter both for the teacher and the class. Two other lads joined them, making twelve in all. A couple of chuprassies were told off to keep them out of mischief and prevent their running away.

Six months later Ramke, disabled by his broken arm for labor in the fields, was allowed to accompany Reban's father on a visit to the school. He was delighted with what he saw, and begged hard to be admitted, but the teacher was unwilling. Then up spoke Omed, pleading that his arm was no hindrance to his head, and that the rest would share their rations with him until permission for him to stay had been obtained from the deputy commissioner, who thought that there were already too many boys from one village. Omed continued to press his suit, and in the end Ramke's name was added to the roll.

Two years went by with no apparent progress. At length Omed and Ramke went boldly up to Lieutenant Agnew's bungalow on the top of the hill, and declared that if they stayed in the school twenty years, under such a teacher, they would never learn. The pundit was called into the " presence " and instantly dismissed. The next man appointed soon won the affection of the boys. " He taught us splendidly," they said. " We shall praise him till death."

After a while it was thought advisable to enlarge their ideas by taking them in a steamer at Government expense, to visit Gauhati. A regiment of sepoys was stationed there, and proved a great attraction to the boys. Jongrin and Ronja enlisted, and Omed was asked to join, but refused. While he was hiring a boat to take them back to Goalpara, a native officer called him, and asked his name. When he had given it, and answered some other questions, the officer said, " Now you have given your name, you are a sepoy," making the youth feel that dire penalities would be visited upon him if he withheld consent. Caught by this trick, though, perhaps, not altogether unwillingly, Omed became a sepoy, and stayed behind at Gauhati, while Ramke went back to school.

IX

THE SWEEPING OF AN EMPTY BUNGALOW

OMED'S life as a sepoy lasted fifteen years, all spent in Gauhati. He steadily rose in the ranks and was a favorite with the officers. The savage blood in his veins made him an ideal soldier for the frontier, now that his spirit was disciplined and tamed. There was a force, alertness, and fearlessness about him that commanded respect. But he was trained for service of another sort; he was to become the first Christian of his tribe and the first evangelist of his people.

Nothing seemed less likely when he enlisted. There was no mission to the Garos. The evangelistic effort for that people had died with Scott nearly twenty years before. Nobody now seemed to think them worth troubling about religiously, except Major Jenkins, on whom Scott's mantle had fallen. This officer had written to a missionary of the American Baptist Board in 1837, recommending the establishment of a station at Gauhati, with a particular view to the Garos; but the claims of larger tribes farther up the valley seemed of more pressing importance. Nevertheless, it was by the means of that same American Baptist Foreign Mission Society, and at this very place, Gauhati, that the first Garo converts were gathered in. Gauhati had been one of the stations of the Serampore Mission, and Mr. Rae was sent there as early as 1829. He was joined in 1836 by Mr. William Robinson, but shortly after, funds failing in Serampore, Gauhati was reluctantly abandoned. Mr.

Robinson, with the consent of the Serampore missionaries, transferred his services to the Government, remaining as master of the Government school.

Meanwhile the Baptist Board, with a flourishing mission in Burma, had sent off their men, on the invitation and with the generous support of Major Jenkins, to open a station at Sadiya, and to them was resigned the whole field of Assam by the English Baptists in 1838, in the hope that, if possible, they might here repeat the successes of their Burman mission, and perhaps open a way to China.

Five years later work reopened at Gauhati, and in February, 1845, a small church was formed with seven members, but its influence scarcely overflowed the mission compound, its energies being directed rather to self-discipline than to self-propagation. Active preaching indeed there was for the Assamese, but little notice was taken of the representatives of other races in the community, or of the hardy men of the hills, who formed a part of the regiment in the lines.

On the other hand the sepoys lived apart in a world of their own. They did their daily drill and strutted about the bazaar, with the temple gongs clanging in their ears, and Hinduism obtruding itself at every corner, apparently quite unaware of the feeble flicker of Christianity close at hand.

One afternoon some years after his enlistment, Omed was told off to guard an empty bungalow on the mission compound. The sentry trod his beat, looking curiously into the house as he passed up and down. Some Bengali tracts were strewn about the floor, and he wanted to pick them up and read them. But his havildar (native sergeant) had warned him not to touch them. When it was added that any breach of this prohibition would receive discipline, Omed's appetite was fully whetted. Who does not long for forbidden fruit? He restrained himself, however, till evening, when the sweeper, coming to clean up the place, whisked out the papers with his broom, some of them falling at Omed's feet. Watching his chance he covered these, picked them up, and tucked them into his uniform, carrying them to his quarters to be read by stealth.

One of the tracts thus acquired was entitled "Apatti Nashak," or "The Destroyer of Objections." It explained the Christian faith and disposed of different objections to its acceptance. The stray booklet made a profound impression on Omed's mind. He kept it carefully to the end of his life, and, though willing to lend it, was always anxious and restless until it was returned. Some of its pages were worm-eaten and polished black with use, but their number was complete. He often showed it with much affection and told how the reading of it had opened his eyes. "I saw," he would say, "that Hinduism, apparently so powerful and seductive, was nothing, Mohammedanism nothing, and resolved to become a Christian." This rapid leap to conviction was characteristic, as was also the tenacity with which he clung to it through the years that followed, until conscience and heart had been stirred to the same conviction, and the whole man gave himself up to Christ. During this time he was gaining ground in the regiment, and looking out for an opportunity to make himself better acquainted with the subject.

Then came the great mutiny, and nothing was talked of until it was over; meanwhile as drill-sergeant, afterward as schoolmaster and havildar, under Major Campbell, he had charge of the magazine, and kept this post for years. On a certain day a suboverseer, Samuel Loveday, who had been appointed to superintend some repairs on the building, applied to him for the key. Some one remarked, " That's a Christian," and Omed's curiosity was immediately aroused. " I picked up an acquaintance with him," writes Loveday,

> and began to talk with him about the Saviour of the world. He used to listen to me very attentively whenever I spoke to him about Jesus Christ. We had several conversations during a period of some months, when a day was fixed for a final discussion with a subahdar, a jemadar, and other inferior officers. This meeting opened with a very hot debate with the subahdar, and it was evenly kept up for two hours. The result was a victory for Christianity. When Omed saw that I had won, he expressed before me the earnest desire to embrace this victorious religion. He at that same time told me that as I was a boy—my age then was about seventeen—he would like to have a talk with one who was older than I. I therefore referred him to Kandura Babu, who was thirty at that time.

Together they went on this search for truth, and that evening, a rare thing for him, Omed was late at roll-call. It was after midnight before he returned to the lines. Every Sunday thereafter he attended Kandura's ministry, with Major Campbell's consent, and was exempt from muster.

We must now go back to Goalpara and see by what steps Ramke had also been drawn into the circle of Christian thought.

X

WHAT'S IN THE LOOM?

RAMKE was still a lad only half-way through his teens, when he bade his uncle good-bye, and stepped into the boat that was to take him back to school. But he was a lad of meditative spirit, to whom the great river would make its own silent and solemn appeal. Clouds of mystery brooded over the face of the waters, and over the blue hills in the distance—the hills of his native land. What fierce passions were there, of man and beast! Was there no promise of better things? Were the souls of men really at the mercy of demons? What then were those other voices that spoke home to his heart; the ties of kindred, the calm of the evening, the stillness of the stars? Above all, what was this new hunger after goodness, and a Being worthy to be loved? The questions remained unanswered. Enough that he had asked them. The Lord's angel was troubling the deeps of an immortal soul.

School life went on as usual. Ramke, quick to learn, soon became proficient in Bengali. On the playground he was handicapped by his crippled arm, which doubtless encouraged his mood for solitude. He loved to stroll quiet paths alone, and think and muse. The Hindu doctrine of repeated births gave him great distress. A new fear was taking the place of the old. In the free life of the jungle, he had a chance, even in spite of demons; it was possible to elude them. They could at any rate be appeased, and a man is a man always. He could be brave and strong; he had personal interests and a personal identity which death could not touch; his relatives and his friends were his forever. But this new teaching stripped him of all these. They belonged to the lowest scale of being, and were doomed to an endless succession of changed and enslaved existences. The whole soul of this Garo rose in revolt. His affection for his relatives was warm and deep. Their love for him was the one thing he was sure of in life and in death. And now it was all slipping away. To whom could he turn for comfort; to whom tell the trouble that weighed down his heart?

Meditating on the statement that, after death, I must be born again and again; sometimes, not of man, but of pigs and cattle, birds, worms, grasshoppers, grass, and trees; being worried I got great distress. The cause of my distress was this; if truly there is repeated birth, then I shall not know my father, mother, family, and relatives. They also will not know me. Now they love me, and I also love them very much. That is to say, my mother loves me. I also love her. These affections will surely be lost. These other *Jats* (races) love not, but hate, despise, and associate not with me and my relatives. I also, and my relatives similarly treat other Jats as unknown faces. If it has always been so and will always continue to be so, what worse misery can there be beyond this? Thinking of all these things, my mind was very unsettled, and not seeing any way to escape these evils, I got more and more distressed.

In the hour of his utter loneliness he lifted up his face to God. I can not explain it. I will not attempt to explain it. He had heard no preaching. He had read no religious books. There were no sacred memories to guide him. The little he had learned had but confused his intelligence and flung a deeper shadow across his path. In his sore need he appealed directly and intuitively to the Father of spirits, and thenceforward knew that "God is, and that he is the rewarder of them that diligently seek him."

The circumstances were such as to seal this faith upon his mind with unusual distinctness. He sometimes related them but always with a certain reticence of speech as of one who had seen and heard what it was scarcely "lawful for man to utter." On one of his solitary walks he had felt the sudden impulse to hide himself in the jungle and fight his pain. There in the quiet he poured out his soul, his long pent-up feelings finding vent in sobs and tears. But the bitterness was already passing. A gleam as of sunshine on a stormy day lightened his heart. "There must be," he thought, "there must be some spirit, better, stronger, wiser, and greater than the demons. If He please he can make opportunity to give an everlasting blessing." That cry of faith went up to heaven and was surely heard. In the hush that followed, a sense of healing touched him, pure and sweet as the falling dew. And he knew that he was not alone, that Another was near; One in whose presence no demons have any power to hurt or destroy; in whose being lie the sanction and surety of all our human love. To this untaught savage, as to the Hebrew singer of long ago, came the great discovery—the radiant truth that transfigures life: "All my springs are in thee."

A longing for fellowship filled him, and he began to pray:

> O Thou who art wiser, greater, better than all! Thou knowest my unrest of mind, and thou knowest the cause! I believe that if thou pleasest and choosest, thou canst rescue me from this distress and grant me an everlasting blessing.

There was no answer. No sound broke the stillness—either then or on the following day, when at the same hour and in the same solemn manner, he renewed his request. But he was willing to wait. And he had not long to wait.

> Having prayed thus for three evenings, on the last evening, there stood near my place of prayer a tall, dignified Person, and there sounded in my ears, as if spoken, the words, "Thy prayer is heard!"

We need not pry too curiously into this strange experience. It may never have happened to us. We may never have needed it to happen. "Blessed are they that have not seen and yet have believed!" But the reality of it to this poor Garo can in no wise be doubted. The vision he saw was not less vivid than that which came to Jacob at Bethel, and the voice that spoke to him was no other than that which Paul heard on the road to Damascus, and Cornelius, in his home by the sea.

Ramke's vision had freed him from fear. He continued at school, his outward circumstances the same, but inwardly everything was changed. Thought of demons sometimes recurred to him, but he knew their power was limited. They were held in leash, and could only go the length of their chains. Above them all and master of them all, was the one God Spirit who had said "Thy prayer is heard." To him, rather than to the spirits of evil, or to the beasts that perish, were men allied. They could commit themselves to his care. They were safe in his keeping; in him all souls were one. Whether savage or civilized, it made no difference; Garo or gosain,[1] black or white, a man was a man "for a' that." He belonged to a larger brotherhood than clan or race.

Thus released, the lad eagerly sought for fresher proofs of the Great Spirit's presence and working in the world,

[1] A Hindu religious mendicant of great authority.

and here new problems arose. What was he to think of the religious life around him? It was pretentious and subtle, sensuous and showy, but also mystical and unworldly; on the one hand pandering to the worst passions, and on the other preaching purity of heart, encouraging among the ignorant the worship of millions of gods, yet holding in reserve for the more spiritual a doctrine of divine Oneness that is all, and the goal of all. The bazaar at Goalpara was a hotbed of Hinduism. Painted idols had a niche in every shop and were worshiped in every house. Tawdry shrines stood at the street corners, while the black image of Kali, standing on the body of her husband, with lolling red tongue and necklace of skulls, looked out from the doorways, as before her yellow-robed priests, wearing the white thread across their breasts, moved to and fro, offering flowers and lights, muttering their *mantras,* waving their censers of incense or clanging the temple gong. By the steps outside could be seen a fork of wood, painted vermilion with blood just spilt in sacrifice, or a black kid might be tied to it waiting the hour of its fate. In sheds here and there stood cars of *Jagannath* (Juggernaut), scaffoldings of dirty wood, ready to be dressed and decorated for the annual procession of the stumplike image. At other points, on the side of the road or by the wall of a house, the *tulsi* bush set in its smooth-smeared clay pedestal like a plant in a pot; or greased pebbles and perhaps a *lingam* (phallus) at the foot of some old tree, bore witness to the daily homage paid to their gods. In certain seasons groups of images made of straw coated with clay and gaudily painted, might be seen set up in open spaces, surrounded by admiring crowds who brought lavish offerings to the priests sitting in front. Such was Hinduism as it caught the eye, the religion of the temple and the street, the faith of the populace and of the ignorant rapacious priests.

But there were devotees of a different sort, holy men who sat under the trees in rapt contemplation, oblivious of passing feet, and ascetic monks who lived in secluded *akras* (shelters of reeds) outside the town, and gave themselves up to prayer and to the study of sacred books. To these the heart of the lad was drawn, and as time went on he made their acquaintance, and told them of the vision and the voice. They did not despise him as others had done. They saw in this son of barbarism a spiritual soul, and took pains to instruct him, to make him a child of the faith. They lent him some of their books, and he spent his holidays poring over the Ramayana and the Mahabharata, those strange legendary epics so full of movement and color, in which gods and men play their part on the earthly stage in " one jumble of the true and the false; of absurdities and fine-sounding sentiments, of noble portraiture and impure imaginings, of wise sayings and grotesque marvels."

As he read he was much impressed by the story of Vishnu, the world-preserver, who is held to have repeatedly manifested his benevolent spirit to deliver men from the tyranny of their foes. His greatest incarnation is Ram, the hero of the Ramayana, a kingly figure of pure character, gracious spirit, and strong self-restraint. Very naturally the Garo lad learned to identify him with the object of his vision. " After I had mastered the school-books, I read the Hindu scriptures, thinking that the spirit called Ram or Vishnu was that greater and better One; I trusted in the hope that he was the one who had heard my prayer." Enamored thus of Hindu worship and Hindu ideals, he now sat at the feet of the Brahman gurus, and gave them unbounded reverence. But the true light was soon to be revealed to this earnest seeker for the day.

The Rev. Ruprecht Bion, a Baptist missionary at Dacca, afterward known as "the apostle of Eastern Bengal," was accustomed to spend several months of each year in visiting the neighboring districts with his colporters and preachers. It was laid on his heart to make still longer journeys to the distant parts of Assam. One of the first of these was in progress during the cold season of 1856.

The little flotilla touched at the various markets and bazaars on either side of the river, and in due course arrived at Goalpara. The missionary began to preach in the bazaar. With him was his Bengali evangelist, Ram Jivan Babu, father of Samuel Loveday, of Gauhati. Each held in his hands a bundle of leaflets and tracts which were given away at the close of the preaching; and there was an eager scramble for copies. The tracts of those days were pointed, uncompromising attacks on the falseness of the prevailing faiths. The sacred books were taken seriously, their errors refuted, ther insufficiency and harmfulness clearly exposed. These tracts left a smart, but produced a healthy reaction. Sounding a sharp challenge, they cleared the air, brought matters to a head, and released many minds from the thraldom of superstition and sin. They addressed themselves with irresistible arguments to the thought of the day; there was nothing namby-pamby or pietistic about them; they were virile, not to say vehement; and they frequently carried all before them by their vigorous contact with awakened minds.

At last, tired, hot, and hungry the missionary and his evangelist returned to their boat. Mr. Bion, quick and observant and with a ready pen for incidents, found nothing worthy of special record in writing his diary. But much had happened.

They left behind them a wrangling crowd. As the tracts were examined a great hubbub arose. Some were torn in pieces, others were trampled under foot. The priests running out of their temples cursed them, extending the curse to all who should read them, meanwhile snatching the papers from unwilling hands. But all this fume and fury set the bystanders thinking, and tended to put a high value upon the few that had not been destroyed. There must be some strange power in the little books, else why such anxiety to be rid of them? Why this opposition so loud and shrill? Presently the crowd dispersed, the missionaries' boat edged off the shore with a prayer that some good might be done; and the first act in the little drama was over.

The next takes us to the Garo school. One or two of the boys had heard the preaching and secured copies of the tracts. The priests had neither dared nor cared to interfere with them. The leaflets were triumphantly displayed and lots cast for some, while pice were offered for others. There was a brisk competition for them among certain of the boys. Ramke, now a young man of about twenty, purchased one for two or three pice. The reading of it completely unsettled his mind. In a pathetic passage he says:

> I got the book called "Apatti Nashak." This book showed many proofs that those things trusting in which the Hindus hoped to obtain heaven were all untrue. Then the trust I had in Ram was also gone, and my mind was again lost.

His visits to the gurus ceased and he was more unhappy than ever. Some relief came in his appointment to Rongjuli for a year as a teacher in the primary school. This kept him busy, but what a change in him since the time, when as a wild boy from the jungle he ran about with hunger for education in his heart, and a wistful look in his bright black eyes! And with what altered feelings he now regarded his kinsmen, as they came to him in their savage state, and told him stories of drunken revels and hairbreadth escapes from the demons!

When the year was over he went back to Goalpara, and one day, to his great delight, received a letter from Omed. "I have found a Christian," it ran, "and there is much to talk about. Come to Gauhati as soon as you can." An opportunity presented itself almost at once. There was at Gauhati a normal school for further training. Ramke applied and was admitted. He went to Gauhati and lived with Omed. Talking over their separate experiences, the younger as of old leaning on the judgment of the elder, said at last:

> We Garos have no religion, but it is certainly necessary for us to seek some way of obtaining good after death. Which of the three religions—that of the Hindus, Mohammedans, or sahibs—is it best for us to receive?

Omed's answer was characteristically shrewd.

> We do not know the Mohammedan religion; the Hindus observe caste, and if we take their religion we must forsake our people; the sahibs do not observe caste, therefore to receive their religion is good in every respect.

Then they two went together to hear Kandura Babu, and to learn the sahibs' religion.

Their progress was naturally slow. It was a new and strange step they contemplated, and it behooved them to be cautious. The Christian religion did not seem to be popular, yet it drew them insensibly on. But there was to be still another break.

After less than a year together Ramke was sent for by Deputy Commissioner Becket, then at Goalpara, and set over a small squad of frontier police at Nibari Market. The work was entirely uncongenial, but his request for another term at the Gauhati school was denied. This was the saddest period of Ramke's life. Four months at Nibari were followed by three years at Jira. "In that way," he says,

> our first endeavor to get a religion was lost. After I left probably Omed thought no further on the subject. I, also, doing police work, did many bad things, and fell entirely into sin.

But he was not forsaken; there came a day when his sense of sinfulness sharpened his sense of need. Instinctively he turned to the Christian books, and rummaging among them, picked out one which Reban had given him some time before, having received it as a prize in school. It was a tale of suffering under persecution of a little girl, called Elizabeth, whose simple faith and quiet heroism had saved her parents from death. It showed the power of Christ to make a life beautiful and strong. As Ramke read it touched his imagination and kindled his love. He was not far from the kingdom now, this Garo policeman; indeed it was already in his heart.

XI

THE BRIDE OF AMJONGA

EVENTS began to crowd upon one another in quick succession. Ramke was transferred to Damra, another market at the foot of the hills, and there, after some months of further service, his career as policeman ended.

But before this happened, he married. Let us step aside to listen to the pealing of the wedding-bells, which, translated into Garo, means fierce beating of drums, and to watch the merry jostle of feet. The scene is laid in the lovely village of Amjonga, six miles away. The village stands a little apart, half-hidden and embowered, a most refreshing nest of shade and coolness after the hot glare of the white dusty road. Green clumps of bamboo dangle their graceful fronds over the roofs of the houses, and all about green grass carpets the ground. This is the home of the bride, a blithe little Garo lassie, whose name is Suban. When I saw her thirty years later, she was small, with soft face, gentle manners, and a pleasant voice. Her eyes sparkled as she talked, and she must have had at some time a very winsome smile. It was of that time we were thinking as we talked—of the days when her heart was young, and the bright face and girlish figure drew longing looks as she flitted among the trees. I guessed that there were other swains in Amjonga who had reason to envy Ramke.

She told me the story of their courtship and early trials. It was a simple story, very briefly told, but touching in its artlessness, and not without a spice of mother wit: "I first met him when he was doing police work there in Damra." That was how it began. That is how every love in Garo ought to begin, for the maidens do the wooing, not the men. It is always she who meets him, and not he who meets her! She went one day to the market, the center of a light-hearted circle of relatives, and the merriest of them all. Perhaps she had often been before; certainly she would often come again. She enjoyed it immensely; the hum of the market-ground, the haggling of buyers and sellers, the unwonted excitement and animation ran like wine through her blood. She liked to be in the midst of these moving scenes. She liked sitting behind her basket of fruit, to watch and wait, while others of her party went in and out about their business. The living panorama was many-colored, and quick to change. Like bits of glass in a kaleidoscope, the people slipped back and forth, every fresh movement grouping a new picture, brighter than the last. And she chatted and laughed incessantly, making shrewd comments and happy hits, as she scanned unfamiliar faces, and caught scraps of busy talk.

Nothing escaped her. Least of all the person and self-possession of a young man in uniform, who seemed to be wanted everywhere, to whom disputes were referred, and delinquents brought, whose very presence breathed authority and calm! How patiently he listened and how pleasantly he spoke! Would he come again that way, she wondered? Had he noticed her as he passed? Her eyes followed him with approval till the market broke up, and maidenlike, she asked skilful questions about him on the homeward way. What else is there to tell? When a woman wills, she wills, at all events a Garo woman will. "I met him," she had said, as one would say, "I came,

I saw, I conquered." Having met him, and knowing him to be the man for her, she straightway chose to marry him. What could be more simple than that? Why linger over the intermediate steps? She took a fancy to him, and then she took him. There you have the whole story!

Certain preliminaries must, of course, be arranged. He must know and understand and desire it himself. The market had quite a new attraction for her now. She sat in the old place with her basket, but the old loquaciousness was gone. She let the crowds pass and missed a thousand chances of repartee. But if a turban and a tunic came near, she photographed every movement, and laid up in her memory every word. It soon got wind. There were plenty of birds to carry such happy news. Barkis was willing, and the wedding took place. There was the usual sacrifice of cock and hen, the usual feasting and drinking, the usual beating of drums and noisy revel. But it was Ramke's last concession to demon-worship. There was one in that merry company, and he the bridegroom, out of all sympathy with the coarseness and the clamor, though full of gladness at the thought of his little bride.

When it was over he told her of the things that had long lain in his mind. They shocked her, and he was disappointed. But she pondered them in her heart, and the more she thought over them, the more perplexed and distressed she became. It was terrifying to carry such a secret. What would her people say and do if they knew! Her husband spoke, not like a Garo, but like a stranger—he talked of becoming a Christian. She did not in the least know what that meant, but she knew it was something dreadful, something that would inevitably bring down upon them the rage of their friends and the pitiless vengeance of the demons. Thus passed the first months of their married life. But all the while an increasing reverence for her husband was possessing her. She knew that he was wiser and worthier than others, and that he loved her truly. Perhaps this trouble in his mind would pass away. She could not understand it; she would try to forget it. She would make him a happy home, and possibly he would forget it too.

During these months letters passed frequently between Ramke and Omed. She could not read them, but she gathered their drift. Her sky clouded as often as they came. She felt sure a plot was brewing, and knew not what to expect. The end was precipitated by an event which neither husband nor wife had anticipated. Ramke was dismissed. Suban knew by his mood of suppressed excitement that something was wrong. One morning he took tender leave of her, saying that he was going to Jira to get some money from his brother, and would come back soon, but could not tell just when. She watched and waited for him until the days lengthened into weeks and still no news. Evening after evening she would stand on the road looking afar for the figure she knew so well. But each time as the sun set her hope set with it for another day. Body and mind would chill as the night mists crept round and wrapped her like a shroud. At last she heard that he had passed through Jira to Goalpara, and from there gone by steamer to Gauhati. Perhaps she had an inkling that other than human power was spiriting him away. At any rate that was the truth. He had heard the voice that came to Abram: "Get thee out of thy country, and from thy kindred, and from thy father's house, unto the land which I will shew thee." And having heard he could not rest until he had obeyed. A fire and burning was in his bones. In a spiritual sense "he went out, not knowing whither he went."

The fragrance of Suban's love was never sweeter and fresher than in those days when she was left alone. Report came that Ramke had declared himself a Christian, and therefore denied his kindred. Her parents tried to persuade her to give him up. But she would not listen. Nothing they urged against him moved her. Not even when bluntly they said that he had deserted her, and would never come back. Her trust in him was perfect, and she elected to wait. This was very hard, but hardest of all when their first child was born—and died. But the brave little mother nursed her grief in silence, and had great store of patience. At length came the welcome news that he had obtained employment at Gauhati, as writer in the commissioner's court, and that he wished her to join him without delay. With a glad heart she went, her troubles for the time over, her trust justified and blessed.

Long afterward, as she reviewed her life, she saw that her faith in her husband was God's means to bring her to himself.

XII

THE BAPTISM AT SUKHESWAR GHAT

LONG before Ramke joined him, Omed had made up his mind. He was going to be a Christian, and it was not a matter that would brook further delay. On the very first opportunity he meant to be baptized. His letters to his nephew were full of this one theme, and the earnest entreaty that Ramke would also decide, so that if possible, they might be baptized together. He had always been the leader; he was the leader now.

The spirit of the Christian Scriptures, the influence of the Bengali suboverseer, young Samuel Loveday, and the preaching and winsome conversations of Kandura, had worked this change in the man. He was no longer a spectator, looking at religion from without; he was a disciple, looking at it from within. Christianity had attracted him from the beginning. Now it had won him. This made itself felt both in bearing and conduct; he had lost none of his directness and vigor; he was as smart a sepoy, and as cheery a comrade as ever. But he was a different man. A spell was upon him that altered his attitude in the old relationships and created new ones. It was a spiritual attachment; he was a lover of Jesus Christ. The effect was humbling and yet exalting. He saw himself loosed from his sins, and was perpetually thinking of the debt he owed to his Saviour. And living in faith in the Son of God, he was conscious also of a dignity independent of earthly conditions that no ribaldry could reach and no threats destroy.

As a man of action, he was ready for any discipline and any service. On a hint from Mr. Bronson he had entirely abandoned the use of liquor—perhaps the severest test a Garo can undergo. His instincts were soldierly. The lowliest of learners in the mission church, he was yet the most contemptuous of critics in the idolatrous bazaar. He had strong and ardent affections. With the courage of his convictions and a fine sense of his natural gifts, he strove incessantly to bring his comrades captive to Christ. But it was an up-hill fight. Some listened and were almost won; others derided and denounced him as a renegade; many thought him mad. He wrote letters to his early associates, and sent them copies of the little books. To Ramke he disclosed his heart, and nothing gladdened him more than the coming of his friend. They went together to Kandura's house, and there Ramke was led, as Omed had been before him, into the full knowledge and acceptance of the truth.

It was the crowning distinction of Kandura's career, that he played so important a part in ushering into the kingdom these two Garos, the first of their tribe. We ought to know more about him than merely his name. Born an Assamese, he was now a young man of twenty-five or thirty years of age, well educated, good-looking, and able to speak more or less in three languages, Assamese, Bengali, and English. He had come to Gauhati four years before, 1857-1858, for a clerkship under Government on a monthly salary of forty rupees.

In 1843 Mr. Bronson had started an orphan institution at Nowgong, which, though discontinued in 1856, was one of the most effective agencies for the kingdom ever planted in Assam. Kandura entered this in 1848. Mrs. Stoddard, then in charge, says that she saw him first at the gate, a little beggar boy with a bright face, leading his blind father by the hand and asking for alms. She took a fancy to him and asked the father to give him up. They were miserably poor and there was a younger brother who could act as guide; so Kandura was allowed to come. He was soon a favorite with Mrs. Stoddard, teaching her the sounds of Assamese while she gave him lessons in English. The boy made rapid progress, delighting in his books, and most of all in the Bible. It opened a new world to him, chained his imagination and fed the springs of his thought. After two years he was baptized, and given the name of Smith, "which it was reasonably hoped he might live up to!" As he grew older he developed a good business capacity, and obtained the post in Gauhati. There he became a leader of the church, and at last resigned the clerkship for the pastorate, on a stipend of fifteen rupees.

Omed and Ramke were now ready for baptism, but there was no missionary in Gauhati, and Kandura had not yet been ordained. The nearest help lay in Nowgong, a hundred miles away. Word was sent to Doctor Bronson, who had been particularly anxious that Gauhati, the headquarters station, with its beautiful mission premises, "on a site unsurpassed in picturesqueness by any place on the wonderful Hudson," should be immediately remanned. He could not understand the continued neglect of the Board or the apathy of the home churches. Had he but known it, this very news from Gauhati was the morning star of that brighter day of recognition and encouragement from the missionary board. And in the good providence of God it was given to him, as a fit reward for his faithfulness, to witness its rising and herald its light.

He made haste to come, but by the time of his arrival, the candidates had been kept waiting nearly a year. Mrs.

Photo by A. E. Scallon.

Bungalow at Goalpara

Photo by W. Carey.

Scene of the Baptism of the First Garo Converts.
Sukheswar Ghat. Gauhati

Bronson and Mr. and Mrs. Scott accompanied him. The first to meet them was Omed, who instantly presented his request. "What testimonials have you?" said the missionary. "None," said the sepoy. "Ask my major." The major spoke of him in the terms of highest praise. Other credentials were forthcoming, and Omed passed. It was now Ramke's turn. "Take him," said the uncle, "if you take me." And in the end they took him. There were three more to be examined, and all were approved. One was Bhupati, an Assamese, brother to Kandura's wife, Itee. He had been greatly enraged at his sister's acceptance of Christianity and had forcibly tried to prevent her baptism two years before. The others were Kandura Bairagi and his wife, an elderly couple of the Kachari race.

The baptism took place on Sunday, February 8, 1863. There was first a service in the beautiful little brick chapel by the riverside, built by Messrs. Danforth and Ward. After the service the congregation passed out by the gate, along the broad road in the shade of the fine old trees, and stood on the steps of the Sukheswar Ghat. A white tent had been erected close by. The river shone in the noonday, relieved by the dark bank of well-wooded rocks on the other shore. At the right, a little up-stream, rose the island of Umananda—sacred to Siva—two of its domes peering out above the trees at this unwonted sight. The temple gongs seemed to sound a challenge across the stream. Close at hand the arched gateway of the ghat reared itself in stately beauty, white, against the background of green. It was a picture for the artist's brush with its focus on the living group near the water's edge. This consisted of an inner circle of Europeans, with Kandura and the candidates in the center, and a crowd of lightly clad spectators hemming them around. Sepoys in uniform stood by watching the scene. A hymn was sung, and Mr. Bronson went down into the water, and stood facing the gap. The first to follow was Bhupati. Omed came next, every inch a soldier, with head erect, and steady, unwavering steps, then Ramke, and last of all, the two tottering pilgrims, hand in hand. Five times over the waters parted in token of burial and of reunion with Him who rose again from the dead. The temple bell was answered. The mighty current, with its secret, flowing half around the Garo Hills, rolled on its way.

That afternoon, for the first time, erstwhile savage Garos sat down at the table of the Lord, and in holy fellowship with him and with those who had pointed them to him as the Lamb of God who taketh away the sin of the world, they partook of the emblems of his broken body and poured-out blood.

XIII

BACK TO THE HILLS

AFTER the baptism the two Garos considered what they would do next. " Is there no missionary for our people ? " said Omed to Mr. Bronson. " If one will come I will take my discharge from the regiment and go with him."

Thus early did the work for which he was destined call him. The whole world he knew was " lying in the wicked one " waiting for the redemption of Christ. But that part which was especially his, how dark it was! With what added circumstances of grim terror and complete subjection were his poor tribesmen found in their wild, and to other than Garos, as yet inaccessible hills! On him surely, the first to be freed, lay the duty of proclaiming the liberty purchased for all.

But the way seemed barred. No missionary was available to give direction and encouragement. He had not yet faced the possibility of going alone. For a whole year the project lay in abeyance. Meanwhile his purpose grew. Ramke was ready to accompany him, and thus these two men were more closely knit together by their common resolve. But it was a difficult task to win over their wives to an enterprise so hazardous and amazing. Epiri, the wife of Omed, being an Assamese, could not share the racial sympathies of her husband. And neither she nor Suban was willing to avow herself a Christian. They had disapproved the recent baptisms of their husbands, and both had declined to be present.

It was hard for them to be reconciled to the thought of alienation from all of their friends. But they could not withhold admiration for the spirit and conduct of their husbands, and little by little they entered into sympathy with their plans.

Mr. Bronson kept in touch with the converts by means of correspondence and reports. In November he paid them a visit, and found that they had been subjected to reproach and many temptations, but were still immovable, bearing their cross humbly, and laboring to bring others to the Saviour. They said:

> If there were a missionary here we would strike our names from the government list and go and teach our people. But we are too ignorant now to go forth. We are often worldly and wicked during the week, but when we come on the Sabbath and hear brother Kandura explain the Bible, our hearts get happy and fixed.

Major Agnew, the commissioner, gave these two Garo converts a good character, and offered them the chance of special training at Nowgong, together with six dollars a month for their support. Ramke was willing, and so was Omed's wife. But Suban and Omed held back. " I am too old," said Omed, " to learn more. I had rather go and teach what I know." There was a deadlock, but events proved his wisdom.

A few months later Mr. Bronson was again at Gauhati. Omed's will had prevailed. When they came to state their decision it happened that the one man best able to help them, Captain B. W. D. Morton, was present. Zealous to reclaim the Garos from barbarism by all the means at his command, he was particularly interested in this indigenous effort; and as he himself was a consistent Christian, he was able to appreciate the motives and share the hopes of these first converts from the tribe. Entering warmly into their proposition, he offered every assistance, and promised to contribute to their support. So the die was cast. Application was immediately made to the commissioner, Colonel Henry Hopkinson, in whose office Ramke was a writer, and to Colonel R. Campbell, commanding Omed's regiment, for their discharge. Both responded with Christian courtesy and with expressions of interest in the undertaking. Colonel Campbell wrote:

> I am sorry that Omed wishes to leave the regiment, as he is a very steady, well-conducted sepoy, but I, of course, can not keep him against his desire, as there are no reasons that I could at present urge for doing so. Consequently he will be free on the next proximo, March, 1864, to go and commence his mission, in which I need hardly say I sincerely trust he will succeed.

In due time they received their appointment as "mission assistants," with the promise of maintenance from Mr. Bronson, who fortunately felt free to act without waiting for sanction from home. The only instruction given was to confer with Captain Morton as they passed through Goalpara to the hills.

After some delay the little party of seven, Omed, his wife and three children, Ramke and Suban, took boat down the river and arrived at Goalpara on May 10. The two men, now thoroughly committed to their enterprise, went immediately to Captain Morton, who spoke encouragingly to them, and duly reported the interview to the missionary at Nowgong. "If God prosper the work," he wrote, "who can tell to what this small beginning may lead?"

Their first endeavor was to gain the good will of their relatives. Two of these, Reban and Fokira, the first a cousin, and the second a brother of Ramke, and both nephews of Omed, were then at Goalpara. Reban was employed as interpreter at the court. Fokira had come as a witness in a case. On explaining the object of their mission, Reban would have nothing to say to them; but Fokira was friendly and willing to help. It had been arranged that Ramke should open a school at Damra, as a sort of base for the mission, and Omed tour among the villages on the heights above. For the one was a born teacher, the other a pioneer. Arrived at Damra, they spent a few days at the *tana* (police station), astonishing the policemen by their presence, and still more by their words. At the market they preached. It was the first time that a Christian advocate had spoken there. Then while a schoolhouse was building they all went up to the hills. Their objectives were Matchokgiri Dambora, and Watrepara. As men after a long sojourn in far lands, come back to revisit the scenes of their childhood, so they went up with beating hearts. The deep silence of the jungle wrapped them around, laden with haunting memories. They lingered by the streams and pools to cool their feet, but ever the old tracks lured them on. They paused at familiar places to recall forgotten events, and quickened their pace as they breasted the last ridge that hid from them the sight of home. How little changed it was after all these years! How well they remembered some of the faces in the doorways, and some of the workers in the fields! But these looked at them askance, as if they had been intruders, and answered them curtly, wondering at their altered appearances and new accent of speech.

It was in truth a rather doubtful reception, with latent hostile possibilities. They felt as men feel in an enemies' country, though it was their own. And they had a message to deliver, which they knew would tax all their resources of faith, patience, and skill. The news of their coming had outstripped them, and a strong feeling of resentment was already aroused. Even their relatives were half afraid, and not a little reluctant to give them shelter and food. But the time had come to test their courage, and they did not flinch. They spent a day or two going from house to house preparing the way, and then, having prayed much for guidance, invited the whole village to come and hear.

What a sight it was, that first gathering of wild Garos in their mountain home to hear the Galilean story! The setting was a crescent of bamboo dwellings, poised on a cliff-point, in an emerald hollow of jungle-covered hills. An excited crowd gathered about the *nokpante* (village bachelor-house), and made a deep ring on the open space in front. The chief sat in the place of honor, and other leaders on either side. Swords were stuck into the ground before them, for the gathering had all the formality of a council, and representatives from other villages were present. All squatted on the ground, their black eyes shining under bent brows, fixed on Omed as he rose to speak. It was a moment to try the nerve of the bravest. But the speaker knew the way to their hearts. " Brothers," he said,

the Garos believe in demons, but there are no demons. At any rate there are no demons that have power to hurt us. God alone has power and God is good. But, as for us, we are not good. We have sinned against God. Therefore we are all condemned, and the great power of God is against us. What shall we do? We can do nothing. But there is One who has done everything for us. He was a man like ourselves, but he was good like God. And he sent him to save us. He willingly offered himself a sacrifice for our sins, and all who trust him are forgiven. He rose again after death, and is now alive in the presence of God. His spirit possesses those who love him so they too become good. And when they die they go to be with him forever, where there is no more sorrow or sickness or sin. This is the true religion. We, your brothers, who believe it, have great joy in our hearts.

And this joy is for all the Garos if they give up the worship of demons and turn to God. Therefore we have brought you the message.

When he had finished there was instant clamor and a burst of pent-up indignation. "What," they exclaimed,

you a Garo, born of a Garo mother, do you presume to know more than the whole Garo tribe, and to teach us, your elder relatives? How did you dare to come here, slighting the demons, and trying to deceive us by pretending that they have no power to hurt or to kill? They have heard your words, and they will have their revenge. Beware lest some sudden calamity come upon you! We follow you indeed! We are not such fools! Who cares for your religion, and who will accept it?

It was a fierce rejoinder and must have blanched the cheeks of the feeble disciples who heard it. It was one thing to think calmly of these things in the chapel at Gauhati, or in Kandura's house among sympathetic friends; and quite another to utter them in the demon-haunted hills, with every natural fear, quickened by the anger of the people, tugging at their breasts. But Omed was not a soldier for nothing. He stood the fire bravely and stuck to his guns. And there were some, when the clamor had subsided, and the crowd mockingly dispersed, who drew near in the gathering darkness for further talk. "They thought much in their minds, and were pleased, saying, 'The word is truly good.'"

Thus was their mission begun, and had they done nothing else they would have proved themselves worthy of a place among the heroes of the faith. In a few days Ramke returned to Damra, taking his youngest brother and two other boys with him as a nucleus for his school. He taught them the Scriptures, and every evening they gathered for prayer. His deep religious spirit imparted itself to his scholars. They too learned to pray, and, once a week, voluntarily to fast.

XIV

THE HUT AT THE FOOT OF THE PASS

IT is a poor little hut at the foot of the Rajasimla pass. Omed and his wife have made it of bamboos and grass, clearing a place for it in the jungle on the banks of a stream. They are quite alone. Wild beasts prowl around at night. The dark mountain looms up behind, black as jet, with jagged edge, clear against the sky. The moon rises on the other side, but takes a long time to top the edge. But lustrous stars hang over and shed soft radiance down upon the open space and the little hut. The waters of the stream catch it as they go gliding by. In the hut the man and wife are sleeping; now and then they start in their dreams. What has happened, and why are they here?

Six months have passed since they first went up to Watrepara. They stayed there as long as they could, working from that center to the villages near, talking, preaching, persuading. They were ridiculed and reproached. At last they were driven away. The cholera did that: there were eight deaths within two or three days. Their own child was taken. The neighbors said it was a judgment; a judgment on the village for harboring their presence, and on them for their disbelief. They turned their steps sorrowfully away, the few of whom they had hopes now deserting them, and came down to the foot of the pass. For three weeks they slept under a tree, taking turns at watching, while they were cutting the jungle, and building their little hut.

Have they abandoned their purpose? Not at all. On the contrary this spot has been chosen skilfully to further their plan of campaign. The little hut stands in the angle on an elevation of ground, overlooking the point where two paths meet, as the two valleys cross, and the Garos pass and repass on either side, as they visit the markets on the plains. Omed can hear them coming, and, if he pleases, join them as they go by, or wait and watch for their return. He has calculated well. It is pleasant to have a resting-place, where one can put down one's load, for a chat or a smoke, sure of being kindly entertained. The hut is already a "house of call," where everything is free, and every one made welcome. The gleam of its tiny light can be seen through the jungle, and belated home-goers hasten on less afraid. Round its cheery fire, blazing in the open, savage groups come often to squat, men and women sitting far into the night, while the talk runs deep.

The little hut is also a house of prayer. It stands a silent witness to the simple, satisfying faith. There are no bamboos stuck around it sprinkled with blood. No priest of the demons goes there to practise his magic spells. No drink is brewed. But there is much reading of a sacred book that sounds good to hear, and much reverent yet familiar speech with the Good Spirit, such as falls, even upon a wild man's heart, like a whisper of peace. All this must needs be explained, and Omed loves nothing better than to tell and commend his trust. His wife is one with him now; bravely and without complaint she is sharing his life. Still it is very lonely; but a soldier on picket duty must not think of that.

A year goes by. The little grass hut has grown, and four more stand by it. A larger clearing has been made, and the banks of the stream are sown with crops. One by one, seven of Omed's people have cast their lot with him. They have ceased the worship of demons. They are learning the new religion. But this has angered their friends, and there is a ferment in the village above.

The excitement is increased by a failure of the rains. The hill crops are beginning to burn. The streams are running dry. Weeks have passed and still no showers have fallen. Sacrifices are offered, doubled, multiplied, but the demons pay no heed. They have shut up the rains. The priests say it is because of the new religion. The feeling thus aroused is intense and spreading. The settlement is regarded with evil eyes. The temper of the people is dangerous. A single spark would set the whole neighborhood in a blaze.

The spark is lighted by Omed, whether unwillingly or of set purpose, it is difficult to say. He is bold enough to do it on purpose. Perhaps it is his answer to all this cringing talk of the demon's power. At all events there is a Samson-like grotesqueness and contemptuousness in what he does.

> I have told you there are no demons. You say they have shut up the rains. Bah! I will show you what I think of them. You shall see for yourselves what bogeys they are.

All this and much more may be the meaning of what he is about to do. He will put the demons to open shame, and he will choose a conspicuous mark. East of Rajasimla and towering above it, wreathed in the mists of the morning, is a black peak that rises nearly two thousand feet. Its name is Koasi, perhaps from a root meaning mist or fog. The mist spells mystery to the savage mind. A powerful demon haunts the mountain. His seat is on the summit. He is greatly feared. A rude stairway leads up the steep ascent. It is strewn on occasion, with little cages, in which puppies and poultry have been taken up to be sacrificed. Dark stains smear the steps and spatter the little bunches of leaves set up here and there at the sides. It is an ascent of blood. At certain seasons there is a constant succession of pilgrims toiling up. The trees on the summit are sacred, and sacred stones lie at their roots, which have been watered with blood. A litter of sacrificial relics lies all about—egg-shells, feathers, tufts of bamboo, blood. The worship of this demon dominates the country round. No mere godling of the glen, or sprite of wood and the stream is he, but a powerful fiend whose voice is thunder, whose tread shakes the earth. Not a bamboo may be cut on all his sacred hill. Omed deliberately goes up and one or two with him. Scornfully, scoffingly, they ascend the steps, not deigning to kick aside the empty baskets on their way, their eyes fixed on the summit, their swords held firmly in hand. They gain the top, seize the stones and scatter them about. They plant their feet where the stones lay, slash the trees that overshadow them, and cut a bundle of bamboos as trophies from the grove. The Garos come out of their villages like hornets, whose nest is disturbed, with an angry buzz and ready to strike. Some visit the desecrated spot. Others hold a council of vengeance. The offended demon must be quickly appeased, or their lives, as well as their crops, will perish. They determine to kill the Christians.

Plotting begins. Plans must be carefully laid. Responsibility must be shared. The villages concerned must be sworn to secrecy and must act with caution. For these men are known to Government. Their massacre would be avenged. An expedition would be sent, the murderers demanded, and, if not given up, hunted, and their villages burned. The sahib at Goalpara, Captain Morton, had already hunted many, and they were caught and hanged. There are conflicting counsels, and it will take time to arrange all.

It is market-day at Rongjuli. Omed and others of the Christians are there. Some of the wilder bloods, maddened at the sight of them, suddenly make a furious attack. The police rush to the rescue, and arrest the ringleaders, but Garos from many parts interfere, and many run away, for they have no fancy of being shot down in the open. There is a fierce altercation, a rough scrimmage, and the market breaks up in confusion.

The Christians have escaped with a few knocks and bruises. But they know now that their lives are in jeopardy, and secret information is obtained that a raid on Rajasimla has been planned. They go back to the settlement with anxious hearts. Those who have been left behind are trembling with fear, for they have heard alarming accounts of the occurrence from passing Garos going back to the hills. Some have cursed them and cast evil looks. Others have called out, "You can't escape, you will soon be killed, and we shall have your heads."

The danger is imminent. They know what a raid means; the stealthy approach at dead of night, the sudden shout and swoop, the firing of the houses, the prod of the spear and the hack of the sword, before the victims are half awake, and the ghastly sawing at the throat. They know that no one is spared, man, woman, or little child. So they set a watch both day and night. Fires are lighted all around the small circle of huts. Every precaution is taken. But how few they are, how feeble and defenseless! If the Garos attack in force they will be overwhelmed in a moment. For three days no one can sleep. All night they watch and listen. Every sound makes them start. The strain on body and mind is great.

Meanwhile, news of the affair has reached Goalpara. The Rongjuli head constable has sent in his report. A messenger from Omed has summoned Ramke from Damra, and gone on to Captain Morton, with a letter from Ramke. The captain takes instant action. He starts for Rongjuli with fifty men of the frontier police.

Ramke is at Rajasimla. Omed had told him what had happened. He understands the deed done on Koasi Hill. But it seems to him an indiscretion. Omed too, perhaps, regrets now having put all their lives to such needless hazard. But all trust him, and all admire the boldness and challenge of the deed. It is not like him to be incautious. He says it was an impulse; he could not do otherwise and good is bound to result. But at present all is at stake. They wait for the expected attack. They are nervous, uneasy, and much afraid. They take turns to watch, and do not forget to pray. Ramke says, in telling the story, "We watched through the nights for a week, without sleep." One thing cheers them. No one who joined the settlement before the outbreak now runs away. During this very week others come, regardless of what may happen.

Again it is market-day at Rongjuli. The deputy commissioner is present. The chiefs of the neighboring villages are called to stand before the sahib. A ring of spectators is formed.

"Do you want to kill these men?" he asks.

"Yes," comes the answer, while a murmur of approval goes round.

"For what reason?"

"Because they are Christians and do not fear the demons."

"What reason is that? I am a Christian too. Do you want to kill me?"

"They have brought this name into our country. We have never heard it before. We do not want it."

"It is not good to be ignorant. Consider what they say. They also are Garos."

"We will not consider. The demons are angry. They will wreak vengeance upon us."

"Be it so then. But why interfere with these men? They live apart. Let them alone."

"It is they who have angered the demons. Their coming has brought cholera and shut up the rains. As long as they live we shall suffer. They must certainly die. The demons will see to that."

"Well, let the demons settle it. They have done nothing yet, have they, though Omed defied them? But mind you keep your hands off, or I shall have to settle with you. You have made a mistake. You think there are only two Christians in the world. There are thousands. They will come and punish you if you touch these men. Demons or no demons, we'll not have murder."

A silence.

"You clearly understand?"

"We understand."

"Then remember and obey."

The chiefs are dismissed. The gong sounds. The market is open. The sahib's words are carried from mouth to mouth, and from stall to stall. They are quoted a hundred times, turned over, discussed, and retold, as the people file off from the grounds. They are carried far up into the hills, and told again in a dozen villages by the evening fire.

Thanksgiving is offered around the hut at the foot of the pass. The little settlement is still anxious but less afraid. Captain Morton has saved them for the time. But it remains to be seen whether his word will be obeyed.

Rajasimla is not in British territory; it is just over the line. The Garos may yet carry out their threat. They have raided often; they may raid again. But the chiefs are tributary. They acknowledge fealty to Government, and know that the sahib keeps his word. Moreover the fifty sepoys will stay at Rongjuli until the danger is past.

Suddenly there is an abundance of rain. The surprise of this turns the current of the people's thoughts. The demons must be less powerful or less angry than they feared. It is a token to be taken note of, a sign that the sahib's words are approved. The idea of a raid is abandoned, and the settlement is safe. The little hut becomes more than ever a star of hope and a standard of victory.

XV

RANGKU TO THE RESCUE

MEANTIME, far away on the other side of the Brahmaputra, among the mountains of Bhutan, a third Garo was being prepared to become the comrade of the first two in their pioneering work. The border between Bengal and Bhutan had long been harried by the mountaineers, and in 1863 Mr. Ashley Eden, afterwards lieutenant-governor, being sent as envoy to demand reparation was grossly insulted, and forced to sign a dishonorable treaty, which the viceroy on his return at once disavowed.

Among the sepoys who served throughout these troubles was a young Garo named Rangku, a brother of Reban, and nephew of Omed. He had visited Omed and Ramke when they were in school at Goalpara, and asked to be admitted as a pupil. But the deputy commissioner had advised him to return home and work with his hands, desiring no more boys from that particular part of the hills. Rangku, much disappointed, remained however with Ramke and Omed for a time, and they taught him the alphabet. Ramke also taught him to say on rising and sitting, "Ram! Ram!" and on retiring "Harisal!" declaring it would make him happy. Five years later, hearing that Sadrag, a brother-in-law of Omed, was about to visit him at Gauhati, and being still ambitious for an education, Rangku resolved to accompany him. The two tramped the five days' journey, sleeping in the jungle and cooking their food by the roadside. This was in

1857 before the trunk road was made. He remained with Omed for six months, then asked to join the regiment. The commandant said, "Why, you're only a boy. You can't be more than fifteen. Can you lift a gun?" Immediately he shouldered one. "All right," said the commandant; "go to the doctor." There was another candidate for enlistment. The two were set to run. Rangku beat and was accepted. Nine months later the mutiny broke out, and being then fully accoutered as a soldier he was sent to Saporino to patrol the road. In due time he returned to Gauhati, where he spent the next seven years, learning much from Ramke, who recalling their former conversation, told him how he had come to disbelieve in the Hindu gods and to accept Jesus Christ as his Saviour. Bit by bit he was taught to read Bengali and a little English. Later, and shortly before the baptism of the other two, he was drafted to Bhutan, where he assisted in piling and burning one hundred and thirty bodies of the slain. Throughout this he carried in his knapsack the little hymn-book in Assamese which he had purchased on the mission compound at Gauhati. When the war was over he took his discharge and sought out Kandura. The latter urged him to come and live with him, and after a few months wrote Mr. Bronson that there was a believer waiting to be baptized. Mr. Bronson replied, "Send him here," and, on his arrival, gave him work to do, a little room to stay in, and an Assamese New Testament to read, with the injunction, quite unnecessary in the case of a Garo, not to be afraid to ask questions. After a month or two, on April 6, 1866, he was baptized. Mr. Bronson, taking him by the hand, said:

> You are my brother. From today the responsibility of God rests upon you. You know it. You know his commands. We love to make these known. Don't be ashamed. Don't be

afraid. If in any way you turn or change it will be very distressing.

His one wish was to join his countrymen in the work they were doing. The Bronsons were delighted and surprised to find him so well grounded in the doctrines of the Bible.

We have reason to think that he gave his whole heart to God soon after hearing the truth for the first time. He has won our love by his humble deportment, patient study of the Scriptures, and thoroughness of character. I cannot, I dare not keep Rangku back. I shall send him if I have to support him out of my own pocket.

Mrs. Bronson wrote,

He is a jewel. His talents are of the highest order. But his Christian character is what gives us most satisfaction. The influence of his example has been most salutary on the members of the school and church. His faith in God, his vivid conception of spiritual things, and his consecration to the cause of Christ give him a weight, a momentum that exceeds anything we have seen among this people. We are so accustomed to halting, timid disciples that it is an unspeakable satisfaction to find in this man a valiant for the truth. We trust he will prove an apostle indeed to the Garos!

Just then Ramke wrote Mr. Bronson word which had just reached him from Rajasimla, that the Garos had decided to exterminate the Christian families. Rangku was told of the affair. Rangku tells how Doctor Bronson, after getting Ramke's letter, came to him with tears rolling down his cheeks, saying, "You must go and help them." And when Rangku remarked, "Suppose they kill me," Doctor Bronson replied, "You go on, the Lord will take care of you." "Let me go at once," he said. If it had not been night he would have started to walk then and there. Mr. Bronson asked if he was not afraid. "No!—but am I to kill them if they kill our people?" He said he could account for ten or a dozen he thought. Bidding him good-bye Mr. Bronson told him about David and his sling and stone. "God will be with you. Perhaps the trouble has blown over. Anyhow go and be brave." And he was gone. All night he searched for a boat. Before dawn he was off, and arrived at Goalpara in two and a half days. Leaving his luggage there and walking on, he reached Rajasimla at sunset. Omed and Ramke were glad to see him, and to receive his help in this time of greatest danger.

For thirteen years he preached through the towns, at Rajasimla, at Damra, and finally settled at Nisangram, thus fulfilling Mrs. Bronson's hope.

XVI

A DAY OF DAYS

RAMKE kept Captain Morton informed of all that was going on both at the Damra school, and in the settlement at the foot of the pass. He took the liveliest interest in these reports and sent them to Mr. Bronson with expressions of cordial approbation.

About this time Mr. Ayerst, Government chaplain at Gauhati, proposed to establish at Goalpara a mission to the Garos in connection with the Church of England. He wrote to the deputy commissioner asking for his assistance, but Captain Morton informed him that Mr. Bronson had already " cut the first sod."

Rangku was a welcome reenforcement at Rajasimla, but the converts no less than Mr. Bronson longed for the appointment of a missionary from home. Some one was needed to take command of the enterprise, to do a hundred things that the Garo pioneers were helpless to attempt alone. Omed had suggested this from the first, and now Captain Morton was urging it. Doctor Bronson was perplexed. It was clearly absurd for him to continue the direction of affairs at a distance of two hundred miles, and yet there was no one else. All he could do was to send home fresh appeals and bide his time. To add to his solicitude he had just received a letter signed by eight Garos representing different villages:

To the Teacher Sahib at Nowgong, with respectful salutations. This is our request. Our brethren Omed and Ramke have come to us bringing in their hands a Holy Book, which tells that Jesus

Christ the Son of God, took the nature and form of man and made an atonement for the sons of men. At first we paid little attention to their words, but our brother Omed ceased not to explain to us the many evidences of the power and attributes of the great God and of his love to us sinners. He also showed us the folly of worshiping senseless idols. Then we gave our minds to examine this subject, and we saw that by all our sacrifices and idol worship we should gain nothing in this world, or in the world to come; but that on the contrary, evil would be the result. We also saw that by worshiping senseless idols we were throwing contempt upon our Creator. In this way we can not tell how much we have sinned against our Creator.

Thus we are lying under the displeasure of God. Our two brothers have pointed out to us that through Jesus Christ we may find the forgiveness of our sins. Believing their words to be true we have come together from our several villages and are listening to the teaching. We are trying to follow their teachings but the path they point out we only faintly see. Thus we are in a sea of anxiety and doubt. We have left the superstitions and customs of our people and have taken the name of Christ, therefore we are much hated and despised by our people. We are like sheep exposed to wild beasts. Therefore we make request that a missionary be sent to be our guide. Otherwise we may stray into wrong ways. Omed and Ramke have found the right way and we have sent them to teach our countrymen. Through their instruction we believe in Christ, and wish to confess our faith. Do not cease your efforts for us. This is our prayer.

Signed:

WANET, village of Dilma,
CHAKIN, village of Dilma,
NEDHA, village of Dilma,
KANGORA, village of Dilma,
BANENG, village of Bangshi,
NATA, village of Dambora,
SAGA, village of Dambora,
FOKIRA, village of Khotopata.

To a man of Mr. Bronson's spirit such a letter as this was like a spark of tinder. It set him aflame. There was something of the seer about him; he was able to look with clear eye into the future. He had a great heart, ready to take in all Assam; a strategic mind, quick to see points of vantage, and a will that takes tenacious hold. He had baptized the first Assamese, the first Garo, and the first Mikir. "I often feel great delight," he said, "in the work of the Lord. I would rather kindle up the fires of Christianity among those long-neglected tribes, than occupy the most honorable position at home." But of all his converts the two Garos had given him the greatest joy. He thought of them as Paul thought of the Galatians, and longed exceedingly to visit them and see their work. Rangku's letters further fanned this desire, and at last the way opened and he resolved to go.

The trip was the gladdest surprise of his life! Going first to Goalpara, he started thence with two elephants, lent by Captain Campbell, on Friday, April 12, 1867. It was a long day's journey in the heat and dust, but Damra was reached at five o'clock, and all fatigue was forgotten as he chatted with Ramke and examined his school of fifteen boys. They talked and sang till bedtime, and the next morning set off early, arriving in the afternoon at Rajasimla. His diary of the tour tells the rest.

This is a lovely spot at the foot of the hills, with a fine stream of water close at hand, and plenty of land suitable for cultivation. A crowd was waiting to receive us. We found a village of forty houses, new and orderly arranged. The largest and best is a place for Christian worship, recently built by the people themselves. Every Sabbath it is crowded with listeners. A house, very clean, was placed at my disposal, so that, although I had a small tent, I never pitched it. As soon as I could I went to the chapel, which I found crowded with people ready to hear from me the word of God. I spoke to them as simply as possible in Assamese, which was understood by some, the three evangelists interpreting to the hills people who understood only Garo. It was deeply affecting to me to witness their fixed attention and deep interest as I spoke to them of Christ and told them that he died to save even poor Garos. It was soon evident that the story of the Cross was familiar to them, and their hearts have begun to melt under its mighty power. At last I put the question, "How many of you love this Saviour, and, abandoning all your heathen worship and practices, worship him alone?" Twenty-six, all residents of this village, arose. I closely questioned them as to their motives, explaining to them what it might cost them to become Christians, ridicule, reproach, opposition, perhaps death. They replied, "Yes, we have thought this all over; we expect opposition; we have decided to become Christ's disciples and be baptized." The evangelists speak of their changed conduct, particularly in their abandonment of their old rites of worship, and in the disuse of drink, which has cost some of them a great struggle. They were therefore received as candidates for Christian baptism. It was late before I could retire to rest and then I left them still assembled.

Sunday, 14th. A day of days! Early morning worship; also at ten o'clock; after which we repaired to the beautiful stream dammed up for the purpose, where I baptized in the name of the sacred Trinity twenty-six Garos, men and women. A crowd of wild savage people stood on the bank, but all were quiet, respectful, and serious as though accustomed to the scene. Among their first ingathering of Garos into the fold of Christ were the aged, middle-aged, and youth. Several of these were a few months ago angry opposers. The case of one of them affected me very much. He had learned to read and write in the Government school at Goalpara, and speaks Assamese well. He is a mountain Garo and one of the first to leave off opposition and join Omed, since which he has been unable to walk from a diseased foot. He said with much feeling: "I am Christ's disciple, but I can not walk. How can I be baptized?" Seeing his earnest wish I told Omed to have him brought to me in the water. You should have seen his delight. This man when asked if he hoped for worldly gain, answered with spirit: "No; is it to fill our bellies that we become Christians? It is salvation we want!" At another time he said: "My heart burns to go and tell my people on the mountains of this religion. Only let my foot get well and I shall go."

Thus the total baptized on this first day was twenty-seven, of whom thirteen were women. Among the men, Maljang, the son of Wanet, who was a brother of Omed, and Chakin were afterward ordained. Of the women, the first was Epiri, Omed's wife, and the second Rangku's mother, Agong. Another was Ramke's sister, Ware, with her husband, Ringbong.

The house of prayer was again crowded in the evening. After preaching I explained that, in the apostles' days, they were wont to form the disciples into churches, and to appoint one of their number as pastor. Which of the three native assistants would they choose as their pastor and preacher, to baptize, to bury their dead, and perform their marriages according to Christian customs? They unanimously chose Omed, from whose lips they had received the gospel. I then and there, in the presence of them all, laid hands on him, and told him to range the hills, to preach, baptize, to do the work of a Christian pastor, and be faithful unto death. Now this is very unepiscopal, but I feel that it is no time to stand on human ceremonies and formalities in the work of God. The Garos have been too long benighted. They are perishing in the darkness. They are just opening their eyes to see this. A good, faithful, cautious native like Omed can do more than a dozen new missionaries just now. There are twenty other Garos, away at present, who desire baptism. I can not stay among them. It is necessary that their preacher and guide should be empowered to preach, baptize, marry, and bury their dead, and it is good for them to feel some responsibility from the first. Let those who will contend for routine and forms. My one work shall be to make the native churches independent of foreign teachers as soon as possible. It is in this way only that Christianity will take root and grow in this country.

Monday, 15th. Gave orders to start early for Damra. We went into the chapel to say a few words, when Omed mentioned to me that ten more in the village were unwilling that I should leave without numbering them among Christ's disciples. One of the number was crying like a child and saying something in Garo. I found on inquiry that he was appealing to the native assistants to witness that, when his life was threatened because he cut a few bamboos on a mountain where the heathen sacrificed he did not recant. Why could not he confess Christ as well as the others? His whole body was shaking with emotion. Others spoke in a similar strain. I saw I had more work to do. I called in the church and baptized ten, one of whom was Suban, Ramke's wife. I baptized alternately with Omed, thus introducing him at once into the work for which he had been set apart. This showed the Garos that baptism by his hand or mine was the same. He used the baptismal formula in Garo, I in Assamese. Thus in one village there is a church of forty Garo Christians, including the assistants. Most of them have been a year or two in deciding, and I believe they will stand the test of opposition.[1] When no one was raising his finger to help the Garos, God put it into the hearts of Omed and Ramke to come and beg to be sent to teach their fellow countrymen. I saw their earnestness. I saw God's hand in it, and although I had no funds, I dared not say, No. I sent them. But I confess I am myself astonished and rebuked by my want of faith. I can only say, "This is the Lord's doing, and it is marvelous in our eyes!"

[1] Here are some extracts from a letter written by M. C. Mason from there forty years later:

RAJASIMLA, January 14, 1908.

I am today on the spot where the first visit by any missionary was made to the Garos; and where at that time there were thirty-six converts baptized, a church of thirty-nine members organized, a pastor ordained, and the little flock left to themselves in this wilderness. Many at home would be glad to know how such converts held out. I have the records before me. It is forty years ago last April that these converts were thus baptized and organized, so that they have had the test of time.

I find that thirty-three of them were faithful unto death, and have gone on to their heavenly home. Five of them became ordained preachers. Four of the thirty-nine are still living faithful lives. One other is still living, but not faithfully. . . This leaves but one other, who was the wife of the first convert, and not a Garo. She remained but a short time and left the place to roam as she pleased among her own people. She was excluded soon after. Only three others have been disciplined and excluded, but afterwards restored. . . Eight hundred and thirty persons have since been connected with this church. The heathen of the adjoining country are now but a fraction of the people that were. . . The present membership stands two hundred and sixty-four, over two hundred have been dismissed to organize and join other churches. But few can imagine the difficulties and the adverse conditions under which these Christians have to live in such a country and amid such surroundings as these.—*Record of Christian Work, June, 1908, p. 371.*

XVII

A NEW BEGINNING

NO general reconnoitering the enemies' position and estimating his own resources, ever felt more sure of victory and more confident of the means to compass it, than this white-haired missionary as he rode back on his elephant to Goalpara.

The road skirted the hills, and, with his face turned that way, he had plenty of leisure for thought. The great creature ambled along, lifting his trunk to pluck down branches of leafy trees, or lowering it to twist up clumps of grass, which he flicked against his forelegs to shake out the dirt and then placed it in his mouth. As the sun rose higher, he cooled himself by sucking up water from the mud and squirting it over his wrinkled sides. A douche of dust occasionally varied the water-spray. The second elephant, bearing the unused tent, kept close behind. Now and then, when the mahauts sitting astride their necks, with naked legs tucked in behind the great flapping ears, struck them with the *ankus* or *guwakh* (a heavy iron crook) or dug its point into the thick skin of their foreheads, drawing a drop of blood, the animals trumpeted and quickened their pace. But no pace could equal the quickness of the rider's desire, or the eager flight of his thought. "In twenty years," he told himself, "these hills will be vocal with the praise of God," and his brain was busy with plans for hastening that day.

Two things he saw must be done at once: first, arrangements made for a separate mission to the Garos, with headquarters at Goalpara, for which funds would have to be found in India till the churches in America could be aroused; secondly, one of the two missionaries just arrived from America and on their way up the river from Calcutta, assigned to this special service and put in charge. With these ideas clearly fixed, he unconsciously followed the rhythmic movements of the giant beast, now devising earnest appeals calculated to open the pockets of his friends, and again marshaling irresistible arguments with which to bear down all reluctance on the part of the travelers up-stream. Arrived at Goalpara, he sought out officials and other European residents, and told them his exciting story, his plans, and his hopes. One and all promised help. It is pleasant to think how David Scott would have welcomed this missionary enthusiast so full of life and vigor in spite of his length of days, and so interested in these wild sons of the jungle, the late commissioner's own favorite folk! It so happened that on the top of the beautiful hill overlooking the river, the most eligible spot in the whole town, a fine house stood empty—the one built and occupied forty years before by David Scott himself. Doctor Bronson determined to have it. With him to think was to act. What was the price? Only eight hundred rupees. A surprising bargain! A second round among his friends, and enthused by his spirit, one thousand one hundred and nineteen rupees are in hand before night, and the house is the property of the mission.

The following day, April 18, 1867, he returned to Gauhati, to find that Mr. and Mrs. Stoddard, just back from furlough, with Rev. M. B. Comfort, a new worker, had already arrived. He put the whole case before them. He told them the story of Ramke and Rangku, and of the settlement at the foot of the pass, the founding of the

Doctor and Mrs. Stoddard
1867

Rev. Miles Bronson, D. D.

Sir William Grey
Lieutenant-Governor of Bengal
1867

Samuel Loveday

first church, and last, but not least, the purchase of the house at Goalpara. Such indications of divine leading could not fail to make a deep impression. The Stoddards especially felt the pull of the facts. Had not they been the means of leading Kandura to Christ? And was it not through him, chiefly, that Omed and Ramke were in turn taught to believe? It was soon decided that they should give themselves to the work, and go into residence at Goalpara at the end of the rains.

Indeed, before coming up country, Mr. Stoddard had had an interview with Sir William Grey, the lieutenant-governor of Bengal, of which he gives the following interesting account:

I returned to Assam in 1866, expecting to work among the Garos. At that time the lieutenant-governor of Bengal had Assam and the hill tribes in his territory, and on Fridays gave a breakfast to Europeans who had reached Calcutta during the week past, from sea or land, as he wished a friendly interview with all tea-planters, indigo, opium, and timber speculators, river-boat captains, and missionaries. About twenty breakfasted the morning I was there. When breakfast was well under way, the lieutenant excused himself and stepped into his office. Soon a servant appeared, inviting all the tea-planters to an interview: about eleven o'clock the missionary's turn came.

"Mr. Stoddard," said the governor, "you say you are on your way to the Garos of Assam?"

"Yes."

"Do you know the Garos?"

"Not much."

"Allow me to kindly advise you and warn you. They are a bloodthirsty set of savages, and deserve extermination. Government is now considering that question."

Then followed a long, fearful account of their annual raids into the plains for human heads of British subjects to pacify the evil spirits, secure good crops, etc. The expenses of Government with an army to punish them was dwelt upon, after which he continued:

"Now, Mr. Stoddard, be advised and warned not to go into the Garo independent territory, to lose your own head and cause the Government trouble. But success to your mission elsewhere and let me know if at any time I can assist you in any way."

I thanked the lieutenant-governor and expressed my utmost confidence in the glorious gospel of the blessed God to "tame the savage."

This then was the task to be accomplished, and there were sympathizers in high positions to render help. Here, too, were a man and woman fitted by temperament and by ties of association as well as by strong personal inclinations, to attempt the task. And Goalpara became the new base of operations, and the Stoddards the first missionaries to the Garos from Western lands.

XVIII

THE STODDARDS AT GOALPARA

DOCTOR and Mrs. Stoddard were charming people. Doctor Stoddard was born in 1820 at Eden,[1] Erie County, New York. His father was a minister, who died, full of ripe wisdom and the gathered harvest of his people's love, at the age of eighty-six. His mother lived to be ninety-nine. He was graduated at Madison, now Colgate University, in 1845, and in September, 1847, having completed a theological course, he was ordained, and the same year was appointed a missionary to Assam by the American Baptist Missionary Union. Before sailing from Boston he married Miss Drusilla Allen, a cultured lady who, after graduating at a famous school in Troy, was in charge of a mission school among the Seneca Indians in the Cattaraugus Reservation. Among her pupils were the children of "Two Guns," "Silver Heels," "Big Kettle," and other braves.

Mrs. Stoddard was a year younger than her husband, of Scotch-Irish descent, and brought up in a Quaker household. Mr. Stoddard had a poor opinion of the Quakers, she tells us, "until I taught him better." The matter was often discussed in the years before the marriage, and at length, being convinced after proper research of the rightness of Baptist views, she adopted them as her own. Their voyage in the "Cato" lasted four months, with many hardships. After reaching Nowgong

[1] Doctor Stoddard still lives in Plainfield, New Jersey, U. S. A. (1915). Mrs. Stoddard passed on in 1913.

and acquiring the use of the Assamese language, they for nine years conducted the Orphan School. But repeated attacks of fever at length drove them home, where for ten years they threw themselves with characteristic zest into the life of the Central University of Iowa. After the financial depression and suspension of operations that followed the Civil War, Mrs. Stoddard and her husband put their time and strength as well as money into the saving of that college, and in two years all debts were paid, its future assured, and they again turned their faces eastward to meet the problem of the Garo mission. Beyond all telling they were less needed in Iowa than in benighted Assam.[2]

They arrived at Goalpara October 3, 1867. The view from the bungalow which Doctor Bronson had secured was fine. Northward sheer down over the tops of trees, with a ribbon road showing through, could be seen the court-house, treasury, and record office, outlined against the stream. Westward a patch of green sprinkled with brown huts, hugging the base of the hill, showed a bit of the bazaar spreading itself a little way on the long stretch of sand, like a small oasis in the desert; beyond the sand, the white gleaming river with a dark line of Lilliputian boats marking its edge; beyond the river, on the horizon two miles distant, the "Gates of Assam"; and beyond these, on very clear days, the white dome of Everest, two hundred miles away. At the back of the hill, southward, winding leafy paths led to the houses of other European residents a hundred feet below.

Hardly were the Stoddards settled when a company of Garos from a distance came in upon them. Several were boys from the Damra school accompanied by Ramke and

[2] The story of Mrs. Stoddard's life and of their work in Iowa is found in "A Beautiful Life," by Mrs. Anna Clarkson Howell.

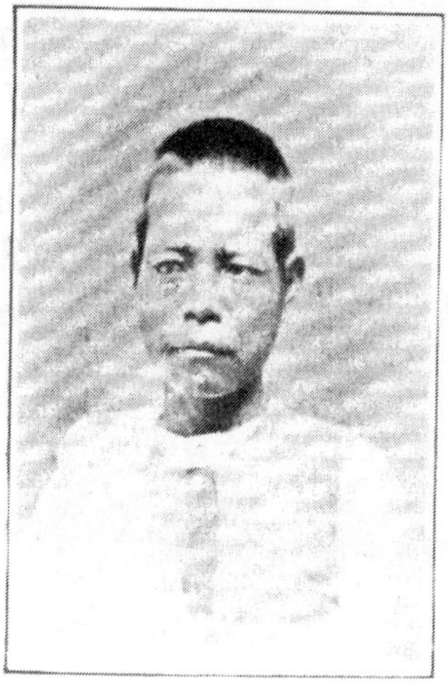

Ramke in 1872

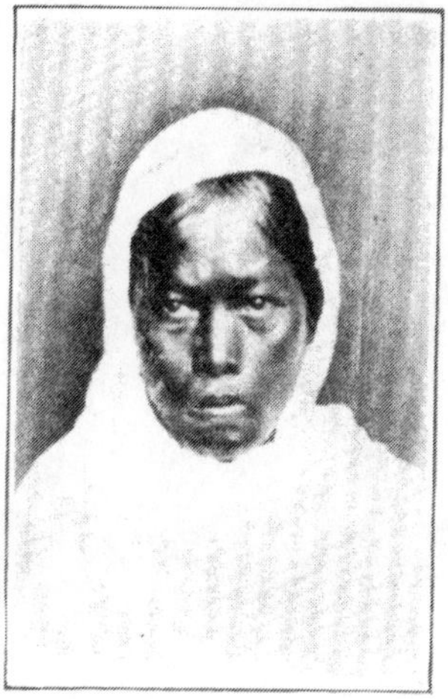

Suban in 1872

Rangku and His Wife in 1872

Rangku. The latter with one or two of the boys was retained to help the missionaries in acquiring the language. The young men were eager to learn English, and Mrs. Stoddard soon had a class of eight or ten.

" Sabbath evenings," writes Mr. Stoddard,

we spend in prayer, singing, and conference, and I will confess to emotions such as I seldom have experienced. Bura Kandura, the Bairagi baptized at Sukheswar Ghat, leads in prayer. He is old, nearly blind, and lame, but having found Christ at last, his soul has put on eternal vigor and youth. "O Lord," he prays, "just like a decayed, rotten thing, utterly worthless am I before thee. Save, Lord, or I perish." A verse is sung and Naran, brother of Suban, and a young Christian, is on his feet. He has just returned from a visit home. He says, "Brothers, pray for my parents. It is not yet two weeks since they decided to be Christ's disciples. I am very glad. How they opposed me a few months ago! Now all the village is angry with them and threatens to stone them from the place if they do not go back to devil worship." Chejing prays. He is not a Christian but desires to be. He uses this forceful language: "Pity me, O Lord! If you do not save me no one can. I have one leg in hell now." All join in singing "The Penitent Thief." Then Bangkill speaks. He has but recently arrived and talks only Garo. We can not understand a word, but Rangku is our interpreter. We learn that the young man lives near the Garo church, is a relative of the Christians, but has been an opposer until now. This is his first confession. He says he has stopped his fight, and all the devil worship with it. He will now serve and obey Christ.

Before we can strike a tune, Rudram is on his feet. He speaks out very earnestly and we feel that he means all he says. "I have not been baptized, but I love Christ. I am a Christian at all hazards. Nothing shall turn me from this new religion. I am happy. My people are among tigers because they have recently confessed Christ. Pray for me and for them."

We can but feel greatly interested in this young man who after a few weeks of instruction now talks, prays, and acts like a child of grace. What wonder of wonders is this Christian religion! Rudram and his mother had come to the station on foot in a single day from their village, a distance of twenty-five miles or more. She was a tall, strong, noble-looking woman. "This is my only son and child," she said to Mrs. Stoddard. "I bring him to you that he may learn wisdom. We Garos know nothing, not even God, only devils." When asked to remain a few days, she replied: "By no means. My husband is lame and cannot wait on himself much. No one in our village now will even cook rice for him, for we have ceased to worship demons, and worship Christ; and we receive great abuse from our neighbors and friends." At dawn she was up and away.

Reports now came in from various places that many had commenced the worship of Christ. The missionaries were begged to come and see them. Mr. Stoddard was petitioned by some to call on Government to stop the persecution that met every one as soon as they decided for the new religion. Wherefore persecuted? Because they ceased to pay the customary share for sacrifice to the demons.

Much attention was given to plans for educational work, and a grant of two hundred and fifty rupees was sanctioned by Government for the preparation and printing of Garo books. Also a monthly grant of fifty rupees was made for the school, now called "the normal class" at Damra, and fifty-two rupees for village schools.

Mr. Bronson, on the occasion of his visit in April, had opened a school at Rajasimla, and appointed Fokira as teacher. He soon had a class of seventeen young Garo men, a class of thirteen small boys, and a class of Garo girls. "But do you want your girls taught?" he was asked. "Yes, the girls as well as the boys." Here was a foundation which led the missionaries to say, "Other schools will follow, and we will soon have plenty of good Christian Garo teachers who will preach while we teach."

Soon Mr. Bronson had in process a Garo primer and reading-book of some sixty pages, and the first catechism. The missionaries in reducing the Garo language to writing were free to choose between Bengali, already familiar to the Christian leaders as it was used by both the Bengalis and the Assamese, and the Roman character which would introduce them to the English vocabulary. The Bengali unfortunately was chosen and retained for years, but has recently been discarded in favor of the Roman.

Thus the missionary spent the first three months at Goalpara, getting acquainted with the people and problems of his strange, wild parish. Then, conducted by Mr. Bronson, he went out on his first Garo tour.

XIX

BRONSON AND STODDARD ON TOUR

IT is early morning. Bronson and Stoddard are astride their stout little ponies. Their wives bid them Godspeed and they canter away in the brisk February air. Halting at Damra with its beautiful lot for school and chapel on the bank of a mountain stream, they find thirty Garos in the Normal School. Another two hours' ride brings them to Amjonga, where they pass the night at the house of a pensioner sepoy, who had called together his friends to hear the gospel. "I shall never forget," wrote Stoddard,

> the eagerness with which that crowd listened to the truth till long after midnight and then dispersed with great reluctance. Long before day the old sepoy and his wife were up and talking over the events of this wonderful night. In the darkness we heard them profess to each other their faith in Christ, and we heard their voices in prayer.

There the missionaries found erected in a beautiful grove temporary buildings for their accommodation. After thirteen had been baptized they sat down to the Lord's Supper for the first time in that village. Among the baptized that day were the old sepoy, his wife, uncle, and son. Their Christian course was brief but very bright. In less than three years all four had died, but each rejoicing in Christ. After the death of the wife, the husband, though quite lame, trudged thirty miles to Goalpara to deliver her dying message to the missionaries.

She had exhorted her friends not to weep for her, but to believe in Christ who could make them smile at death. And, contrary to Garo custom, she had taken the ornaments from her neck and wrists, and begged that these might not be buried with her but sold and the proceeds sent to the missionaries for the purpose of preaching the gospel to her countrymen. The old man told his story with tearful eyes, rejoicing in the calm triumph of such a death. She had no fear; Jesus was with her. She loved to pray, and many a time went by herself to talk with Jesus. She was still talking to him when she died.

The son, Rudram, after his mother's death, spent two years more with the Stoddards, "trusty in all his work, a devoted and growing Christian." At his death his own villagers desired to offer sacrifices that his life might be spared. But he forbade them, for, since Christ was his hope, he had no fear of death. When he became unconscious, hurried preparations for a sacrifice were made. He awoke just in time to stop them. "Listen," he said,

> I have been to heaven. I saw my mother and a vast multitude all full of joy. I saw Jesus our Friend. It was a beautiful sight. Believe in him. I am going to him.

And with these words on his lips he passed away.

Is it any wonder that Mr. Stoddard in writing of the baptism of such converts exclaimed:

> How solemn and unspeakably delightful are all these scenes! Tongue and pen can not describe them. Here I saw as never before, how easy it is to "believe and be saved." Simple, confiding faith in Christ saves the soul.

Leaving this new interest, the travelers rode on farther to the Christian village at Rajasimla, where the entire population, cleanly clad and with smiling faces, met them at the entrance of the town, drawn up as if in military array. "This is the Lord's army," said the missionaries. Omed repeated the words. "Yes, we are the Lord's sepoys," came the response all along the line.

A goodly sight were these men and women and children, a Christian village in this wild place! Only a day's march from this point into the hills and the people were savages, where they take a man's head with the same delight with which we would kill a mad dog.

Omed pointed out the little grass hut, still standing, where he and his wife lived for nearly a year almost entirely alone.

Here a week was spent holding meetings morning and evening. Once when Omed was interpreting, forgetting all else but the interest in the subject, and treating it in his own way, he spoke rapidly with intense earnestness for half an hour, and held spellbound his astonished audience and the superseded missionary!

Half of each day was spent in correcting and revising the books that had been prepared in Garo by Mr. Bronson, their greatest perplexity being to fix upon proper terms for God, heaven, sin, and other similar words.

After hours and days spent in hard research and inquiry, we were overwhelmed with the solemn thought, Here is a people so lost that they have no word for God, the Creator of all things, no word for sin, only as we would say bad man, bad horse or dog! No words for heaven and hell above the tradition that after death the mind remains some six days in a delightful tank within the Garo hills, during which time it becomes a living creature again.

"Who is the Creator?" "We do not know." "A female gave birth to the sun and moon. Another gave birth to water, another to vegetation, and so on." "But who gave birth to those females?" "We have no knowledge." Such is Garo theology!

During this week twenty-five men were examined and baptized. On either side of the narrow alley where the village stood was a mountain stream. A dam had been thrown across one of these, about twenty rods from the chapel, to form a baptistery.

The sun shone bright and clear between the high hills upon that quiet scene. The entire village lined the banks of the stream clad in their clean white garments. Here and there were groups of wild, almost naked Garos from the hills, on their way to a market on the plains. They paused to witness the ceremony. Omed, the pastor, being unwell, the ordinance was performed by Mr. Bronson and myself baptizing alternately. As we passed in and out of this Jordan, engaged in this delightful task, we sang in Assamese.

In the evening of this day we observed the Lord's Supper. It was witnessed for the first time by most of the seventy-two Garo Christians present. One year ago only three baptized! Now eighty-one in all, awaking from ignorance and darkness most profound! Look at this company around the Lord's table, seated upon mats on the ground! As I pass the elements assisted by Omed, what silence reigns! Nothing but the beating of my heart is heard and the sobs of one or two women as I approach them with these sacred emblems. Is it possible that hearts so ignorant and dark only yesterday can be melted thus at the first sight of a Body, broken and bruised for us! "Let there be light, and there was light." Thus instantly can the grace of Christ change the heart of a savage to a saint. To God then be all the praise, now and forever, world without end, amen.

"This was one of the most interesting tours of our whole life," wrote Mr. Bronson.

The church has doubled the last year. Some of the members are from the mountains several days' distance. They have literally left all for Christ. On the evening that we celebrated the Lord's Supper some rose and with tears of gratitude gave expression to their thoughts. One said: "How unworthy I am to be here, I whose sun has almost set, and have known no worship but that of devils! How wonderful that I should have been called to hear this new religion, and be numbered with Christ's disciples." Another said: "I have lived a wicked life here. I have many evil desires. Help me to be a true disciple." Still another: "I am ignorant, but when I heard that Christ had died for sinners, I felt that I was such and now I have left all worship of demons and believe only in Him." Every day something new and of thrilling interest occurred. We were enabled thoroughly to go over our Garo books, and take the language from the lips of the people. We closed our visit by a pleasant Christian wedding. Two couples had requested to be married, and the native assistant wished to see how Christian marriages were performed.

Last of all the church presented three of their number, who were anxious to go and break another field where they thought a teacher and a preacher would soon meet with success. Two of them whose names were Chakin and Posallu, were to go as colporters, on a salary of eight rupees a month. The third, Ramsing, lately a head constable, who was receiving from Government fifteen rupees per month, was to serve as Bible reader and colporter on ten rupees. We have entertained their request, as we must at such a time as this put every man at work, trusting to our brethren at home to sustain us.

On the tenth of February they left Rajasimla amidst many tears, and returned to Damra, where several days were spent in preaching and looking after the interests of the Normal School. They superintended the erection of a building to be used as a chapel and schoolhouse, the lads of the school doing most of the work. They also attended the Damra market where thousands listened with "all curiosity and attention." "The scene was enough," wrote Bronson, "to move the soul of any one who has a heart to feel anything. We have enjoyed good health thus far, and would not exchange this labor for any other."

All the Garo assistants, including those newly appointed, rejoined the missionary party at Damra to accompany them for the rest of the tour. This led from market to market, where the Bread of Life was offered to hundreds of hillmen. But at last Doctor Bronson falling ill with fever, returned to Goalpara, and left Mr. Stoddard to go alone to Tura, at the heart of the hills.

XX

BLAZING THE TRAIL

AS a base of operations Goalpara had many advantages. The nearest Garo villages could be reached in a morning ride, and half a dozen important markets were within a fair day's march. Many Garos, having business at the courts, were easily attracted to the house on the top of the hill.

Still its position was that of a solitary rock, standing off from the coast, rather a post of observation and a tower of defense than a fort for effective attack. It commanded a view of the outlying spurs of a country to be won, but even these were not in range, except at favorable times. Rajasimla was at least thirty miles away and could only be visited during the cold season. The new converts, whose number was constantly increasing, needed instruction, and Mr. Stoddard was anxious to be in closer touch with them and the work.

As an experiment he tried living at Damra, where he had already secured a desirable site on the bank of a stream navigable by country boat the whole way to Goalpara. Here a good building had been erected for the Normal School, and the place was intended to become the educational headquarters of the mission. But he had reckoned without his host. The deadly miasma, lurking at the foot of the hills, made him ill before a month was out, and with his family, he soon, and wisely, retreated to the house on the hill, at Goalpara.

Five young men in the Normal Class soon applied for

baptism. There were seven candidates from other villages, and all were baptized on Sunday, June 28, 1868, in the Dudhnai, which flowed past the school grounds, "thus consecrating another mountain stream to Christ." Unfortunately, soon after the Stoddards left, one of the baptized students, Magua, committed an outrage, which might have had a serious effect upon the mission. It was an act of mistaken zeal, probably due to an emulation of Omed's spirit and a desire to exhibit his new-found freedom, perhaps also to retaliate upon his former tormentors. There was a place of sacrifice upon a jagged rock some miles from the school. The rock was a sort of shelf overhanging the cliff, and on it lay a ring of pebbles spattered with blood. This spot, sacred to the demons, was held in utmost awe by the Garos for miles around; none but the priests would have dared even to touch the mystic circle of stones. Magua went up, pushed the pebbles into a heap, and then flung them one by one over the edge of the cliff. It was an act that called for immediate revenge. He was tracked, caught, and beaten almost to death. Worse than all, his teacher, the inoffensive Ramke, was held partially responsible for the deed, made to pay a heavy fine, and regarded with extreme disfavor for months to come.

Notwithstanding this, Damra continued to play an important part in the development of the work. Lying as it did, on the road to Rajasimla, it received a good deal of attention from the missionaries when on tour. They made it their first objective on starting out, and their last halting-place on the homeward journey. The number of converts increased to fifty in two years. Many of these were heads of families and persons of local repute, who came from villages in the neighborhood, and met for worship at Damra.

The Normal School continued to flourish under varying conditions and received much fostering care. It was supported mainly by Government grant, but the great problem was that of missionary supervision. Mr. Stoddard found it impossible to spend an adequate amount of time at Damra during the touring season, and for the rest of the year malaria warned him away. A compromise was effected with the permission of Government to transfer the institution to Goalpara for the four months during the rains. This arrangement was carried out in 1870 and again in 1871 with encouraging success.

Every Sabbath, whether at Damra or at Goalpara, the students went out two by two, to spread in the neighboring hamlets the knowledge they had gained. At the end of the first five years, October, 1872, there were twenty-two students in residence, in age from thirteen to thirty; while among their countrymen, as teachers, vaccinators, evangelists, another twenty, who had finished the course, were already at work. No less than forty out of a total of forty-two had been baptized.

Meanwhile Lieutenant Williamson, having built his stockade and established himself at Tura to get a grip on the whole group of hills, found that his position was made tenable only by the presence of armed police. The clans immediately around him had submitted, but their temper was uncertain, and the central masses were still obstinately sullen and opposed. On the other hand his sporting instincts and strong, tactful personality admirably fitted him for the task of holding them in restraint. Thus far no rupture had occurred to mar the policy of patient conciliation.

In July, 1870, Mr. Stoddard had met for the second time the lieutenant-governor of Bengal, Sir William Grey, on whose mind the success of the Goalpara mission, par-

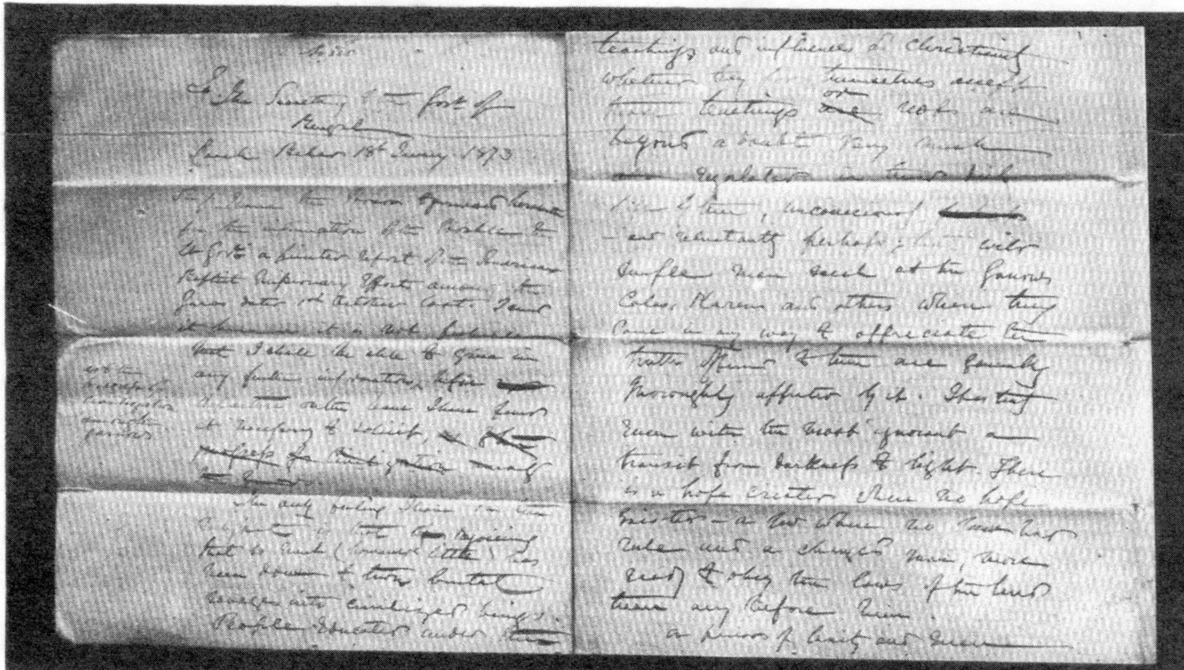

Letter of Lieutenant-General J. C. Haughton

Showing attitude of Government officers toward mission.

ticularly in the matter of Garo education, had made a pleasing impression, all the more pleasing because of his gloomy prognostications three years before. As the son of a bishop, he could not, as time passed, fail to be impressed by the evidence of a spiritual movement at the heart of the educational enterprise, accounting for its success and controlling its policy and aim. He was anxious to induce the mission to settle at Tura and had suggested in his review of the Commissioner's Annual Report for the year 1869-1870, that encouragement be given to the American missionaries in their efforts to educate the Garos. Colonel Haughton forwarded a copy of these suggestions with a personal letter to Mr. Stoddard.

My dear Mr. Stoddard:

You will see by the enclosed that there is a clear field at Tura, and you will not doubt that I will give to the American missionaries every encouragement in my power. I should think you could do better in every way at Tura than at Goalpara. . . A cold and healthy station from which, when the season permitted, you could descend to all parts, invigorated rather than enfeebled by the hot season, is an advantage, not, I think, to be despised. Hoping you will continue well, believe me,

Yours sincerely,

(Signed) J. C. Haughton.

Such a communication naturally excited very strong desire, and Mr. Stoddard was at once possessed with a passion to capture this stronghold for Christ. It was not in the nature of things that such an offer emanating from the head of the Government should escape the notice of the foster-father of the mission. As soon as the news reached him, Doctor Bronson wrote to the Board, "The Garo mission needs the very first and best man that can be sent out."

This offer was freely discussed by the Garo leaders and in the Normal School. Volunteers were called for who should go up at once and spy out the land, while Mr. Stoddard and other missionaries would prepare to follow in December, and determine what ought to be done. Three men responded to the call for volunteers, a teacher and two pupils of the Normal School. They started immediately, going around the hills by the beaten track, through the country of the tributary clans, which was now comparatively safe. Arrived at Tura they visited the villages near-by, met with friendly reception, and were eager to stay. The missionaries came up in due time, selected a site for mission premises and decided to recommend the occupation of the station as soon as reenforcements could be sent from home. When they left, the three volunteers remained behind. The teacher was to open the school, and the two others, Ramsing and Chejing, obtained employment as vaccinators, on a small monthly pay to be eked out in other ways. As a passport to the wild men's favor, and an easy means for support, the little inoculating needle was of more value than a purse of gold, while as a protection it was more powerful than the sharpest spear. The commissioner placed no restriction upon them. They could go where they wished and preach as much as they would in their preventive profession. And so the men who started as scouts, with no thought of such a future before them, became surgeon-evangelists, and spent some months roaming over the Garo country. They inoculated thousands of their countrymen with much more than the coveted vaccine.

It was a bold venture for these Garo Christians to penetrate unknown territory without an escort and to submit themselves to the cross-fire of questioning and challenge at every stopping-place on the way. They entered the forbidden section at the risk of losing their heads, and had some fearsome experiences during the first few days. Taken into the presence of a chief, and ordered to give an account of themselves, they stood trembling before him, awaiting their fate. They had no doubt what it would be, for the ghastly skulls of many victims were piled up at his door. They were threatened with torture if they did not leave the country at once, and with death if they returned; but their captors, for some unexplained reason, let them go. Then it was discovered that they had a preventive for small-pox, and the fierce attitude changed to one of hospitality and they were taken everywhere and sumptuously entertained. Thus medical missionaries blazed a track for the gospel through the heart of Garo land.

XXI

EARLY PROSPECTIVE VISITS

THE first visit to Tura was made by Doctor Stoddard alone, in March, 1868. His impressions seem to have been strong, but not favorable to an immediate move to Tura.

The object of Government seems to be an experiment to tame the savage, and thus put a stop to the annual raids into the plains after Bengali heads. Their looks are against them, and I observed that the men always went armed; that, as I passed through the fields they were cultivating, they all had a sword or spear in the ground near-by.

The Government station is situated on the central spur of the Tura range. This spur is shaped something like a crescent, and is about two thousand eight hundred feet below the summit of the mountain. Mt. Tura is some four thousand one hundred feet above sea level. Nokrek, about ten miles east of Tura, the highest peak of the Garo range, is four thousand six hundred and fifty-two feet above sea. From this lofty eyrie on a clear morning the Snowy Range is distinctly visible, and the silvery Brahmaputra can be traced for a hundred miles, while the view extends on the east to the Khasia group; on the west and south the plain of Bengal is before us; on the north we see the Bhutan Hills and the eye rests with fixed delight upon the pure and eternal snow of the Himalayas. Between the station and the spur on the south is a large gorge, up which the winds blow at nearly all seasons of the year. When the site was first occupied, the buildings, constructed of wooden posts, bamboo mats, and thatch, were a small bungalow in which the deputy commissioner and the district superintendent of police lived, and a long building which was made to serve as court-house, guard-room and storehouse; facing this was a large barrack to accommodate about a hundred and fifty constables, and, in line with it, the hospital. These buildings were all enclosed by a stockade outside of which were a few huts for cooking purposes, and the parade-ground. On the top of the mountain was a small outpost station.

At sundown when the stockade was closed and the guard had been set, a log fire was lighted in the center, and the two white men sat down to palaver about bringing the mission to Tura. All around them lay the impenetrable jungle as if asleep, in a silence that might be felt. As yet the experiment of Government was in its initial stage, and Lieutenant Williamson discouraged the idea of an immediate move. There were persons enough already in that little stockade, and a missionary added to the party, might, in case of uprising, embarrass the fighting force.

Mr. Stoddard grasped the situation, and within a fortnight of his return, wrote:

> Garos in great numbers may be found in all the markets at the foot of the hills, bartering their cotton in a friendly way for the products of the plains. There are the most favorable places for the visits of the missionary. The Garos are so exceedingly jealous of strangers penetrating to the interior of their hills, that it would be an unwise measure for missionaries to attempt it at present. For all practical purposes they are accessible at these *hats.*

Three years elapsed before the next missionary visit to the Tura stockade. Meanwhile the Normal School demanded personal supervision, and in consequence had been moved permanently from Damra to Goalpara. The Garo markets were found to be less fruitful as ground for the gospel seed than the jungle village and the jungle school. It was therefore increasingly clear that Goalpara was too remote and apart to remain a suitable base for work whose natural expansion would lead it ever farther away into and over the hills. During the cold season, on January 7, 1871, Doctor Bronson, in "his little canoe about thirty feet long and five feet wide," was on his way to join Stoddard and Comfort at Goalpara, on a tour of the mountain Garos, with Tura as an objective. "Who knows," he writes, as the dug-out glides down the stream, "but the time may come, in reference to this people, for the Lord's house to be 'established on the top of the mountains?'"

The three men left Goalpara on the evening of the ninth, in the boat which bore them in two days to Singimari. There they trudged on foot in the hot sun the first twenty miles, doing the remaining twenty on the ponies which had failed to meet them earlier. They reached Tura on the twentieth.

The bamboo shanty within the log enclosure had given place to the substantial wooden buildings in which both the officers and their wives could be comfortably housed. Outside the stockade, the police had built lines (barracks) for their families, and the settlement was beginning to grow.

A busy week in most delightful weather was spent reconnoitering the ground, asking questions, listening to the talk of the people, and forming an estimate of the facilities for the mission work. Considering the best site for a bungalow and a school, they chose the present parade-ground—a knoll which rounds off the spur on which the station is built, forming the southern end of the crescent, and holding a commanding position in relation to the surrounding hills. Its bluff sides rise up sheer out of the depths, and its summit, now level and grass-grown, would make a striking situation for a fort. A beautiful spot it indeed was, but by no means suitable for the purposes of the mission, as will be subsequently shown.

Before leaving Tura, the party rode their ponies up the steep zigzag ascent to the top of the mountain, two thousand eight hundred feet above. The bridle-path led through the "forest primeval," tall, straight trees with very little grass jungle beneath, but moss hanging in abundance, showing the dampness of the climate. Numerous "black, tailless monkeys laughed, screeched, and scampered, and beautiful golden pheasants flew up as they passed." From the summit, with powerful field-glasses they had a splendid view "of all the world and the glories thereof."

Leaving behind a Christian pundit to start a school, the trio bade farewell on January 27, and returned to Goalpara on horseback, halting at the markets by the way. Then sped the message to America:

> Where is the man for Tura? Must he be drawn from the present force in Assam, or shall a new man come out, designed especially for the Garos? The station *must* be occupied.

Another three years slipped by and no missionary set foot in Tura. In the meantime in March, 1871, the treacherous murder of a survey coolie at Rongmagiri, resulting in the march of an avenging force in the following cold season, and the arrest of the murderers in May, 1872, led to that inner rising of the independent class grouped in some sixty villages which compelled the annexation expedition of 1872-1873.

Writing on the eve of his departure for America, under date October 21, 1872, Mr. Stoddard says:

> Government has decided that the entire Garo country shall be annexed. A formidable expedition is organized, the land is explored, surveyed, and mapped. The messengers of peace may follow, and the good news be published to every one.

On January 27, 1873, Mr. Keith reports:

> The whole Garo country is open. No doubt our preachers can now go from one end of the hills to another. . . This event oc-

curring at such a stage in the history of the mission may be justly claimed as a part of the divine plan. It is not the first time in the history of missionary enterprise that the forerunner of the Messenger of Peace has been the herald of the law, "the highway of our God" prepared by means of the sword.

Immediate advantage was taken of the new conditions, and Garo preachers went up unmolested through the open doors. They were followed by Mr. Keith who, accompanied by a government military escort, went not so much to see Tura as the state of the country lying between. He found the people morose and sullen but with a very wholesome dread of the new authority lately imposed upon them. The journey is thus described:

> In January of the present year (1874) it was my privilege in company with the native assistants to traverse the hills to the northern frontier, visiting many large villages of the interior, where the missionary had never been before. But we cannot say that the people of any of the newly opened places did more than tolerate us. These evidently cherished a too vivid recollection of the energetic measures taken a twelvemonth before to teach them loyalty, by the representatives of Her Majesty's Crown, to care to take any confidences with foreigners. Indeed they seem to regard it as a doubtful matter whether or no they had any solid title to their own lives. Every question, as to whether they would like to have schools and teachers, was referred with dutiful submission to the "Great King" at Tura, meaning the deputy commissioner. "If he ordered them, they would have them, otherwise not." One chief, to whom we offered a small book as a memento of our visit, threw it away in great horror lest it should be found in his possession by the "raja," and should occasion his displeasure. Such is their present state of mind. They have a low opinion of white foreigners, and submit to their intrusion only because they must. But all this will by degrees pass away. And then, what a fine class of people upon which to expend effort for the enlightenment of Christianity! I can truly say that I have never seen finer specimens of the physical man than I saw in the interior of the Garo hills.

They have not the receding forehead, high cheek bones, and other facial angles indicative of the low, brutal savage. In fact, barring all their filth and numerous skin diseases, they are in physical development and symmetry of shape, well-nigh perfect.

Their dwelling-houses in their size and the material of which they are constructed indicate no little enterprise. Real skill and ingenuity is shown in their manner of bridging the mountain rivers, on the banks of which their villages are usually built, and which often separate them from their fields. Two large trees, growing on opposite banks, throw their branches well forward over the stream. To these they make fast strong vines of creepers, which form stout cables. To these, again, strong bamboos are fastened, and, on this foundation, as much extension, floor-laying and side-fastening as is thought necessary is done. And thus we have the veritable suspension bridges, thirty, forty, or sixty yards long.

And these are people only just made accessible to the gospel. Ignorant indeed they are. They have no more conception of God or a book, or what writing or reading mean, than a blind man has of color. When some of the simple facts of revelation were made known to them—such as the creation of man, the birth, death, and resurrection of Christ—they received them with outbursts of uproarious laughter. They are as ignorant as were the sturdy highlanders of Scotland three centuries ago. Like causes produce like effects. The power of the gospel is one, because its living principle is one unchanging Spirit, one Mind. May we not therefore expect that, here in these hills, will yet be seen effects as glorious as those that have followed the introduction of the gospel into the mountains of Switzerland or the highlands of Scotland?

With all this interest Mr. Keith does not seem to have contemplated moving to Tura as the best means of giving the gospel to the Garos. We shall see later how the matter shaped itself in his mind. For the present, let it suffice that the third prospective visit of the missionaries ended like those which had gone before, in further delays.

XXII

"TO BE OR NOT TO BE"

Mission to the Garos. Messrs. Mason and Phillips, with their wives, are now on their way to this Mission. One or both of them may go to Tura as may be deemed best on arriving at Goalpara.—*Baptist Missionary Magazine, November, 1874.*

WHAT to do about Tura—this was the great problem when the new arrivals came.

It seems a simple enough problem after this lapse of time. What else was there to do but to go there, and establish the mission in the very heart of the hills? There had already been unaccountable delay. The move might have taken place six years earlier. It was not completed until four more had passed.

There would seem to be room for trenchant criticism when an action so vital to the enterprise took ten years to accomplish, especially in view of repeated encouragement and offers of help from Government. But no missionary board is always wise, nor are the men and the means always forthcoming when a right decision has been made.

The point of contact with Government lay in the development of educational plans. A beginning had been made at Damra with the Normal School, and some of the teachers trained in the institution had been planted out among the villages near. Primers had been printed, and the work was proceeding satisfactorily with generous aid from Government funds. But it was local, not central, and an effort confined to the northern frontier, having in it no promise of enlightenment for the Garos as a whole. Such an arrangement could only be a compromise at the best, and must sooner or later give place to the wider plan.

The period of transition really dates from December, 1867, when Lieutenant Williamson boldly advanced through the hills and established himself under the shadow of the Tura peak. The movement was strategic, and as we have seen, immediately successful. It opened a way into the wild heart of the country. It focused the interest of the several clans. It set up a visible sign of authority on the highest of the interior ranges, and thus took advantage of a natural watershed from which the rivers and streams of influence might flow down easily, by a hundred channels, to every corner of the land.

From the day when the lucky officer built his first stockade, set its back to the mountain, and looked out over the strange rough territory he had come to govern, it was a foregone conclusion that the mission would have to follow. To stay outside on the isolated rock at Goalpara was to lose grip of the greatness of the task, to sacrifice permanent and imperial opportunities for the temporary convenience and absorption in the duties of the hour.

The men on the spot saw this. It haunted their imagination and controlled their thoughts. But innumerable difficulties presented themselves, by no means the least of which was the knowledge that little could be expected by way of adequate help from home. To the Board in Boston Assam was but a small and disappointing part of their Eastern field, the Garo Hills an insignificant and malarious fragment of Assam, and the Garo Mission, though fruitful, an embarrassing undertaking, not of their own choosing, yet seemingly committed to them in the providence of God, and involving responsibilities neither to be lightly regarded nor hastily assumed.

It is difficult from the records to account for the attitude of the mission during these years. It was hesitant and uncertain, when a bold policy, a straight and confident course, seemed to be demanded. But "near-cuts" in the jungle are notoriously deceptive, and the longest way round is quite likely to prove the shortest way there. The move to Tura was not an end in itself, but a means toward the Christianization of the tribe; and there were elements in the circumstances which forbade the too hasty assumption that this, the ultimate aim, was necessarily retarded by the slowness of the Board.

For one thing, the work in the Normal School and on the northern frontier flourished and spread. It was self-propagative, following natural lines of extension, while claiming ever more and more of the missionary's time. To transplant the school to Tura meant more than finding the necessary funds. It meant overcoming the prejudices of the teachers and students, who clung to the familiar region of Damra and Goalpara, and were not eager to take up residence on the interior heights. Moreover, it was very improbable that pupils to take their places could be drawn from the new neighborhood for years to come, whereas there were applicants in plenty at near range, as the school was situated at present. Obviously, this was a work that must go on; the seal of the divine approval was upon it; it was both the training institution for all future Garo teachers, and a nursery for the Garo church. To imperil its usefulness, perhaps its existence, by any sudden removal, was a step which well might seem immature both to the missionary and his staff, and to the committee at home.

And this difficulty involved another—namely, the weakening of facilities for acquiring the language, for developing the beginnings of Scripture translations, and the preparation of suitable books to be used in the village schools. For here again the most important factor was not the Government grant, however timely and generous, but that body of Christian leaders, who had all been drawn from the northern border, and were there most readily accessible and conveniently placed for aiding in the work. Mr. Keith was especially endowed for this undertaking and entered into it with great enthusiasm. He may well have looked askance at the proposal to transfer his workshop to Tura, leaving half the tools behind.

The health and smallness of the mission staff were also obstacles that barred the way. Had Mr. Stoddard's health permitted his remaining on the field, it is possible that either he or Mr. Keith might have proceeded to occupy Tura as an additional station.

The Government officials, however, held divergent views which were reflected in their dealings with the missionaries, and this accounted, in some measure, for the uncertainty of their plans. But the hand of God guides the world, not excluding the actions of these human governors, to whom he has committed the temporal well-being and destiny of the races over whom they rule. When mindful of his authority, and sympathetic toward his work, they are as much his servants as any priest or prophet, missionary or herald of the Cross. The gift of administration is theirs, the grasp of affairs as a whole, the genius for large enterprises, and a wholesome impatience with all that looks petty and parochial.

With the peaceful subjugation of the Garo tribes an accomplished fact, the Government was desirous of promulgating educational plans which should really cover the field. Convinced of the value of missionary influence, as the best means for the purpose, the lieutenant-governor, Sir George Campbell, following in the wake of his predecessor, Sir William Grey, definitely proposed to commit the entire educational interest of the district to the American mission, and provide the necessary funds. But the condition was absolute that the base of operations should be moved to Tura, and that some assurance should be given of ability to cope with the large demands of the work.

Accordingly Mr. Keith was asked to give explicit answers to the following inquiries: Will the mission undertake the management of a normal school at Tura, to be opened at once? Will they undertake to find teachers for, and to open, village schools in the interior? How many teachers, competent to instruct in Garo and Bengali, would be available yearly from the Goalpara Normal School?

With these questions came the offer of five thousand rupees for the "entire education of the Garos," coupled with the demand for an immediate removal to Tura, which involved great expense. The mission was, perhaps, a little too contented with things as they were, and here was something likely to prove a very effective spur.

Mr. Keith acted with Scottish caution and sent a diplomatic reply. The commissioner reported to the Government at Bengal, August 29, 1874, that Mr. Keith was of the opinion that the mission was able and really ought to undertake the whole work; that books and teachers were available and a fellow worker expected soon from America. Moreover, that although he could not at once visit Tura, he could send native assistants to open a central school there, and could also find teachers for other schools in the interior at the rate of about four schools per annum.

The commissioner stated that the mission had gained the confidence of the people around Goalpara, and he felt that to break up the Normal School at Damra and to withdraw mission aid from the northern Garo boundary would be very unadvisable. He also expressed the opinion that the work was too urgent and important to be left to the possible chances of American philanthropy, and suggested that such grants as Government might be able to devote should be expended through Mr. Keith for schools on the Goalpara frontier and through the deputy commissioner for the central, eastern, western, and southern portions. Further, that an intelligent educational officer be deputed to Tura to start a normal school; or if it were possible to obtain their services that one or two subinstructors of schools be appointed from the primary schools on the Mymensing frontier and placed under the orders of the deputy commissioner, and that their services be retained until a missionary should arrive from America to take up the work. He also recommended that a bungalow be erected at Tura for the convenience of the inspector, "which accommodation should always be reserved for members of the American mission."

In later correspondence it is the bungalow that bulks most largely. The move to Tura was a necessity, since the Government would have it so, but how was the missionary to live there without a house? On this rock the project for a time went hopelessly aground. There was no building available, and Mr. Keith had neither the means nor the strength to construct one from the depths of the jungle, without official resources. His wife was in failing health; his work at Goalpara pressing; what could he do? His visit to Tura, far from minimizing the obstacles, only showed them to be greater than he had at first supposed. There were no workmen to be had, and even the deputy commissioner was, on that account, sometimes in straits.

He therefore made a final appeal to the Government, but with disappointing results. Captain Williamson wrote that he was quite unable to give him any encouragement. "I hope soon to commence the schoolhouse that has been sanctioned," he wrote.

> Government has allowed me five hundred rupees to build a house to be available for their educational officers, and which the missionaries may occupy when not in use. This is the only sanction I have for any building for the mission. I could not promise you the same aid, in constructing the houses for the mission, that is offered to Mr. Cawley, neither could I bind myself to provide you with labor, which is the great difficulty at Tura, as I am already underhanded myself.

Thus the way was blocked. Meanwhile the Board had approved the transfer and was preparing to send out two new missionaries, Messrs. Mason and Phillips, for the Garo work. The news reached Mr. Keith in August and he refers to it thus:

> I thank the Executive Committee for the permission to go to Tura. I should like very much to go. But I should not at first have a good house. That, together with the change of locality, might prove too much for the already enfeebled health of my wife. If I remain here on this hill, with its river air, I have hope that my wife will be able to stay for several years, or until I complete my translation of the gospel into Garo. Then a year or two in America may fit her to return for another term of service here. And since the receipt of the intelligence that two new families are designated to this field I have thought that it would be better perhaps for one of them to go to Tura. That would secure all the aid from Government that we can hope to get, and satisfy the conditions on which Sir George Campbell made this generous offer. There would also be certain personal advantages to be gained by a new man going there directly. He could learn the language there more easily than here, and lay the founda-

tions to suit himself. Two families at Goalpara, one at Tura, and a young lady teacher, are what we now need for the work.

But the pressure from Government, exerted at the critical time, did really put the wheels of resolve in motion, while the long delay served another purpose in the good governance of God. It gave place and opportunity for the trial of lesser expedients than the gospel as a means of "taming the tribe," and brought into strong relief the ancient and eternal truth that it is "not by might nor by power, but by His Spirit" that human hearts are changed.

XXIII

THE TRUE YOKEFELLOWS--MASON AND PHILLIPS

I

MEANTIME, at sunset on December 19, 1874, the two young missionaries arrived at Goalpara to give themselves to the Garo work. Their coming is a sort of hinge upon which subsequent history turns. From that time onward the mission set itself seriously to the task of proclaiming the evangel through the whole Garo hills. It ceased to be the local effort nibbling at the northern edge, and struck for the center, establishing itself by degrees at Tura, and thence burrowing into the jungles on every side.

For such a work there was a providential preparation. The two men had much in common. Both were born in the "Empire State," with the difference of only a year and a half in age. Both were farmers' sons. They studied in the same academy and afterward became college chums. Their wives were sisters; they married on the same day, at the same time and place. They were designated to the same field, and made the voyage in company. What more could be added to fit them for the double harness?

Marcus Clark Mason was born near Strykersville, New York, on June 6, 1844. Soon after his birth his parents consecrated their lad to the Lord, in accordance with the ancient law—"the first-born of thy sons shalt thou give to me." He spent a breezy boyhood on his

Fidelia Howes

Marcus C. Mason

Ella Howes

Elnathan Phillips

father's farm, tending the cattle, helping to make the dairy produce, and driving to market. The market town was Buffalo, twenty-five miles away, and this gave him early glimpses of the outside world. Once he went as far as Niagara. He attended for many years the district school about a mile from home. He was keen in driving a bargain, and very proud of the rate secured from some of his annual contracts in the market town. It was an open-air life of zest and freedom, head and hands, from the first, being trained together. His father, a stern man, master of himself and every one and everything about him, taught him courage and strength of will. The farm life gave him a sturdy physique.

His conversion was characteristic. In that revival of religion which swept over the United States in 1857 even little hamlets shared. Meetings were held in Strykersville, and for many it was the first awakening of spiritual life. Marcus Mason, then only thirteen, felt the power of the preaching, and in the preacher's phrase, "came under conviction of sin." There was struggle of his will—he knew what was the matter with him—but he would not yield. One day in the early spring, the time of "the maple woods, the crisp February days and the sugar-making," his father sent him to the sugar-bush to gather the sap.

It was a day such as sometimes came in the idyllic times, a day of storm and tempest. There was a wild wind blowing, and when he entered the forest the great hemlocks were swaying and soughing in the gale. The noise was terrific—it looked as though at any moment some of them might come crashing down. It must have been an unusual occasion, for the strong lad was not easily scared. But a fiercer tempest, even than that without, was going on within. Death seemed imminent, and he was not ready for death. There was an account to be settled first, a submission to make, and a reconciliation to seek. The fury of the elements seemed to be wrapping him round and singling him out for destruction as if it were the wrath of God. It was impossible to stay. With a frightened face, he turned and fled back into the open. There, leaning against a great tree stump, he battled with himself, wondering what to do. He could neither go home, for he dared not disobey his father, nor yet venture under those tossing trees. "What has made such a coward of me?" he thought. Yet he knew. Presently the hardness within melted, and, all reserve giving way, he fell upon his knees and quietly gave himself to God. "I don't deserve anything," he murmured between his sobs, "do with me just as you are of a mind to." And the sweet old truth of redeeming love that God is more ready to forgive than we are to ask, flowed into his soul like balm. What could the storm do? The dove of peace was in his heart. He rose up and trod the shrieking forest without fear.

It was not long before Elder Kneeland baptized him. To the ministry of that good man the boy owed more than he could ever tell. "Marcus," he said on giving him the hand of fellowship, "remember that we should feel very bad if you should in any way go back." And then, like a wise pastor, he set him to work. A class was given him in the Sunday School. The church needed another collector, and he was enrolled. There were little meetings to organize for prayer and fellowship among the new converts, where he from the very first was taught to lead an active Christian life.

The missionary idea took shape in his mind. As in so many other instances, it was a missionary from the field who first planted the seed. Mrs. Bennet from Burma, sister of his pastor, visiting the Sunday School, exhibited an image of Buddha, and gave an address. This and another address from a missionary with the appeal "Six Men for Arakan" left a lasting impression, though it did not lead him to think of the work abroad in any definite way. Later, in college, he wrote in his diary:

> As I expect to live, but am always ready to die, so I expect to be a missionary, but am always ready to do anything else the Lord wants.

He spent the winter of 1865 teaching school at Waterloo, Iowa. Then came an unusually hard season at the farm, followed by typhus and inflammation of the lungs. He had a constitution like iron, but all this strain and toil was beginning to tell on his health.

In 1866, attracted by an advertisement, he went to study at Hamilton, a little town in "one of the healthiest and most beautiful regions of central New York." Hamilton was the seat of Madison, now Colgate, University, from which an astonishing number had gone forth to evangelize the nations.

In the academy young Mason spent two years, then took the full college and seminary courses. Many of the students had to earn their way. Marcus was one of these, and had a rather hard time at first. He cut wood, sold soap, did clerical work for the Institution, anything to turn an honest dime, at times boarding himself and cooking his own food. His friends urged him to be content with a partial course. But this was contrary to his secret covenant with God, that he would go on as long as sufficient money for the barest necessities could be found. Sometimes he did well, earning from forty to eighty dollars a month. But there were days when he was tempted to give up.

The soap manufacturers, for whom he did a little business on commission, offered him a post as wholesale agent by which they assured him he could easily net seven thousand dollars a year. It was a tempting offer. By taking it he could earn enough in a year or two to pay for a good and full education. But held by his promise to God he turned the offer over to a chum who kept the agency for many years. This test of fidelity strengthened the roots of his manhood.

On another occasion his last cent had been expended, and he had eaten the last mouthful of food. He rose in the morning and went as usual to recitations, but at noon when he crossed to his room, he realized there was nothing to eat for dinner. Hungry, and with a heavy heart, he took his basket and walked down to the grocery store intending to ask for work enough to pay for a meal, and then turn his back on the town in which his hopes of an education had so long been set. On the way it occurred to him to call at the post-office and see if there were any letters. There was one. It was handed to him. He opened it and found inside a five-dollar bill. There was no message, no signature, no clue as to who had sent it. Not a scrap or a word. What wonder that the ball rose in his throat? Help so direct, timely, and unexpected, could come from only one source—from Him who "knoweth our down-sitting and uprising, and is acquainted with all our ways." His faith thus encouraged, he went on to the store, filled his basket with provisions, and knew he had a Father in heaven.

Long afterward he heard how the money came to be sent. An old schoolmate had married and settled down. Knowing the struggle Marcus was making, the friend had it in mind to send him an occasional gift. But time went on and the matter was forgotten. One night, however, he could not sleep. The impulse was upon him to do something at once. He woke his wife and told her how he felt. "Marcus wants money, sure," he said. "I feel like sending some right away." "Why don't you do it, then?" was the kindly, practical answer. So the next morning, he rose early, went to the barn, harnessed his team, and drove to Strykersville, and posted the envelope with the five-dollar bill.

II

Meantime Elnathan G. Phillips had arrived at Hamilton, joined the college, and was studying with Mason in the class of '72. Phillips was born in the township of East Bloomfield, Ontario County, New York, December 6, 1845. His father was a well-to-do farmer, and the principal supporter of the local Baptist church, which was situated at Bristol, some miles away. The easy circumstances of the family made hardship for the lad unnecessary, though he was brought up to love work, and led a strong, healthy life. His parents were of a sturdy religious type, and this character was their son's best inheritance. In early childhood a dangerous illness almost carried him off. They prayed very earnestly that his life might be spared, and should the prayer be answered, solemnly vowed to give him wholly to God.

When eleven years old Elnathan, moved by the meetings held in Bristol as in other places during the "Great Revival," knelt one day in the hayloft, alone with God, intending to pray. The thought suggested itself that he was too young and ignorant to know what he was doing, that he had better wait. It was not until three years later that help came to him and he ventured to make a fresh start. No one in all that time seems to have guessed his need. The word of release was spoken by a stranger, a young student preacher, who had come for a Sunday to fill the Bristol pulpit. It was customary on such occasions for the "supply" to be met at the station on Saturday and driven over to the Phillips' farm. This duty was entrusted to Elnathan. It was a pleasant drive, with plenty to engage the interest and conversation of the visitor in the natural features of the country and the character and idiosyncrasies of its people; but this stranger, attracted perhaps by the winsomeness and modesty of his boy companion, sought to use the opportunity for the highest ends.

They had driven far and chatted about many things, when at length, turning quiet eyes upon the lad's face, with a look of kindly and serious meaning that seemed to read his heart, the visitor asked him the question that impelled decision. "What are you going to do with your life?" The boy flushed and hung his head, but the next instant looked up and made a vow which, once made, is irrevocable as the word of a recruit enlisting in the services of the King. "I am going to give it to God." Then followed a helpful talk and presently they reached the farm. The stranger kept the lad's confidence sacred, and no one in the household got any inkling of what had passed between them.

Elnathan led the horse to the stable, and having attended to its wants, prayed for forgiveness and right guidance. Even as the thoughts came to be expressed he was conscious of infinite Love, enfolding, comforting, answering the cry of the heart, with a whispered "What is there between me and thee? Thou art mine, child, today and forevermore, and I am thine."

The joy of discipleship and the liberty of decision had now become his, but natural timidity and reserve still held him back from the duty of open confession. One day while working in the field with his father, they two being alone, he managed to tell him, after a painful struggle, that he wished to be baptized. The announcement was received in silence; a silence grave and deliberate, at once a challenge to sincerity and a reverent recognition of the sacredness of the divine seal and touch. But the lad, now that his secret was out, felt intense relief and understood that a new bond of sympathy had been formed between his father and himself. In due time the boy was baptized.

His school days were spent at Canandaigua. Nothing eventful happened during the years preceding college, but Christian character was forming, and, at length, with the avowed purpose of becoming a preacher, he set out for Hamilton. His parents had never forgotten their vow of consecration, but neither had they done anything to guide him in his choice of a special calling. It was not their wish to bring any influence to bear on their children which might lead them to act in advance of their own convictions. But when, after another struggle, Elnathan declared his resolve to give himself to the work of the ministry, in obedience to what he felt was the call of God, they gratefully welcomed the purpose and helped him all they could through the long period of preparation.

What his mother's thoughts were from that day onward, she told him for the first time in a letter written only a few years ago at the age of eighty-five. She had, it seems, a clear prevision that he would serve on the foreign field, though the young man himself entertained no such thought until long afterward. These were her words:

When I first knew that you thought of going to college, feeling that this would be only preliminary to becoming a missionary

I felt the wish to hinder you. It almost seems that it was not quite so easy for persons to go to the foreign field then as now. When you went I felt as though I had buried you, but when we received your first letter, I did not have that feeling any more.

At the close of their college course, before entering the theological seminary, both Mason and Phillips were moved by a loud call for men to send in their names as volunteers for foreign work. The offer was conditioned on the judgment of the Society that it would be wise for them to forego the advantage of theological training and go out at once. Happily better counsel prevailed.

All the traditions of Hamilton were such as to encourage the missionary idea. A former student, William Dean, D. D., of Bangkok, Siam, thus wrote of his alma mater, as he remembered it in the early days:

The prevailing characteristic of the Institution was the spirit of missions, and to this work, perhaps more than anything else, may be attributed the prosperity of that "school of the prophets." Hamilton men, whether they have gone abroad or settled at home, have generally been missionary men. From the campfire of Hamilton Hill has been kindled a light in many of the dark places of the earth.

This statement is strictly true. The very first student of Hamilton, Jonathan Wade, was a missionary to Burma; and the record shows that seventy-five missionaries went out from the Institution in one period of fifty years. Among these were many for Burma; two for Bengal-Orissa; Samuel S. Day, founder of the Telugu Mission; and Jeremiah Phillips, father of Dr. H. L. Phillips, late Secretary of the India Sunday School Union; a few for Assam, including Miles Bronson and Ira J. Stoddard; and two for China.

Such being the history of the Institution, the decision of Messrs. Mason and Phillips, on the completion of their theological course, to offer themselves for the work abroad, was received alike by the faculty and the Mission Society with the utmost satisfaction, most particularly because for thirteen years not a man had gone out thence to the foreign field. The letters of Doctor Bronson and Doctor Stoddard, giving full account of the movement among the Garos, had lately been powerful factors in arousing a livelier interest and desire.

The candidates were called to the "Rooms" of the American Baptist Missionary Union in Boston, examined, accepted, and designated to the Garo field. They were married the day after Commencement and set sail three months later. The double wedding took place at Hamilton on June 18, 1874, in the presence of hundreds of fellow students and guests. The weather was fair and the air musical with the peals of bells. Ella Howes was united to Elnathan Phillips, and Fidelia to Marcus Mason.

The two sisters were sadly missed when they went away. They had rare qualities of mind and heart, and had received a thorough education at the Ladies' Seminary of the town. Gracious in manner and earnest in Christian life, with natural sympathy and tact, and plenty of wise womanly wit, they were well prepared for the missionary life before them.

XXIV

EPOCH-MAKERS

THE task before the two young couples demanded a strong mental equipment, sound knowledge of the Scriptures, ability to manage men, much wisdom of heart, and great powers of physical endurance, with courage. A literature had to be produced, beginning with early school-books and going on to the finished translation of the New Testament, in a language of which little more than the rudiments had been learned by their predecessors, or written down for the tribe; journeyings made unattended through the roughest interior country and friendly relations established with a sullen and savage people; teachers trained, the raw material being the wild Garo boy or girl, and when trained, sent back into the depths of the jungle with torches lighted at the central fire; the beginnings of interest in a score of far-scattered places watched and fostered; and churches formed and guided to a right exercise of discipline and an earnest advocacy of the faith.

All this, however, lay in the dim future that evening in 1874, when the two couples stepped off the steamer at Goalpara and shook hands with Mr. Keith. He had been watching for them all day from the bungalow on the top of the hill, and, at the first sight of the trail of smoke in the west, had hurried down, bringing coolies and palanquins to take them and their luggage across the broad stretch of sand. Long before casting anchor they could see him, a solitary figure, pacing up and down the bank.

Wedged between the two flats, the steamer Success made a pretty picture coming up the stream in the warm evening glow. The little group at the prow were glad to be nearing the end of their journey. Their eyes scanned with eager interest the quiet beauty of the final reach; the broad surface of the stream, its race past sedge and sand; a native boat paddling inshore, with the turbans of the rowers showing white against the reeds and swaying grass; the mountains banked behind, with long forest-covered spurs, stretching like the arms of a starfish toward the river; and right ahead, detached from the tip of one of these, the isolated rock of Goalpara, like a wooded Gibraltar, at the water's edge. On a nearer approach, the western face of this cliff being lighted by the setting sun, they could see the Government buildings nestling at the foot, the paths zigzagging up the hill, and the mission slope and the mission house at the summit outlined against the sky. An hour later, they had climbed to its hospitable porch, and found Mrs. Keith on the veranda waiting to give them welcome.

In a little more than a year after their arrival they were left alone at Goalpara. And ever since, with untiring devotion, the two colleagues have toiled to accomplish their task, to build up, among the crags of the jungle, a "spiritual house," a temple whose walls are salvation and whose gates are praise. They may be reckoned in truth the makers of the mission as we see it today.

The contrast in the appearance of these two brother missionaries is strongly marked. Doctor Mason is of the broad, burly type, thick-set, with a fast-hardening frame, and large gripping hands. His face is a rounded oval with no rugged lines. The dome forehead has a slight fringe of dark gray hair, the mustache is full and gray. The cheeks, soft and almost chubby, grow a close-cropped whitening beard. Called out of his study, you may see him any morning standing squarely on the veranda, in shirt sleeves, a light, open waistcoat, with spectacles on the end of his nose, and kindly gray eyes looking over them—a picture of Puritan manhood, subtle sagacity, and benevolence. His manner is quiet; it gives the impression of subdued forces in reserve. Neither voice nor laugh rings. But few men have a larger fund of humor or can tell a story with better effect. A whimsical light generally plays about the eyes, but they are clear and serious, and, on occasion, can be cold or stern. Under stress of moral indignation there is a sudden revealing of hidden fire. The voice has a thrill of passion in it, especially when speaking of the Garo converts and their love and fidelity to the Saviour; the eyes swim in a shining mist, indicating an open, elemental nature, well disciplined, abounding in vitality, with plenty of pushful resource.

Doctor Phillips is of a military type, slim, wiry, well groomed, alert in movement, with erect, finely poised head, and strong, clear-cut face. He might be the colonel of a regiment. The profile shows a clifflike brow, with overhanging, bushy eyebrows black as jet, a Roman nose, thick, drooping mustachios, and (in summer!) a clean-shaven chin. The complexion is pale and there are deep furrows on the cheeks. But the eyes, intensely dark, flash at you with a wide-awake brilliance, which is bold and almost startling. *Pince-nez* in a gold frame soften this expression, while heightening the general refinement of the face. A man of soldierly caution and reticence in speech, Doctor Phillips is more retiring than his colleague, but has the same keen sense of humor, tactful personality, and strong emotional nature.

Their very names are now inseparably linked. To think of one is instantly to recall the other. You can no more dissociate Mason and Phillips than you can Martha and Mary. Unlike in disposition as they are in appearance, and often taking the opposite sides in questions of debate, yet as often reaching cordial agreement by interchange of views, they have lived together all these years in the happiest relations of mutual respect and affection, pursuing with singleness of mind their common aim. A pair raised of God on farms in Western New York,[1] with which he might more fully answer that prayer of Ramke for knowledge of the truth; a pair called of God to work with that other pair of men whom God raised in the jungles of Assam. In their carrying out of this their mission work they have stamped the enterprise with those qualities of vigor, strength, and sound judgment, which belong to both, but with no idiosyncrasies, no individually aggressive personal ear-marks. There is a fine breadth and balance about them, a full roundness of character that does not attract by single outstanding qualities, but makes its impression whole. Neither has a following, or his own exclusive line of work. No one says, "I am of Mason," or "I am of Phillips." Their achievement is one, because each is the complement of the other.

As a fitting crown to so perfect a fellowship and so fruitful and united a life, their alma mater conferred upon each of them in June, 1906, the degree of doctor of divinity. There appears to have been no precedent for the bestowal of this distinction upon two men of the same class together, but it was felt impossible to distinguish between Mason and Phillips in any public recognition of the honor they have done the University and the esteem in which they are held by the churches.

[1] Doctor Phillips, Doctor and Mrs. Stoddard, Doctor Mason, and Miss Stella Mason were all from Western New York; the last four from the Buffalo Association. Mrs. Bronson, Mrs. Mason, and Mrs. Phillips were from the town of Madison, Central New York, Doctor Bronson and Mrs. Harding were from Norway, Central New York.

One of the first problems for these newcomers to solve was the selection of a position for their head-quarters. Tura as a favorable location was of course mentioned, and in September, 1875, the two went together up to Tura to consider its advantages, and if advisable, to select a site and settle plans for the future. It was decided that Mr. Mason should for a while further carry on the work begun on the Goalpara site and that Mr. Phillips should open a new station at Tura.

At Tura they were the guests of Captain Williamson. He showed them the site chosen by Messrs. Bronson and Stoddard, but advised them not to take it, saying that it was soon to be made a parade-ground. So they wandered about, clambering up and down the steep ridges and the lower flanks and spurs of the mountain, in search of a better plot. It was all jungle then—jungle that smothered the irregular contour of the ridges and shut out the view. But they found the very patch to suit, a fine bulge on the northern spur, about a mile from the Government lines. It was draped with forest and rose up boldly between two streams, a ravine on either side. From the rough cone at the top, its skirts slope down to a broadening base, gently lifted at one end, to form a beautiful knoll, facing the open, from which pleasant glimpses could be had of Rangira, the plains, and the far, shining river. They climbed up a tall tree, like any settler out West, and peering about, spied out the land.

Apart from the convenience of the site itself, with its rolling surface, ample space, and perennial supply of pure, fresh water rushing down from the heights, its situation has proved to be of the utmost value to the mission. It stands aloof from the town, yet astride the only path of entrance from the whole northern frontier, from the Khasia Hills boundary on the east to Singimari on the west. The routes from these points, picking up innumerable tracks, as they come through the hills, converge on the edge of the mission plot and pass through it to the station and the market-ground, thus bringing ceaseless streams of Garos from the remote interior villages into touch with the mission on every market-day.

The parade-ground would have been small by comparison, its water-supply obtainable only by a steep descent, and its contiguity to the bazaar a continual source of distraction. Moreover, its terminal and isolated position, a sort of land's end promontory, projected from the market ground, would have left the mission cut off from the currents of traffic and deprived of a constant opportunity of intercourse with strangers from the central hills.

The object of their visit accomplished, the missionaries returned to Goalpara, Captain Williamson escorting them to the river. He was no less pleased than they at the prospect of a speedy settlement of the mission at his own headquarters, and continued to be a staunch friend of the enterprise through the future years. It will doubtless be accounted to him for righteousness when the secrets of all hearts are revealed. The two strangers felt the charm of his personality as the wild hillmen over whom he ruled had felt it. They reached the river about ten o'clock on a bright, hot morning, but their host sat chatting with them until two, when, mounting his Arab, he rode straight back to Tura, forty miles, without drawing rein, except to change *dawks*. They knew he had to make the journey in one heat and wondered at his lingering as the day wore on. But the action was characteristic, the sort of swift exercise he delighted in to keep himself in training. The Garos smiled admiringly as they watched his ways. Many a tussle they had with him in tests of strength, but he always won. They would tell how he would challenge them to a race up-hill, and easily outdistance their fleetest of foot; how he would toss up potatoes, by way of teaching them to shoot, and split each one with a bullet as it fell; and how he was quick to reward special service or skill. Very proud was that Garo, Mena, whom he selected to run the whole way to Goalpara and back and bring medicine for a fellow officer; proudest of all when his speed was praised, for he had made the round trip in two days and one night. And he received, in addition, the nice little sum of fifty rupees. Tradition has it that on one occasion the deputy commissioner rode to Goalpara, a hundred and thirty miles, via Garobada and Singimari, in a single day; and then, having bathed and dined, sat down to write his administration report. It also adds that he used eight horses, some of which died because of this work.

XXV

THE PIONEERS

On December 12, 1876, Mr. Phillips writes:

I am at Tura at last. After all the wishing, the talking, and the waiting, there is the prospect that we shall, to say the least, have a mission station here. May the Father of mercies grant that it may speedily become a center of saving influence for the Garos! I left Goalpara November seventh, reaching Dhubri on the following day, where I stopped to get coolies for building, as this is a place to which many Nepalese come seeking work.[1] I arrived here late on Saturday evening. Sunday I had services in the tent. A number of coolies employed here by Government attended besides several others. They listened attentively, I can't say quietly, for they talked nearly as much as I during quite a part of the service! But they came again on Monday, and other evenings that week. I brought one of our Garo preachers with me from Goalpara, and also one of the schoolboys, temporarily as servant. . . It is all new to them; they have not heard a word of the glad tidings. We must take the very beginning of the gospel with them. Their constant reply is *"Aija"* ("Don't know!")

I have decided to put up first a very small house, twenty-four by thirty feet, and we will occupy that while the other is being built. When we are through using it as a dwelling, it can easily be changed into a chapel by moving the mat partition walls. The little house is now well begun, and I hope soon to complete it, and then bring Mrs. Phillips here to our home.

Thus, with his first thought of the kingdom, and his little house from the beginning a "tent of meeting," the

[1] It took him some days there, as non-Garos feared to enter Garo land, and the Garos of the place were not inclined to serve. After three weeks at Tura his force reached eighteen, twelve Nepalese and six Garos.

missionary laid his foundations. The jungle patch soon began to be alive with the sights and sounds of labor. The clearing grew; day by day many-handed work went on; coolies bringing in their loads of lumber which sawyers had been cutting, men measuring the ground and driving in the stakes; trees being felled, rocks and boulders moved out of the way. But there was scarcely an echo of all this in the long letter he was writing home. He was glad to get sawyers but most glad when some of the workmen proved to be seekers after truth. The voices he would have us listen to are not those of the timber-yard and the workshop, but of the little tent at night, with its handful of souls hearing for the first time of God and the Saviour. He dismisses in a sentence the dwelling-house for himself and his wife, but lingers to tell in detail the history of a few inquirers, " stones made ready at the quarry " for another sort of building, even a "spiritual house." As he thinks of the foundations laid for that fair fabric, and of its walls already rising around him, fashioned by unseen hands, it is no wonder that the day's din dies out of his mind.

About the middle of January, having finished the temporary bungalow, Mr. Phillips went down to Goalpara, and from there to Rajasimla, to attend the association meetings. Returning, husband and wife broke up their home at Goalpara, then started themselves, going by steamer to Romari, where they arrived on Saturday, March 17, 1877.

It was a tedious journey after that. The boats with their baggage did not turn up till midday on Monday, necessitating a dreary wait of forty-eight hours in a shanty on the sand. Glad to get away, they set out at once in the hot March sun, for Putimari, a distance of fifteen miles. Nothing could have been more foolish or more hurtful. But we all have to learn by experience. Poor Mrs. Phillips had fever and ague as soon as they reached the rest-house, and spent a miserable night. "Such greenhorns we were!" she said. The next day they moved to Damalgiri, and on Wednesday reached Tura. There, at any rate, a pleasant surprise awaited her. The little bungalow which she had expected to find a wretched bamboo hut, turned out to be a charming "cottage in the wood," with its white walls of wattle and plaster, the great mountain as a background, and the babbling brook close by. Her husband had dissembled in describing the edifice—such are the ways of men—partly to try her resolution and partly to effect this little rush of gladness when it came into view. He had his reward no less than she. They breakfasted with Mr. and Mrs. Cawley and then came over in a flutter of happy anticipation, to settle down in the first Tura mission house.

But on closer acquaintance, it proved to be a tiny, inconvenient dwelling even for temporary use. The prettiness was all outside! Moreover, it "squeaked," making queer sounds at night, which were apt to get on one's nerves, when, at dusk, leopards had been seen playing in the space outside! It proved also to be rather unhealthy. Master, mistress, and servants, all fell ill. The cook lay sick in the cook-house. Mr. Phillips had fever, with "shivers" nine times at intervals of a fortnight. He got to watching for them, they came with such clocklike regularity. It was rather a miserable beginning. To add to the trouble, a letter with disappointing news had come from home, which gave a sad account of the mission funds, closing with a touch of criticism, if not of reproach. But Mr. Phillips sent back a brave and fitting reply.

The first-fruits were gathered on two Sabbaths in May, when six men were baptized, in a clear pool prettily situated in a leafy dell at the base of the knoll on the lower outskirts of the mission site. The pool was a shelving, sandy bottom, and the water from the stream comes rushing down to it, making pleasant music as it swirls among the stones. On the second Sabbath a dozen or more wild Garos were present, attentively regarding this strange sight and listening to the explanation given. Of these converts, two of them first heard the message in the missionary's tent six months before, one ventured as a school-teacher to settle at Chokpotgiri, in the south of the hills, and soon sealed his testimony with his blood, a martyr to the cause.

Meanwhile the present bungalow was getting on. It was to stand on the crown of the knoll, and a small avenue of trees planted up the gentle slope would make a pleasant approach. The change in the appearance of things must have struck Mr. Mason agreeably when he came up, in December, to pay them a visit.

It was now becoming clear that if there were to be but two missionaries the best interests of the mission would be served by their being located together at Tura. The rainy season work could be carried on then in concert, and they would always be able to consult each other on important matters as occasion arose.

On his return trip to Goalpara, Mr. Mason wrote to a friend:

I am spending the night in one of the wildest of places, surrounded by the wildest of peoples, twelve thousand miles from my native home, fifty miles from my family, and a day's journey from a single white face. I am stopping in a large deserted village, situated on the bank of a stream that goes roaring along the gorge, over a bed of massive boulders. The Garo houses, still

Photo by W. Dring.

Tura's First Baptistery

in very good order, are mostly covered with a luxuriant growth of weeds and vines. I have just been through one. Like all Garo houses it is a long, low, dark, smoky thing, built on posts, with grass roof and bamboo sides. The floor is twenty feet wide, and one hundred and twenty feet long. I found nothing in the house but a few old war-shields and two strings of skulls and jaw-bones, of which I counted over a hundred. Just outside, over the bones of the dead who have been burned, stand several poles, loaded with rice and other food intended for the demons. Close by stands a post or a bull-sacrificing fork to which the village priest was recently tied and whipped for allowing a murder here. Two plains people passing asked for guides. Two Garos, thinking it a fine opportunity to obtain a pair of skulls without detection, led them into the jungle and killed one of them. The other escaped, bleeding, and ran all the way back to Tura, about sixteen miles, over the Arbela range. In these wilds, elephants, tigers, leopards, bears, wild cattle, and hogs still find their natural home. In these fastnesses the people have for ages perhaps felt safe from intrusion, but the power of civilization has found entrance, and now we come bearing the Sword of the Spirit, whereby we hope to see them liberated from their bondage of sin, and a change made in all things.

After writing these reflections, the missionary, with a rather weird sense of loneliness, lay down to sleep. Totaram, a Garo Christian helper, kept him company. Both were weary and perhaps a little anxious. The influence of the night and their gloomy surroundings, uncertainty as to the temper of the late inhabitants, who could not have gone far away, were thoughts neither comforting nor restful. They nevertheless dropped off to sleep, to be startled about midnight by blood-curdling cries. At first far off, the strange noises came nearer and nearer, traveling up the gorge. There could be no doubt that they were the shouts of the wild Garos making for the village, as they followed the course of the stream. They listened with strained attention. "In all my journeys over the hills," says Doctor Mason, "I have only twice been startled by people. Once was in that village and on that night." Doubtless the ghastly memory of the poor Bengali who had been murdered here gave them creepy sensations. At length Totaram shouted in commanding tones: "Be quiet, can't you! There's a sahib here!" The effect was magical; instant silence reigned. Then, in the darkness, they could hear the Garos passing around the house and whispering to one another: "What sahib? Where?" Perhaps they thought it was the deputy commissioner come back to inflict more punishment. At any rate, before very long, they took themselves off, and the sleepers settled down again to their rest.

A month later, in January, 1878, Mr. Phillips, having sent his wife by steamer on a short visit to her sister, also went through the hills to Goalpara. These were the first attempts of white men to enter the Garo interior without an armed guard. On the thirty-first, all but Mrs. Mason, whose small baby, Walter, prevented her from undertaking the journey, started for the association meetings held at Resu. That night they camped under a large rubber tree, on the bank of the stream—"My first night in a tent," Mrs. Phillips tells us. Scores of people "clad in clean white garments" welcomed them with a hearty handshake, as they emerged from the jungle and appeared on the Association grounds. There was a marked contrast to the days that followed, as she went with her husband, via Nibari, to Tura. The people then fled into the jungle at the mere sight of a white woman, the first to make that trip across the inner hills.

During this visit to Goalpara an important step was taken. The Government had renewed its offer to make over to the mission the whole educational work of the district, provided the mission would bring the Normal School to Tura. This proposal was definitely accepted and the school moved up in March, 1878. Thus another link with Goalpara was broken. It was the beginning of the end.

The school was held in a shed which the Chinese carpenters had been using. These carpenters, employed in the first instance by the deputy commissioner, when no longer needed by him had been engaged by Mr. Phillips. The shed also served as a chapel for the Sunday and Thursday services, being more convenient than the poky little dining-room of the missionaries' temporary dwelling.

On February 24 two women were baptized, wives of two of the men who confessed their faith the previous year. They were the first women to be baptized in Tura.

In May the little settlement was visited by death. Mr. H. B. Eyre, assistant superintendent of police, came in from camp with fever, and almost immediately passed away. To Captain Peet, the deputy commissioner, and Mr. Phillips fell the mournful duty of selecting the last resting-place and committing the body to the ground. No cemetery had been previously marked out. The site chosen was a high grassy slope above the bridge over the Rengi, about half-way between the station and the mission spur. Near and yet apart, lone and lifted up, with an open prospect that raises the thoughts heavenward, and a quiet slope facing the setting sun, it is a fitting spot for the silent home of the dead. The following day, Dr. J. P. Cromarty, the civil surgeon, who had just returned from a trip to Calcutta, was carried out from the same house and laid beside his younger comrade.

A week later, May seventeen, Mr. Phillips and his wife took possession of the new bungalow, and found it a most pleasant change. But Mrs. Phillips was almost immediately prostrated with fever, which lasted a fortnight.

On July 1, Mr. Phillips reported a much brighter outlook.

> We are comfortably settled in our new bungalow. The carpenters and coolies have been dismissed, and I begin to feel free for genuine evangelistic work. I am glad to say that Mrs. Phillips has entirely recovered, and we are both now enjoying good health. During these days of heavy rains we find it no small source of comfort that our house has floors clear from the damp; and that with windows having glass we can shut out the storm without shutting out the daylight. Such a house will, I am sure, contribute to retaining health.

But alas, more sickness was ahead. On the thirteenth he began a course of instruction which was to last three months, taking two evenings a week.

> The pupils seemed interested, and I anticipated pleasure in teaching them, but on the very next day I was taken sick with remittent fever, and on the twenty-ninth was obliged to dismiss the school. We have had excessive rain. On account of the swollen rivers and land-slips blocking the road, no rice could be brought up from the plains. The price in the bazaar trebled, and finally the supply failed entirely. . . On the last day Mrs. Phillips fed the boys with biscuits and the next day they were off.

Her husband's attacks of fever seemed to have been severe and frequent. And she was naturally alarmed. There was no doctor and no other lady in the station. July 28 was a sad Sunday. Abdul, the doctor-babu, came over in the morning and gave some medicine, but the patient fell into a stupor and lay all day. Was there to be a third grave opened in the little cemetery on the hill? The poor wife suffered an agony of fear. "He was very near the Border-land, and I was quite alone." But she continued to pray and trust. The attacks lasted, with intermissions, till October, causing great debility and quite unfitting him for work. But as often as possible the

Sunday service was maintained, and, at last, on October 17, the school was recalled. The pioneers were not to be daunted or driven off the field. While any strength remained to them they would stay at Tura and continue the work so well begun.

XXVI

THE NEW SETTLEMENT TRIED BY FIRE

WE now come to the final stage in the process of removal—the breaking up of the remaining home at Goalpara, and the joining of the two forces at the headquarters in the hills.

Approval of this step had been received from home, and Mr. Mason was authorized to sell the Goalpara house. After days of toil and trouble, arrangements having been completed, just as darkness was covering them, the family crowded with their goods and servants into Bengali boats, and pushed from shore out into the broad, dark, deep, boiling river, and for three days in that bark and four days of varied land travel they made a never-to-be-forgotten journey, and reached Tura November 27, 1878. At Tura they occupied the little hut first built by Mr. Phillips while a second bungalow was in course of erection. The joy of the two sisters and their husbands was great in thus being reunited after their long separation, when so much of the time had been spent in anxiety.

The mission was about to be strengthened by the arrival of a lady for work among the women and girls. In expectation of this Mrs. Mason wrote:

> It will be a happy day for us when we can see something being done for these poor women and girls. Many of them are as bright and pretty girls as you see anywhere. I have one in mind now that no one could help loving at first sight.

Miss Russell reached Tura on January 2, 1879.

Mr. Phillips, visiting Samnagar in October, sketches the progress of the work:

You see I am not at Tura, though as I sit writing, I can see the blue top of Tura mountain in the distance. Yes, we are getting quite a settlement of our own at Tura now. Miss Russell has men sawing lumber for her bungalow and schoolroom, men cutting posts, and others digging holes, and so forth. Brother Mason's bungalow is nearing completion; they hope to occupy it within a month, I think. That bit of ground in the Garo Hills certainly has a different appearance from what it had when I went there three years ago next month. Then it was wholly jungle; now we have a community of our own—"The United States," as our English friends over at the station sometimes say. I trust that in this building the Lord built with us and that we shall be prospered.

Mr. Mason had chosen a capital site for his bungalow; just the place for a spider who means business to spin his web. The road that comes around the bulge cuts the compound in two, and forms the starting-place of a green, switch-back hollow, that slopes down, and then up, in a graceful curve to the Phillips bungalow, set endwise on the top of the knoll. As you pause at the edge of this slope you face beautiful jets of water rising from an artificial pool, used as a baptistery, built in memory of Mrs. Fidelia Mason; the meeting-house stands to the right and the Mason bungalow to the left, each flanking the entrance, with a broad space between, each conveniently placed, just below the road, to catch the passers-by. At the end of the vista, in the left-hand corner at the base of the knoll, the dip flows down into sort of a pocket, with Miss Russell's bungalow stretched across the mouth. Miss Russell's bungalow was only just beginning to take shape at the time of which we are thinking and the school building stood then on the site where the chapel stands today.

On December 1, 1879, the Masons took possession of their house. Mr. Mason wrote: "We moved into our new house a week ago last Saturday, and feel like birds escaped from a cage."

With his bungalow finished, the missionary promptly went off on a tour, returning toward the end of the month. So the year closed very happily; the mission staff all together, and all well, the road end of the compound full of new serviceable buildings, and all the work in full swing. At that time Mr. and Mrs. P. H. Moore, just arriving from America for Nowgong, paid this new station a visit of a few days.

Another week and it was little more than a heap of ashes. Mr. Mason was heating some varnish in an inner room when it blazed up suddenly, caught the ceiling cloth, and then the thatch. He rushed outside with a pot of living flame in his hands; but alas, too late. Their beautiful home was burning. In one short hour nothing was left of it but a few charred posts. The Chinese carpenters, in the little dwelling opposite, by the school, and the Government clerks who were living across the road and had a holiday that day, worked with a will to render what help they could; but all was lost. The police came over as soon as possible, but not in time to save any property. The flying sparks and red-hot splinters threatened even the Phillips bungalow on the top of the knoll. Blankets and wet plantain leaves were spread over the thatched roof, and by quick action and vigilant care, that building, but, alas, that building alone, was preserved. Mr. Mason, in great sorrow, sent home the following account:

From Mr. Phillips' letter last week you have heard of our calamity. It is a heavy blow, and you will doubtless feel it severely, but I am sure you can never realize its severity to the ex-

Photo by W. Mason.

A Part of the Mission Compound. Doctor Phillips' House on the Hill

Rev. W. Dring's Bungalow

tent we do here. Years of mission labor are lost. We are thrown far back in our plans of work; how far can only be told by future providences. My hands are useless and will be for some time to come. I am still unable to be out, but I am recovering from the shock of the burns. I cannot therefore, write you full particulars of the fire nor of our present circumstances; but, lying on my back, I dictate a few words to let you know of our wants, and beg for help.

Although we lost all our stores and great part of our clothing and furniture, this loss to us is small compared with the loss of a house. For a long time our only hope of health and a continued stay in Assam has been in the obtaining of a suitable house. The new house seemed to far surpass our expectations. For health, comfort, for pleasantness and durability, it was all we could ask; yet it cost less than any other house in Tura.

Our work seemed to move on with remarkable ease and rapidity. I had spent over two weeks among the churches and heathen villages, and Brother Phillips and myself were about to start on another tour. But I am prostrated; the house is consumed; with it the schoolhouse, dormitory, two pundits' houses, my accounts of every description, records of the mission, every paper belonging to the office, and the Garo Gospels prepared by Mr. Keith, with the exception of the two hundred copies of Luke and John which are in Calcutta. Mr. Keith's Garo Dictionary and Outline of Garo Grammar and nearly all the books we had in Garo are burned. A rough translation of about half of The Acts in manuscript, a Garo Arithmetic of about one hundred octavo pages, ready for the press, to which I had given considerable attention during last summer, besides odd moments for the last three years; much labor in manuscript on the history of the Garo Mission, are all consumed. The Scriptures and most of the other books must be replaced as soon as possible.

My faith is strong, my heart is hopeful; but this calamity puzzles me as to what is the line of duty. We are now staying in Miss Russell's room at Brother Phillips' house; but we know not what day she may be deprived of her present refuge at Doctor Cooper's, and we be obliged to live in a tent or a straw hut.

I will write further as soon as I recover the use of my hands. Please answer by cable, with as little delay as possible, as we can make no plans until we can get a reply.

Such was the sudden calamity that overwhelmed the new settlement. What is there to say about it? There is much to say. Fire purifies. Fire is a test. It tempers the spirit of the man, while it lays waste the work of his hands. And fires are beacons. They light up the whole sky. They draw attention and sympathy in a moment. After the fire comes the " still, small voice."

With characteristic energy, Mr. Mason set himself to the task of rebuilding; and in less than two months he had finished a schoolhouse and a temporary shelter for his family. Mr. Phillips, meanwhile, had been touring among the churches.

When the story of the fire reached home, the Committee acted with instant and sympathetic decision. On March 4, after the week-night service, their cable message arrived. It ran, "*Rebuild house.*" That was all. But it brought intense relief and gladness of heart. Acknowledging the message Mr. Mason wrote:

> The cablegram was received night before last. It is in season to save a great deal of labor and expense. I am now driven to the limit. Beside the correspondence in behalf of the treasury and collecting information concerning the Assam Mission treasury accounts that were burned, I have eighty-two men at work; some here, and some there, but all needing constant supervision. On Sundays, for the last month, I have walked from sixteen to twenty miles, preaching as best I could to the people of a certain market among the hills below us. I have also been able to hold meetings every evening during this week with my workmen. The Christians of the other side have responded to our call for laborers much better than we had expected. We now have a rude zayat (caravansary) near the compound, built with money contributed for this purpose by the Government. We hope to make good use of it for preaching to those who stop there. Just now there is quite a company of them. During the cold season the house will be occupied by people from all parts of the hills coming in on business. We have put in charge an earnest Christian who

Photo by W. Carey.

The Mission Compound from the Road

Showing Doctor Mason's bungalow on the left and the Ladies' Bungalow in the center. The baptistery on the right.

will, I think, to the extent of his ability, improve the opportunity. I hope to get the roof on our new bungalow before the rains, but it will take until January or February, I fear, to finish the house.

In due course Miss Russell's bungalow and the Mason house were completed, and both occupied in the spring of 1881. Thus was accomplished and made permanent the move to Tura, notwithstanding the many difficulties.

XXVII

POSITION OF THE CHURCHES

THAT the north has always been distinct from the south is true even in this rugged patch of country. The clans of the north are *Matchis*—fierce, hot-blooded, set ablaze in a moment: those of the south, *Abengs*—are milder in disposition, manners, and appearance. The Matchis in their wild state were as peppery and pugnacious as possible, loved fighting with a fine scorn of consequence, and clothed themselves with filth as with a garment. With a score or so of old feuds festering in their minds, what recked they of aught besides? These characteristics still prevail, and the Abengs, by no means themselves fastidious in their personal habits, speak contemptuously of the Matchis as people who are always angry and never bathe. The Tura range, then, roughly divides the Garos as it divides their land. But there is a good deal of overlapping, and some other clans are geographically distinct both from the Matchi and the Abeng, such as the Awe, who cling to the foothills of Damra and Nibari, and the Atong, who haunt the beautiful banks of the Sameswari. All, however, are *Achik,* "men of the hills," but their ultimate classification of themselves as *Mande,* "men," not brutes, is interesting. Beasts at best can be tamed, brought to heel, and taught tricks of civilization; but for men there is a higher destiny—men can be redeemed. Sunk never so low, they can rise at the voice of the Eternal, walk in the light of his countenance, hold communion with his liberating

Photo by W. Dring.

Baptizing in the Sameswari, in Southeast Hills

Spirit, and thus become in truth the sons and daughters of the Most High.

The first to hear of him among the Garos were the men of the north. There the earliest converts were found and the earliest churches formed. Of the eighteen "mother" churches on the field today, eleven lie to the north, and count among them nearly two-thirds of the total membership.

But the north means, almost exclusively, the northern edge of the eastern half of the hills—the long spurs running out into the plains, the valleys and lowlands between them, the bigger buttresses of the eastern corner, and the crags and crevices of which they are composed. On the map it is not unlike the wings of a butterfly, folded erect. But the chief beauty lies in the little disks that light up the outer edge. Their gentle radiance on the rough outline of the hills is as pure and ethereal as that emitted by a cluster of fireflies hovering over some jungle shrub. They belong to it. Amid the swarms of other insects, whose home is in the darkened branches, they alone have this gift of light. The little disks represent communities of Garo Christians and Christian schools. Few of them have come far inland, nor has the light spread over the central hills. Even where they seem closest together, they are really scattered, and the sum total is comparatively small. But what joy it is to see them! How wonderful the story of how they came to be!

Let us study the map more closely. A straight line, drawn from Tura to Goalpara, will pass through the length of the long spur, emerging at a point near the tip. That point marks Derek, the most westerly church on this northern edge. Another line, drawn from Tura to the northeast corner, will pass out at Adokgiri, a sort of sentinel church between the Garo and the Khasia Hills. These are the two extremes.

Now join these two lines, measuring the middle point. We shall find it rests at Damra. Damra is on the Dudhnai River in the center of a little plain of its own, three miles square, and almost surrounded by hills. The name is familiar to us already, as the scene of the great market. Here Ramke served as sepoy, and fell in love with Suban. Here, after his baptism, he started a school, which grew to be the Normal School of the mission; the nursery of the Garo churches. Here Mr. Stoddard built a house and brought his family to try the experiment of a residence close to the hills. Here he contracted the fever which sent him home, to stay. But the chief attraction to Damra is its proximity to Nisangram, two miles south, where the largest and best of all the Garo churches witnesses to the power and beauty of the gospel. This is the Christian village that Ramke prayed into being.

Half-way between Nisangram and Adokgiri lies the church of Chotcholja, which was tormented by wild elephants, and by great rocks on the day of the terrible earthquake, in June, 1897. Northeast about three miles as the crow flies, but more than double that in going round, is Rajasimla, the first Christian village—"God's village," as it used to be called by the Garos—the Jerusalem of the mission, as Mr. Stoddard loved to style it. This is "Omed's Settlement." Moving down the valley, on the left, almost in the shadow of the hills, nestles the church of Santipur, "Place of Peace." Then we strike the Grand Trunk Road coming down from Gauhati, and crossing it, enter Rongjuli Bazaar. Here, as we know, in 1847, the first attempt was made to hire hill boys for the Goalpara school. Here Ramke learned his letters, and here the first Christians were murderously attacked

Photo by W. Carey.

Chotcholja

Great rocks shaken from the cliffs by the earthquake, 1897.

Photo by W. Dring.

In the Bamboo Jungle

one market-day after the failure of the rains. Just beyond is the Rongjuli church. It is a typical plains church, enervated, Hinduized, with a blend of bad qualities from mixed blood and vicious surroundings, one of the earliest of the Garo churches, yet it is today the smallest and weakest of them all.

Returning to the Grand Trunk Road, following it westward, we come first to Amjonga, at the south of the Damra Dwar. Here Ramke and Suban were married. This is the home of Naran, afterwards a Mauzadar, living twenty miles south, whose parents, with those of Rudram, were the first disciples of the village. Amjonga figures large in the Stoddard days and its position on the road has always made it an easy place to call. The church, however, is the smallest but one on the Garo field. The principal person of note is Fokira, Ramke's brother. Leaving Amjonga and crossing the Dudhnai, the Tengas, and the Krishnai, all within ten miles, we are in line with the fine, elongated spur between the Krishnai and the Jinjiram. Two of the Garo markets, Nibari and Jira, balance each other over the spur, while cross-balancing are two churches, Kongkal and Resu. The Grand Trunk Road runs on straight another seven miles, touches the tip of the farther spur, and bifurcates, one arm stretching north to Goalpara, while the other bends southward, embracing the hills. In the lower angle lies Agia, where there is a Government rest-house, and below that, Balijana, which is Ramsing's village, and also sacred to the memory of Kandura Bura, the old Bairagi. In close connection with Balijana, about a mile north, is Rangsapara, Jadu's village. I never think of Jadu without recalling another of the same type, Bago. Jadu and Bago are fragrant names in the Garo church. Each heard the truth at a distance, believed, went back to his village, and there, alone as a Christian, set up a building for worship, and began the preaching of Christ. Both were humble, earnest, and persistent. The word of the Lord was as a fire burning in their bones. These two men, of so zealous a spirit, the one here, and the other on the heights above Rajasimla, seemed to signal each other, like shining lights, across the base of the hills. Balijana bulks largely in the early records, as the church name for this region, but was gradually superseded by Derek, as the latter was found to be a more convenient center for the several communities near.

This bird's-eye view of the northern churches is now almost complete. They spread fanlike across the fringe of the hills. Only one remains to be noticed, the church at Rongjong. We shall find it low down in the posterior bulge of the butterfly's wing. It is strangely isolated, a little nest among the cliffs of the Khasia's border, but almost due south from Damra, and overlooking a bend of the Dudhnai.

It must be remembered, in passing, that each of these eleven churches represents a group of villages and sometimes a far-scattered group from which its members are drawn. While this narrative touches only the more northerly churches, a strong work has been accomplished in the south and on the plains.

XXVIII

TURA TO NISANGRAM—A MARCH THROUGH THE HILLS

WE shall best appreciate the conditions under which these churches were born, and now live, if we approach them through their own environment, marching over the central ranges, and coming up to them out of the jungle of their native home.

It is a fairly stiff march, even with a stout hill-pony to carry you, and takes time. For one thing you can not go ahead of your coolies, since they carry your bedding and stretcher, camp-table and chair, cooking-pots, food and clothes, besides grain for your horses, rice for themselves, and blankets for both. All this must be packed in baskets to fit on the back, with a strap of bark round the forehead to bear part of the weight, and toilsomely carried up the steep, slippery paths, through deep valleys, where the high grass almost smothers one, and heavy growths of recent jungle catch the loads. Every man has an *ate,* or bill-hook, for this purpose stuck in the top of his basket, while he carries his sword or spear, and your cook dangles a hurricane lantern, and perhaps shoulders your gun. Moreover, you must halt where the *alda* or rest-house is, or take your chance for the night in a heathen Garo interior, which I could not recommend. The missionaries have done it, of course, and would do it again and welcome rather than miss an opportunity with the people, but there is no need for us as visitors to go out of our way in search of a sensation. These rest-houses are placed about ten miles apart, along the bridle-path, and when you have done that bit you have usually had enough for the day. Your coolies certainly have! I was fortunate in being able to accompany Mr. Mason, in 1898, and we made good time. But it took us five days to get from Tura to Nisangram although we cut a corner and thus covered two marches in one.

We started on the fifteenth of November. All the morning the coolies had been busy, stripping new bark for their baskets, weighing up the loads, putting the baggage in and out with merry vociferation, each trying to choose the least weight or the least awkward share. But the missionary understood his business, and with quiet hand, and some good-humored banter, finally adjusted the partition. Then they trailed off, each with his burden on his back, from which two lively legs depended. A few strides up the grassy slope, a squeeze through the little gate to the road, then they turned sharply to the left, and one by one dipped out of sight, coasting the hills, I watched them from my host's veranda. The last of the line had my steel trunk sticking end up out of the mouth of his basket. It flashed for a moment in the sun, and he too was gone.

Soon after we followed on our ponies. The road nicks into the cleft which marks the boundary of the compound, curls round the bulge beyond, enters a Nepalese village, and then goes off in the direction of Dhubri, past the rifle-butts. We rode for a while on the level, up the mouth of a gorge, then, splashing across the stream, began a steep ascent. The cliffs drew near together. That on the left towered upward in bold curves, with the bridle-path, like a trail of white ribbon, twined about it. All else was greenery, moss, fern, and jungle, draping the gorge, with the twinkle of running water far below. Up we mounted to the top of the Dura Pass. Then down by a similar devious way, many hundreds of feet, into the gap between the two great converging ranges, the main peaks of which, Tura and Arbela, here face each other. A beautiful stream, the *Kalu* or *Ganol,* winds westward through the gap. Deep woods rise up on either side, while the rapid current gleams and foams round the purple boulders in its bed. The water is a clear blue with green pools under the rocks. A neat little bamboo bridge, clean and white, spanned the stream. It would be difficult to find a prettier picture to paint.

But there was no time to linger and admire. Our resting-place for the night lay on the summit of Arbela, three thousand two hundred feet above, and the afternoon was already beginning to wane. Not soon shall I forget that climb. One shoulder rose above another as the outworks of the mountain were scaled. There was no sign of human habitation. The jungle fell below us, and then we plunged into it again. Now we were riding on a high track, like a red streak against the forest, and a few minutes later were wetting our ankles in mud and mush of decayed vegetation at the bottom of the gorge. Finally there was the long spiral to the top. Our ponies panted up the steep slope, standing at every easing of the gradient to recover breath. As we reached the summit, the sun dipped blood-red among the shadows of the far horizon. We dismounted and shivered. What a windy hill! The cold was intense. But alas, our coolies had been left far behind. Only the syces were with us. There was nothing to eat and nowhere to sit. Of all the cheerless shelters that on the top of Arbela seemed the least inviting. We had no lamp and no wraps. Above all we were desperately hungry. Happily some matches were found, and with these a fire could be lit. We went out to the cook-house, a little low shed sheltered from the wind, and sat on a *machang*[1] in the friendly warmth of the fire. But the smoke was pungent, and though we told cheerful tales to keep up our spirits, the points were punctuated with tears. At intervals the syces went out and shouted; but there were no answering cries. Our personal discomfort was forgotten in the anxiety about the men. Not until two hours later did they come toiling in up the track, close together, waving a couple of lanterns, and a little scared, having met a leopard on the way!

The next day's march was short and uneventful. The path had been cleared of jungle. Was not the "bora sahib" (deputy commissioner) expected to travel this way shortly? The fiat had gone forth, "Prepare my way before me," and so we found little gangs of coolies hard at work, chopping down branches, filling up gaps, cutting into the cliff where the narrow track had been washed away by rains, bridging the stream, each little bridge being a stretcher of bamboo overlaid with a thick felting of grass, and making the rough places smooth and the crooked places straight. The system of *begar,* or enforced labor on the roads, is open to small objection in such a country, where the clearing is a boon to trade, as well as a necessity of Government. It is left with each luskar to toll his own circle of villages and provide the required number of men, at the given time and place. And fair wages are paid. But the Garos are an independent lot, and it would seem to be impossible to obtain coolies without compulsion. The system becomes vexatious, however, when, as sometimes happens, labor is not

[1] An undercover platform or floor, usually two to three feet from the ground, upon which to sit, sleep, or place one's belongings.

Photo by Major Playfair.

Suspension Bridge

levied locally, but drafted from distant sections, with scanty consideration for the loss of time and other inconveniences involved. The season for the road-repairing synchronizes with that of the cotton harvest, which is an added drawback.

The men sleep in the jungle by the roadside. Their safety lies in numbers. They are accustomed to this sort of camping out on their long journeys to market. Curled up on a bed of leaves, or light branches, and covered with a blanket, they seem quite happy. A kindly Providence must certainly watch over their slumbers or many more would fall an easy prey to prowling beasts. One man told us of an adventure. They were startled in the night by the approach of elephants. To have shown any fear or make the least noise would have been to create a stampede, in which, most likely, all would have been trampled to death. So, with great presence of mind, they lay prone and still and breathless, till the danger passed. One or two of the huge beasts actually touched them with their trunks, and stepped carefully between their bodies, apparently taking the shapeless lumps for logs of wood or treacherous mounds of earth!

Shortly after leaving Arbela we saw traces of bears. There were deep scratches on the trees and the cliffside, where during the night they had scraped for toothsome food. At noon we reached the rest-house at Megagiri, finely situated near the end of the ridge, from which a sort of rostrum projects commanding the encircling hills. It was occupied by a few police. A line of huts ran along either side of the projection with a yard of sandstone between, where the ground had been leveled and bared. This bit of crude color contrasted most vividly with the forest of young green bamboos growing on the hills around, and the deep blue of the overhanging sky.

Near the bungalow, where the road winds off eastward, a solitary tree had been left standing in the open, with a graceful plume of leafy branches bent toward the road. Perched in the middle of it, about forty feet high, was a fine specimen of the Garo *borang,* or tree-house. A whole family lives there, cooks, eats, and sleeps. If the mother has need to descend, she must come down and return by that springy ladder, with its rungs a wide stride apart, carrying her baby on her back. To ease the spring and prevent a break, the ladder had two stanchions fixed in the ground, while ropes of creepers lashed it firmly to the trees. Other bamboos attached to the topmost branches, held up one end of the dwelling. These strange erections are common and serve several purposes. They give the sleepers purer air than that of the jungle, and protect them from mosquitoes and wild beasts. They usually overlook the jhum, and thus enable the growing crops to be watched. And they foster the sense of personality and pride. What is an Englishman in the castle or an Arab at his tent door, compared with a Garo leaning over the railed platform of his exalted borang, and holding colloquy with callers forty feet below! They seem to love a high roosting-place and have a bird's fondness for being cradled by the wind. Mr. Mason got fever that afternoon, and I was lamed by a thorn in the ankle, which might have been a poisoned tip, it made so bad a sore and took so long to heal. From a village far down at the bottom of the hill, sounds of drunken revelry floated up to us all the evening, and once or twice we caught the glimmer of torches as stragglers from the party went singing home.

The third day was crowded with incident. It was the day of the "short-cut." Our Garo cook got up at four o'clock, made us our usual breakfast of hot porridge,

Photo by Major Playfair.

A Borang, or Tree House

potatoes, rice, biscuit, and stewed fowl in thickened gravy. At daybreak, exulting in the freshness of the clear cool air, we began our journey. After riding about half a mile, Mr. Mason called a halt. At this point the road bends southward to Rongrengiri, the rendezvous of the three invading columns in the expedition of 1872. "If we go there," he said, "we shall lose a day. We have to go over yonder," pointing to the big flanks of a mountain called Chokadam Giri, which faced us almost due east. Between us was a broad open valley lying far below. "There's a Garo track which leads across. I think we will leave the road and go by that."

This seemed an excellent idea, especially as all the irregularities of that smiling valley were hidden under its mantle of green. But when, a few moments later, we commenced a slippery descent, the wet jungle soaked our boots, leggings, and breeches, and the ponies, with fore-legs extended, started to slide down a fungus-covered path, which seemed to curve in on itself, I began to have misgivings. There were snags in the path too, and bits of loose stone. The pony tripped on these and only got his legs straight again by a violent jerk, which left them taut and trembling. "It's all right," said my friend, "you'll get used to it soon"; but I was far from deriving full satisfaction from this assurance. When we had had an hour or two of such neck-breaking scuttle, I really did get used to it and sat in my saddle with a nonchalance that was not a bad imitation of his own! For the benefit of future travelers I have a bit of advice—look well to your saddle crupper!

The climbs, and we had an innumerable number, were almost worse than the descents. Your pony strains, scrapes, and scrambles half-way up a precipice, and then, just where a bulging mass of slippery clay stares him in the face, gets winded, and for a moment you hang between heaven and earth while his bellows work. Before you know it he is rearing again and pawing the obstacle, while you set your teeth, cling to his mane, and wonder when the somersault will come. At last, by a desperate leap, he does it, and the situation is saved. But the strain is tremendous, both on the nerves of the man and the muscles of the beast. But a good hill-pony is as sure-footed as a goat, and you had better trust to him if you mean to try Garo tracks.

Between the ridges are wet bottoms of marsh-land and dank jungle, and little streams meandering over rocky beds. The first we crossed had a margin of black soil, in which a tiger had just printed his paws. It was time, we thought, to put cartridges into our only firearms the smoothbore. It surprised me not a little to find that Mr. Mason, who had wandered about these jungles for thirty years, never carries a gun, either in sport or in self-defense.

We rode through several clearings on the bluffs of the hills, all starred with white cotton. The plants grow only a few feet high, and each soft pendant, or puffy cone, dangles like a snowy tassel from its single stem. Pure as snow and with the freshness of the dew upon them, they glistened in the morning sun.

Our path for some miles lay through a belt of tall, dried-up grass in a deep hollow. The heat was stifling. The soft ground had been freshly trodden into great holes by elephants. They were all around us. We were in a sort of trap. This caused chatter to cease, and we began to talk in whispers. The coolies put down their loads and listened, and then were unwilling to proceed. At any moment one of the gigantic beasts might noiselessly part the grass and come unexpectedly upon us.

We could hear them cracking the branches in the jungle on either side. We sat down, kept as still as we could, and waited. Spears were in readiness, and our one gun, a ridiculous armament, rather worse than useless. Presently two Garos met us, stepping lightly along the path, every sense alert. They were trying to get through without disturbing the herd. They told us that only three days before on that very spot a luskar had met his death. He was going home and had met an elephant in the way. He speared it, and ran; but it turned swiftly, caught him, and crushed him. It was not a pleasant story under the circumstances, but we could not stay where we were, evidently, and as these men had come through safely, we ventured on. The relief was great when we got clear, and out of the grass. In some parts it had all been trodden down by the herd. A village stood on the nearest spur, and the path leading to it was guarded by long, stout bamboos, stuck obliquely into the ground to keep the marauders in check.

All through that hollow we had felt the ground quiver, and there were frequent rumblings like the mutterings of thunder, with occasional loud reports, as if a cannon had been fired from some distant hill. What could it mean? It was simply the lingering throes of that awful cataclysm which did such wide-spread damage seventeen months before! Every day since, so we were told, the earth-tremors had persisted, and these noises had been heard.

XXIX

STILL ON THE TRAIL TO NISANGRAM

THE village of Chokadam Giri interested me much. It was perched on a rough platform or ledge, on the side of the hill. The houses faced each other round an open space, with their backs standing out from the edge propped up by piles. The first had a spacious porch on the side of which was a fine young bull mounted on a *machang*. Opposite, standing on the ground, were *gumlas* or large earthen casks of fermenting *chu*. A woman was pounding rice just outside, with a litter of speckled pigs around her, and a dirty cat was sitting in the doorway. On the roof were tattered squares of simpak, the cinnamon-colored cloth made from phakram (*grewia liliæ felia*) bark, drying in the sun. It was the family stock of blankets! I wanted to buy one, but the woman was so pleased with the offer that she pulled it off the thatch and presented it with a smile. Held up to the light it resembled a threadbare door-mat of cocoanut fiber, only it was as thin as a sheet of old brown paper. A few yards off a man was soaking the raw bark in water and beating it on a log of wood with a stone, hammering it out. A fleshy strip about six inches wide was being beaten. It would probably expand to eighteen or twenty-four inches in the process.

Just outside the village, at a bend in the path, we came upon a wild Garo standing by his *sambasi* or bamboo shrine. He had been sacrificing a sucking pig to *Susumi,* the wealth-giver, and a fowl to *Saljong,* the god of fer-

Sambasi, or Place of Sacrifice

tility, the supreme spirit. Each was represented by a few branches stuck in the ground. There lay the *chapba,* or little basket, in which the pig had been brought. Beyond was a miniature hut half filled with earth. He had probably desired the favor of the deity on behalf of a new site about to be jhumed. His right hand held a large-headed *selu,* or spear, which I purchased for three rupees. But that was a dear bargain as the sequel will show. A few steps farther we were horrified to see three black gibbets standing up against the background of a leafy jungle in a clear space by the road. *They were crosses.* We asked what they meant and were told that they were used for crucifying monkeys as sacrifices to the demons. The sight gave us a queer turn, with its ghastly symbolism of suffering and death, and its awful suggestiveness, in view of that other Sacrifice which alone avails to cleanse the conscience of sin. For a long time after that we rode in silence, brooding over the great mystery, and rejoicing in the revealed power of the cross of Christ to lift those demon-haunted savages out of their misery and sin.

The afternoon was sunny, as, leaving the cross-cut, we climbed to the made-road and cantered down a gentle incline through pleasant sal forests to the little rest-house at Songsak. Some of the coolies had already arrived and as the others came trotting in and relinquished their loads, the spirit of friskiness seemed to seize us all. We chased each other about laughing and shouting, all because we had come through the gloom and toil of that day's march. The finale came, when, grasping my purchased spear, I charged down upon one of the men and made as if I would prod him through. Instantly the men took sides and a tug of war ensued. In the scuffle the spear was drawn through my hand, making a nasty cut. We quieted down a little then, our cook boiling the kettle for tea, and the coolies scooting off into the jungle to get water and fuel for their own evening meal. The wound was washed, and Painkiller, which is Doctor Mason's panacea for all the ills that Garo flesh is heir to, was poured in. We had a grand talk by the camp-fire that night, stretching out our limbs to the cheery blaze with a most grateful sense of comfort and rest.

Breaking camp the next morning at seven-twenty, we followed a path through woods for several miles. Deer darted out of sight, giving us a momentary glimpse of their red bodies and black horn-tips. Monkeys swung themselves through the trees, and peacocks and jungle-fowl crossed our path. I shot a squirrel, two feet long, with a handsome fur, and gave the coolies a savory dish for dinner. Then we reentered the earthquake zone. The bed of the Rongri, a main affluent of the Krishnai, subsided after the earthquake, and we found the valley more or less submerged. It was difficult to find a place to ford, and the ponies sometimes had to swim across, with our feet resting on their necks. How the coolies managed I hardly know. They probably made longer detours. I know the lower parts of the load got wet.

More miles of leafy forest and we came to Cheran, a large heathen village, old, filthy, typical. You want to wash your mind as well as your body when you have seen Cheran. The photographs give an excellent idea of the houses, but they mercifully hide the dirt, the drunkenness, and the smell. The long street is an avenue of nauseating sights. The people who live in those sooty galleries, stinking with rotten fish and putrifying skulls, came out into the sun with heads full of dirt and vermin and limbs disfigured by open suppurating sores. The women, nursing their naked babies, looked more un-

Rest-houses Used by Missionaries on Tour

Photo by W. Mason.

Cheran

cleanly than the speckled sows suckling their brood under the floor of the house. Every child was scrofulous and every cat mangy. Most of the inhabitants were drunk and either sleeping it off with loud snores in their pens—you could see them lying uncovered as you passed the doors—or else leering and lolling about in a half-merry, half-maudlin mood. Every building gave forth the sour breath of *chu.* Even the dust on the ground seemed tainted with lice and scabs, and not a gourd or a post or a basket but had its own skin of dirt. Baking in the sun's glare, the whole place looked leprous, as if it would take a dozen thunder-storms to wash it clean.

What wonder that death is busy in such a spot? Most of the houses have *kimas* near them, either a sheaf of notched poles, or effigies grotesquely carved. Other *kimas* were being rudely fashioned as they lay on the ground. In front of one dwelling we counted fourteen of these memorial posts! At a little distance a few men in the open street were tom-toming round a bamboo fence enclosing the remains of a little girl who had died the day before. No one else seemed to care.

We walked through a fourteen-post house. It had a deep porch, in which a coarse-looking woman was pounding corn. A big beer-vessel and bunches of Indian corn, red ripe, hung suspended from the roof. One long step admitted us through a narrow door. The smell was awful. Two slabs of earth, for fireplaces, stood in the center, some yards apart. Over one of these stale lumps of raw pork were drying on a string. Other pieces were lying on the floor. Black grime was over everything. At the far end was the sleeping compartment of the husband and wife, about six feet square, as odoriferous as the rest. A great heap of crude lac was piled up at the door. There must have been a barrelful. It was caked with dirt and smelled vile. We were glad to get back to the comparatively fresh air outside. But before leaving, we examined some ancient *rongs,* rough brass pans and bowls, which are prized as heirlooms by the Garos, and may cost anything from twenty to a hundred rupees.

Then we visited the house in which the drinking was going on. It stood on a bit of rising ground, up a side street. Sounds of drumming and dancing issued from it. A little crowd hung about the door. If one came out another went in to take the place. We climbed up a notched pole into that revolting interior. It was a long building, with only one opening, that at the door. And the roof came low down, making it a kind of tunnel. It reeked with the smell of uncleanly humanity and the fumes of *chu.* It was full of Garos in all stages of inebriety. They were squatting together on the bamboo floor, shaking their tousled heads and the brass rings in their ears, as they eyed each other in jovial anticipation, and shouted and laughed. Two men, with extraordinarily long arms, stood in the middle, and beat the drums incessantly, and kept time by leaping, dancing, and singing. Behind them stood open tubs of the liquor. Busy servers skipped to and fro, filling their long-necked *pongs* (gourd calabashes) with the liquid and bringing it to the expectant rows of sitters. Each in turn threw back his head, and opened his mouth. The vessel was poised above, and the contents poured down his throat. Only when he could hold no more and dribbled was the stream allowed to stop. Meanwhile the dancers capered wildly after having their share of *chu,* and once more beat their drums in delirious intoxication. Others sprang up and joined them before settling down for another drink. It was a sickening sight. But what must it be when the women unite with the men, as they often do and all get drunk together! That foul tunnel, with its poisoned atmosphere and loathsome plug of besotted humanity haunts my memory still. But it brings to a focus the social life of the Garos without the gospel, and adds a new urgency to our conception of their spiritual needs. May it quicken the sense of responsibility and hasten the preaching of the grace that saves!

Outside Cheran we halted at the *alda,* or traveler's rest-house, for a wash before going on to Simseng. Two Christian lads followed us, one of them rather shame-facedly since he had been drinking too. They stand alone here, except for the mauzadar, Naran, whose house we saw, surrounded by a high, plaited bamboo fence. He himself was away. Mr. Mason talked long and earnestly to the delinquent. And I realized, as I could not have done otherwise, the strength and fidelity required of such new converts to resist the familiar temptation in such a place as Cheran. On the road beyond the *alda,* up a very steep hill, we met a gang of Christian coolies from the neighboring village of Baldam-Dagal. The houses in that village were all thrown down by the earthquake, and this shook the hearts of the people, quickening the sense of sin, and preparing them for the message of the evangel. Over thirty have since been received into the membership of the church by baptism.

Simseng is only three miles from Cheran, but you climb to it over the rim of a very rough ridge. The village clings to the steep inner side of the cliff on the opposite side. It looks down into a sort of basin. The only Christians here are the school-teacher and his wife. The schoolhouse is perched on the highest point of the crag up which the village creeps. We slept in that house. By one sitting on the platform in front of it a fine view was obtained. Drinking was going on there too, at the base of the crag, in celebration of new houses to be built, material for which was being brought in fresh from the jungle on all sides. One man came galloping up the hill to look at us and, standing before Mr. Mason, said, with a knowing wink, "I am drunk." "You don't need to tell us that!" was the rejoinder, which greatly amused both the newcomer and his friends. But when, to cultivate our acquaintance further, he seated himself between us, and looked sideways in my direction, I had had enough. His breath shot me off my perch.

Simseng, however, seemed a much breezier, clearer place both morally and physically, than debased, drink-sodden Cheran. And when at night, the stars looked down from a clear sky, and the camp-fire was lighted outside the school, and we had had our meal, and put on our overcoats, it was a sure pleasure to watch the missionary preach to a circle of eager, interested people, as they came up in twos and threes and squatted on the stony steep about us. It is by such means that the story is told, and the good work spreads. Many, and even our friends of the afternoon, appeared to be sober when they bade us "good night."

The next morning I was astonished to see the size, variety, and trappings of the gaily decorated *kimas* in the porch of a house just below the school. Stumpy blocks of wood had been carved into heavy, square faces, adorned with hair and feathers. Stone necklaces, earrings galore, the apronlike garments for men and women, and many stringed belts of wampum, were all in place. To crown everything one effigy had a once dainty ruby silk parasol fastened carefully above it at a most chic and fetching angle. Where this came from I could not learn, but I smiled as I wondered what the white Miss

The New Church at Nisangram

Kimas

or Mem Saheb to whom it originally belonged would have said had she been able to see it here so tilted in the center of such a galaxy of Garo beauty.

From Simseng to Nisangram is one march. The track led over breezy hills. We ate our usual tiffin of corned beef and biscuits, sitting on a log by the edge of a stream near the village of Bangshi. The water was beautifully clear, cool, and refreshing. Bangshi is interesting as the early home of Thangkan, and the place where he first went to school. Thangkan is one of the finest types of a Garo Christian. Trained partly at Serampore, and partly in America, he stands, in knowledge, intellectual force, and experience, far above most of the other leaders. And in self-sacrifice, simplicity of heart, and zeal as an evangelist, he is not a whit behind any; offers from the Government of a salary five times what he was getting were rejected that he might the better serve his Lord. Bangshi is mentioned only once in the early records, though it must often have been visited, and it is one of the villages from which the first converts baptized at Damra were drawn. There are Christians still in Bangshi, and we rode about among the houses trying to find them, but they were away from home. Leaving this we entered a fine wood of sal trees with no undergrowth of jungle, much like a forest of saplings at home, and had a pleasant canter of two miles, almost on a level, through the slim, straight trees. Their shadows interlaced the path, and protected us from the hot rays of the afternoon sun. Then came a sudden descent to the rice-fields of Nisangram. Before us was a broad belt of ripening grain, widening toward Damra and the plains beyond. A low spur banked this belt from behind, while a line of brighter foliage at its base marked the village site. Facing that, out in the open, a little white bungalow caught the eye. A stream flowed past our feet. It was an arm of the Dudhnai. We crossed it, rode through a corner of the crop, and dismounted at the bungalow. It was Saturday evening, and we were to spend the Sunday at Nisangram.

XXX

"THE SOLITARY PLACE SHALL BE GLAD FOR THEM"

BOTH of the first Garo converts formed Christian villages, Omed at Rajasimla, and Ramke at Nisangram. And each stamped upon the place his own image and superscription.

Their similarities only brightened the contrast. Both sites were tucked up close under the hills, in touch with neighboring clans, and in the path of approach to important Garo markets situated in the plains beyond. Yet each stands aloof and sheltered from the baneful influences of the market-ground, Rongjuli being six miles from Rajasimla, and Damra two miles from Nisangram. Both were reclaimed from the jungle, and both prospered from the first. Something akin to the paralysis that afflicted Omed crippled Rajasimla, checked its energy, and left it weak and dependent. But Nisangram went forward from strength to strength. Whether you regard its expanding population and bountiful harvests, or its wonderful spirit of activity and generosity, it presents one of the happiest fulfilments of the ancient Scriptures:

> The desire of the righteous shall be granted.
> The blessing of the Lord it maketh rich,
> And he addeth no sorrow therewith.

The secret lies in Ramke's walk with God, and continual waiting upon him. " From me is thy fruit found." " He that abideth in me, and I in him, the same beareth much fruit." Omed too was a Christian, and in the early years of his discipleship a Christian hero; but he lacked this habit and attitude of the heart, and so missed his way. He was able, magnetic, impetuous, a born leader, the Peter among the Garo apostles, while Ramke was the John. But, alas, this Peter sadly failed from the want of a perfect surrender and sustained fellowship with his Lord.

> The little more, and how much it is,
> The little less, and what worlds away.

In point of time, Rajasimla takes precedence over Nisangram. Omed made his first clearing in October or November, 1864. It was not until seven years later, in February, 1872, that a new village, Nisangram, was reported as "springing up" in the dense jungle. The words must be taken literally. Many still living remember the great sal forest of hard old trees that filled the valley, and sunk their roots deep into the soil, where now is a broad expanse of waving rice-fields. But the change was brought about with infinite patience and toil. Apart from the exhausting work of felling trees and digging up stumps and roots, it was found necessary to dam up the stream to make the land fit for use. Again and again they did it, and again and again it broke away. There were not enough of them to complete it at the right time and with sufficient speed, and heathen Garos, of course, would not help. But a tiger came and turned the scale. The tiger was hungry and there was a pony belonging to one of the merchants in the Damra bazaar grazing unconscious of danger near the market-ground; the enemy crept stealthily nearer and, with a bound, sprang upon his prey, and went back to the forest. Some one was wanted to kill that tiger, and Rangku was sent for.

"Can you do it? Are you brave, and have you a gun?"

"Certainly," said this ex-sepoy, the third Garo convert and now a Christian preacher, who had thrown in his lot with Ramke. "I will do it tonight."

He brought his gun, examined the "kill," selected a spot in which to lie in wait, and there he kept tense watch till dusk. All was still. No sound came from the jungle, but, just as the light was fading, "stripes" appeared. He marched out with a leisurely catlike stride, ready for his meal, but a little suspicious. Rangku sat waiting for his chance, hand steady, gun cocked, eye glued to the barrel. Presently they fronted each other; there was a loud report, and the tiger dropped dead, shot through the skull.

It was a pretty piece of work. He had done it once or twice before, and would do it many times again. For Rangku was a great *shikari* (huntsman). His record up to 1907 was a "bag" of seventy-five tigers, six elephants, not counting such small fry as leopards, bears, and deer. All these fell to his gun single-handed.

The striped carcass caused high jubilation in the Damra bazaar. The next day the skin was taken to Goalpara, and Rangku was paid the Government reward of twenty-five rupees. With this he purchased sweetmeats and rice, which he took back with him to make a feast. The Garos all around should be invited, and perhaps they would help with the dam. "I can't give you *chu*, but I will feast you well if you will come and lend us a hand." The bait was tempting, in spite of the absence of *chu*, and hundreds came down. In one day the dam was finished. And it never broke again.

But we shall miss the point if we think that toil and patience alone brought the new settlement into being. It was toil and patience plus the blessing of heaven, earnestly sought and obtained. Long before the land was leased from the Raja, or the ax was heard among the trees, this inlet of the mountains was a man's trysting-place with God. It was not superstition that held him; he came not to sacrifice to demons, but to hold converse with the Father in heaven. That it was Ramke, is in harmony with the tenor and spirit of his strong and beautiful life.

Let us glance back to the time when Ramke on returning to Damra as a Christian first opened his little school, in 1864. He lodged at the familiar *thana,* or police outpost, and put up a small building close at hand for a school. It stood on the market-ground. The hill-men came down every week for the Thursday market, and flocked round the schoolhouse to see and hear. It was a capital investment. When Mr. Bronson arrived, three years later, and formed the first church of forty members at Rajasimla, the school was placed on a larger basis as a training institution for teachers and preachers. The following year, February, 1868, when he came again with Mr. Stoddard, there were fifteen students in training, with an equal number of schoolboys. But it was obviously desirable to move the institution to a better site, and provide more ample accommodation. They secured a beautiful lot for school and chapel on the left bank of the stream, about half a mile to the north of the bazaar. It is still pointed out, near the post-office.

The new buildings were soon put up, including the bungalow for the missionaries, and in June Mr. and Mrs. Stoddard with their family came to take their fleeting possession. Ten days of class work and meetings were followed by fever, prostration, and enforced return to Goalpara. But the visit was memorable as the occasion of the first baptisms there and the beginnings of the church soon to be known as the church of Nisangram.

By December, 1868, twenty-five had been baptized. A year later, in December, 1869, there was another notable ingathering. Mr. Comfort, then touring overland from Gauhati, was invited by Mr. Stoddard to join him at Damra. As he writes:

> I reached here by twelve o'clock, and found all the congregation beside the large and beautiful stream that flows by the school compound. As I appeared on the bank they were standing in silence below, with bowed heads and reverent attitude, while Omed was offering prayer in the Garo language. When he had closed, Brother Stoddard saw and welcomed me. His greeting was followed by one equally cordial from the native Christians. I was asked to take part in the baptism, a gladsome service which I was not loath to perform. We buried in the liquid grave sixteen who had been received, eleven men and five women, Omed baptizing alternately with ourselves. Afterward about fifty assembled in the schoolroom to commemorate with glad hearts the dying love of the Saviour who had made American and Garo, white and black, one in himself.

On February 7, 1870, Mr. Stoddard baptized nine more, and he speaks of sixteen feet added to the chapel by voluntary labor to accommodate the enlarging congregation. All about the hills around Damra the interest spread. There was opposition, of course, as when two of the preachers were turned out of a village and refused shelter for the night, on the ground that, after their last sojourn, the Nokma was taken ill; they reasoned that this was a mark of the demon's displeasure at his having befriended men of the new religion. Hence the edict, "No Christian shall ever lodge in this village again." But the work steadily grew.

The man most at the heart of things in Damra was Ramke. Most of the promising inquirers and the principal youths among the early converts passed through his hands. It was he who had trained the teachers and, to a large extent, inspired the preachers to preach. Above all else he showed them an example of a quiet faith in God, bearing its natural fruit in consistent righteousness of life. " He was no ordinary Christian," said Doctor Stoddard; and this was confirmed by all.

Ramke gave one day a week to fasting and prayer. This was a habit with him from the first. Another habit was to go daily to a secret place in the woods, where he could hold undisturbed communion with God. The spot he had chosen was two or three miles from the school, on the present site of Nisangram. It soon became very dear to him. The walk there was a long enjoyment of anticipated help; the walk back, like the aftershining of Moses' face, a realized sense of gladness and calm. Gradually the idea took possession of him that the place was suitable for a Christian settlement, of which there was need, now that the converts were multiplying on the neighboring hills. They would be stronger together, more easily instructed in the faith, and free to develop unhindered their social and religious life according to the mind of Christ. The position was central, the space adequate to provide that material prosperity so necessary to success. He saw the possibilities, and had a prescient conviction that the thing was " from the Lord." The thought began to dominate his mind. It soon became a wish, and then a prayer, that God would raise up a Christian village on that spot. And God did.

So it came to pass that near Damra where there was no Garo village a generation ago, one of the largest of all the Garo villages is found today. And it is a Christian village, marked as such on all Government maps since the survey of 1870-1872.

When the surveyors came upon the settlers, preparing to colonize this corner of this virgin forest, they queried in wonder:

"Who are you?"

"We are Garos."

"Why then don't you sacrifice and drink like other Garos?"

"Because we are Christians."

"Christians?"—in a tone of incredulity.

"Yes, we are all Christians here."

"Why, what is this place then?"

"Christian Para," was the answer, which means Christian Hamlet, and so the name went down. Perhaps it was Ramke who spoke. It would be like him to think that designation sufficient. The settlement was not only for Christians, but Christian. He wanted that to be its distinctive mark and crowning glory. But afterward, when the surveyors had left the district, carrying the name with them, another was substituted for it. The occasion was a visit from Doctor Bronson. Ramke and Rangku took him out to the village and told him its story. The veteran listened, the light of holy joy kindling his face. Fastening his eyes on Ramke, he quoted the benediction of the Twentieth Psalm:

> The Lord grant thee thy heart's desire,
> And fulfill all thy counsel.

Then he talked of changing the name. As the gospel spread over the hills there would be a number of villages equally entitled to be called Christian Para, and this would bring confusion. Why not keep the idea, but give it a more distinctive form? Nisangram, for instance, which means Banner Town. And translating once more from the Psalm, he repeated the exultant refrain:

> We will triumph in Thy salvation,
> In the name of our God we will set up our banners.

That was enough. It struck the right chord, and there was instant acquiescence. Nisangram was Bengali and not Garo, like many other place-names at the foot of the hills, but it was felt to be appropriate and adopted the more gladly because chosen by their father in the faith.

In November, 1872, Ramke was ordained. He had in truth been the virtual pastor of the growing flock from the beginning. It only remained to put the seal of recognition upon the office to which the Spirit had called him.

The chapel was built in due course, a very solid and commodious structure of timber and thatch, and was still in good condition twenty-five years later. In front of it stood two poles with a bell swinging high in the air between them. I had the privilege of worshiping in it; and one of the happiest Sundays of my life was spent attending the services held within its walls. It was filled to overflowing with a congregation of Garo Christians, largely the fruit of Ramke's saintly influence and steady toil. His very presence seemed to pervade the house. The services were conducted by Gongman, his disciple and successor, while a few feet from the place allotted me sat Suban, Ramke's lifelong helpmeet, now white-haired and widowed, but lovingly carrying on his work.

With the building of the chapel Nisangram became the focus of activity for all the interest which once centered in Damra. The settlement added to its numbers yearly notwithstanding some sore trial. It was almost threatened with extinction when an epidemic of cholera broke out and carried off many victims. The faith of the founder was tested. His stock of medicines was exhausted and the people were dying rapidly. In this extremity he called the remnant of his flock together to the house of God, and there they spent the day in fasting and intercession that the plague might be stayed. And the Lord heard them. In the evening, when they went back to their homes, all the sick were found to be recovering, and no one else was afterward attacked. " Many such marked answers to prayer," writes Doctor Mason,

> were among Ramke's experiences. But the most marvelous was the Christlike character given to this man, born and brought up a heathen in the midst of heathenism, with all its sins, its ignorance and superstition. In all my acquaintance with him, covering a period of seventeen years, I never, to my recollection, found a flaw in his character. His word was safe in any capacity. Seemingly there was no desire to stretch or curtail the truth, much less to falsify. His mild and even temper, kindness and wisdom, made him a general friend and confidant. His steady devotion to the kingdom held him to the best interests of the church, even to the facing of intense suffering, and the severing of family ties. I shall never forget the occasion when, as pastor and leader of the church, he had to discipline and exclude the mother of his children.

It says much for Suban that she was not soured, though she was greatly humbled by this experience. His example of uprightness, devotion, and systematic Christian giving will bear fruit as long as fruit grows.

Ramke was head master of the Normal School, both at Goalpara and Tura, and in the prosecution of other important work was frequently absent, and sometimes for long periods, from Nisangram. But his heart was there always, and he gladly returned whenever opportunity offered. Successive missionaries spoke of him as " our best assistant," " our most competent and faithful worker," " our right-hand man." Months and years he spent in direct association with them, translating the Scripture and preparing books for the press. To mention one item only, he put into Garo the definitions of a Bengali dictionary of about forty-five thousand words.

As preacher and evangelist to his own people he traveled widely and baptized many. "On his list were over two thousand two hundred names of those who had been found of their Saviour," in part, at least, through these personal efforts. But it was as pastor of Nisangram that his finest work was done. He gave the life of that church a tone and direction which have persisted through the years. In 1886 the members desired his full time as pastor and to assume his entire support, thus leading on to further self-dependence. And though it meant for him the sacrifice of half his previous allowance, he joyfully consented. At his death this church, which he had led and trained for twenty-three years, numbered two hundred and seventy souls. "He left it," says Doctor Mason, "to the pastoral care of a young man whom he had instructed and trained to become one of the most remarkable pastors I ever knew." This was Gongman.

Ramke was as much a Christian at home as in his conduct of the church. He walked within his house with a perfect heart. In July, 1881, his eldest boy, Dhonsing, was baptized at Tura, with five others from the Normal School. The lad, in giving his testimony, said he had heard the truth from his infancy and could not remember when he did not pray to the heavenly Father and feel that his prayers were heard. His case is the more interesting because he is the first Garo boy to be brought up a Christian. Ramke's love for and interest in him were always marked. He never asked aid from the mission for his education, but made a personal sacrifice to keep him in school, and afterward sent him to Serampore where it is said he rose to be the best Bengali scholar in his class. The missionaries, no less than his father, looked forward with bright anticipation to the work for which he was preparing himself, as teacher in the Normal School. But God had another purpose, as yet mercifully hidden from their eyes. The young man came back from college, apparently in excellent health, and in a few months sickened and died. The pure gold of his father's experience shone forth. In the hour when his heart was wrung with grief, he sent a letter to the missionary accompanied by a gift of one hundred and nine rupees. The letter breathed a spirit of simple trust in the goodness and wisdom of God, and gratitude for the life, the redeemed life of the son taken from him. And it closed with these words:

> If Dhon had lived he would have worked for the Lord. As he is gone I want to give this money to help support some one to preach in his place.

The donation was not given out of his abundance. It represented almost his salary for a year as pastor of the church.

In less than six months the angel of Death entered the home again, and robbed him of his only daughter. She is spoken of as a model girl in every respect. The poor mother was nearly crushed by this double affliction, and the sorrowing father added her burden to his own. But not even then did his trust waver. Doctor Mason was able to write:

> Ramke's faith seems as clear as crystal. He has given me Rs. 66-10-3 in behalf of this departed daughter; thus making Rs. 177-10-3 within a few months, given as a thank-offering to the Lord for his mercies, and as in part a substitute for what the children had hoped to do.

Ramke lived but a brief time after the children's death. His call came on January 25, 1891. Doctor Mason was with him a day or two before. "I think, sahib, I shall go soon," he said. "I do not wish to stay." Suban survived him fourteen years. Her greatest joy was to continue his liberal gifts, and to order her life and interests after the pattern of his own. Through all the term of her loneliness, she regularly contributed a sum sufficient to support two traveling preachers engaged in publishing the gospel of peace among the hills around. The humble dwelling at Nisangram made sacred by a host of memories, continued to be her home to the last. It was there that I found her one sunny afternoon, and there, sitting in the shadow under the eaves of the house, overlooking the beautiful valley she told me the story of the past. When the talk was over, she and Gongman sat for their pictures, with Reban as the center of the group. Reban, an older brother of Rangku, was the first boy to go with Omed to the Goalpara school in 1847. Six years later, on January 18, 1905, Suban went to join those that had gone on before.

Gongman, though still a comparatively young man, had already preceded her, having finished his course on December 3, 1902. Brief though it was, his ministry could hardly have been more efficient or have left a deeper mark. He began his career as a lad in the Tura Normal School, becoming a pupil teacher, and early giving hopeful indications of an interest in personal religion. The influence of heathen relatives, however, and especially of a brother in the police, held him back from making a profession of his faith. Then came the baptism of six, including Dhonsing, which so impressed the school that it resulted, less than a month later, in the decision of two more, the only remaining students still unbaptized. Gongman, though a teacher, cast in his lot with them, and the three "put on Christ" together. His sterling

Ramke

Gongman, Reban, and Suban

character and special gifts soon brought him into prominence. In 1883 he was elected a deacon. One year at Rajasimla, where he did a noble work, was followed by the call to be Ramke's assistant at Nisangram. He was ordained in 1891, a few days only before Ramke's death, and thereafter had sole charge of the church for eleven fruitful years. A double portion of his teacher's spirit seemed to fall on him. He had the poet's gift and composed the best original hymns in his mother tongue, no less than forty of which appear in the current Garo hymn-book, the largest number contributed by any writer.

His death was a heavy blow. " What seems to us," writes Mr. Phillips,

> and to the whole Christian community an irreparable loss is the calling home of the pastor of the Nisangram church, Rev. Gongman. Few men could be missed more than he. No one ever found him in fault. He was a brother to all the Garos, and a tower of strength. A man of meekness and gentleness, but of such undoubted loyalty to Christ, such clear vision in religious matters, such practical wisdom and force of character, that he has, for many years, not only splendidly led the Nisangram church, but has been the constantly sought counselor of the brethren throughout the field and of the missionaries as well. We thank God for such a miracle of divine grace.

Before his death, the church of Christian Para numbered seven hundred members and supported not only its pastor, but wholly or in part, six traveling evangelists, several school-teachers and local preachers. The church has seven times entertained the Garo Association at its annual meetings. On the first occasion, in 1876, Doctor Bronson was present, and Mr. Keith reported an attendance of over two hundred delegates and others. At the one held in February, 1904, so large was the number that a special auditorium was constructed to seat seventeen hundred. The walls and roof were of bamboo and jungle grass, lined with clean white cloth, while the earth floor was covered with fresh straw. Some of the delegates came in families, seven or eight days' journey across the hills, carrying their little ones, their belongings and food. There were five missionaries present besides Doctors Mason and Phillips, who could remember that first gathering on the same spot twenty-eight years before; the youngest recruit being Mrs. Walter Mason, from whose lively account of the proceedings were culled these interesting facts. The literature stall at which her husband presided netted one hundred rupees by sales during the course of the meetings. "The Garos are always willing," she says, "to pay a good price for a good book, and more could have been sold if they had been on hand." Each session was opened with a short sermon by one of the leaders, after which business was dispatched, and with such refreshing expedition as greatly to please the smart little lady just from New York. She was amused, however, when, in a mixed assembly the pastor's wife read a paper on "The Work of Women in the Home," and only one woman took part in the debate. Doubtless many of the sex had thoughts to express if they had had the courage to voice them, but the men seemed to find the subject most interesting, and several of the younger ones, who had not yet become benedicts, gave their ideas most eloquently. It is satisfactory to learn that the ladies had plenty to say for themselves at their own meeting on the Sabbath afternoon when Miss Bond presided, and fully three hundred attended. In February, 1912, the Association was entertained for the eighth time, and two thousand two hundred and fifty-four were present at one session.

For a year after Gongman's death, the church of necessity suffered for the want of a fitting successor. The next pastor was Tuni, who for a long period taught in the training-school at Tura, and was, for a time at least, both able and earnest. The church is still the premier church on the Garo field, with a membership, in 1913, of nine hundred and forty-six, living in fourteen separate communities. A blessing rests on " Banner Town," and its founder's hopes have been more than fulfilled. " What a fine Christian village," exclaimed Doctor Phillips in a private letter written not long ago while out on tour,

> What a fine Christian village Nisangram is! And constantly growing! It has now over two hundred houses, and the majority are Christian homes.

The first chapel built by Ramke has given place to another, erected in 1900, under Gongman. It offers accommodation for a thousand worshipers with seats for about five hundred. When Doctor Mason saw it for the first time, as it was nearing completion, he said it " feasted my eyes." The broad-stretching hospitable roof of thatch, the whitened walls, the solid little belfry and steeple, and the railed veranda, which serves both as porch and vestibule, all give it a handsome and substantial appearance. Apart from the doors and windows, which were made in Calcutta, the work was done entirely by the Garos themselves. It cost the church seven hundred rupees in cash, while the labor was freely contributed by the members.

XXXI

A VISIT TO RAJASIMLA IN THE EVENING OF OMED'S LIFE

IT was getting dusk, on a chilly November afternoon, when we rode into Rajasimla, our boots and leggings wet with wading through many streams, our ponies hanging their heads, and thoroughly jaded after the rough twelve-mile scramble across the hills.

We had breakfasted with the deputy commissioner of Goalpara in his camp at Damra, under the fine old trees planted by David Scott, and afterward borrowed his elephant to ferry us over the Dudhnai. The river was narrow, deep, and muddy, and the water rose to the pad on the elephant's back. The rest of the journey was gloomy, through heavy jungle, with only one clearing to lighten the monotony, and no sign of human life. We came upon a herd of wild elephants. The green leaves they had trodden down were freshly pressed into their circular footprints, like flowers painted in a bowl. We could hear their movements on every side. It was not a pleasant experience with no escort and our only gun gone on ahead with the syce. It is one thing to read of the annual tours of the missionaries, often alone and unarmed, along these dangerous paths, and quite another to travel them oneself and realize the strain on the nerves. Mr. Mason returned by the same route a week later and wrote me this:

I met some sixty odd elephants of all sizes. The hunters had been there and caught thirty. In doing so, however, six men had been killed, and several others have died of wounds. At Cheran I met the *keddah* (elephant catching equipment) at work. They had just caught another herd of fourteen, near where the laskar was killed a few days before we passed. Mr. Clark, the superintendent, told me that this season's haul would bring the number of elephants caught in these hills by the Government keddah up to four thousand in fifteen years.

Entering the Rajasimla valley was like coming out of a cave. The darkness and closeness of the jungle were exchanged for an open sky and clear, pure air. Peaceful hamlets clustered at the base of the cliffs, and level fields, carpeted with tender crops, made soft going for tired feet. As we rode along, the smoke of cottage fires diffused an aromatic fragrance, while a few of the inhabitants came out to bid us welcome, and chatted pleasantly, walking by our side. We dismounted at the head of the valley, climbing a few feet to the grassy strip of high ground which here, like a ship's bridge, stretches across the narrow neck, and commands a pass on either side, with a fine wooded mountain towering up between. The side ranges close it at this point, and their jagged outlines are etched against the sky. Five minutes more, and we were comfortably ensconced by the camp-fire, in the middle of the ridge, near the bamboo rest-house where we were to spend the night. This stood on the site of the "grass hut" which Omed built for himself and his wife when they first settled here, after being driven from the hills. Just opposite, deep in the shadow of the mountain, some Garo houses loomed faintly, one of which was Omed's. The fire-light flickered over its porch as we sat and watched and the crescent moon began to shed a soft light over its roof of thatch.

After our meal, we crossed over and entered the dim interior. Omed lay on a platform at the farther end.

It was pitiful to see him—an old man of nearly seventy, half-paralyzed in body, sick, miserable. His features were indistinguishable in the dark. The one little smoking lamp, which his wife carried about in her hand, merely served to deepen the shadows and accentuate the gloom. The voice that spoke to us from the bed was husky and indistinct. Yet that was Omed—the smart sepoy, the first convert of the tribe, the brave, intrepid pioneer whom God had chosen to be his instrument in founding the earliest Garo church in this romantic spot! With a rather sinking heart I opened my note-book, borrowed the tiny lamp, and, sitting on a *morah* by the bed, prepared to question him on the story of those brighter days.

We conversed in Bengali, in which I found he was quite proficient, though Mr. Mason was at hand to interpret, whenever, in moments of special animation, he dropped unconsciously into Garo. The talk lasted two or three hours, and gave us more than a glimpse of the real Omed, the man as he had been in his prime. Some of the old vigor returned to him as he relived the greater events of his stirring life. His voice gathered force and resonance; his manner became vivacious; his recital was full of mirth and tenderness, and his comments on men and things surprised me by their shrewdness and depth. He had evidently been a magic personality, though now a physical wreck. There was, moreover, a ring of sincerity in his tone when speaking of his personal convictions and the progress of the gospel, which it was refreshing to hear. In spite of the fact that he was then, for the second time, under discipline and excluded from the church, I could not but regard him with reverence, as one who had been called and chosen to do a work for God which for nineteen years he faithfully accomplished, notwithstanding great opposition.

Photo by W. Carey.

Omed and Doctor Mason

Photo by W. Carey.

Scene of the First Baptism

Moving and sacred memories clustered around this place. Perhaps the most joyous of these memories were centered in the little stream to the right of the ridge, at a point not many rods distant west and south of Omed's house. He himself, standing on the ridge, pointed it out, indicating the exact position to a boy sent down for the purpose. I followed with the camera, but before setting it up, I stood for a moment to worship, with head uncovered, by the little grass-kissed rivulet with its margin of sand. For it was here that Doctor Bronson, that Sabbath morning in April, 1867, baptized the twenty-seven men and women who formed the nucleus of the first Garo church; and here too that ten more on the following day witnessed a good confession, when Omed and the missionary baptized in turn. Over this quiet strip of water, and to those echoing but astonished hills, the triune Name was first wafted as the seal of consecration in the Garo tongue.

I thought of the other twenty-five baptized within the year, when Mr. Stoddard came and engaged in the delightful task, and of the hymns they sang as they went in and out of this Jordan in Garo land. One of the candidates that day was Bago,[1] who now stood with Omed watching for our return. How real and wonderful it seemed!

The little lad was persuaded to step into the water, when the photograph was taken, and the ridge of Rajasimla made the background, while the hills above looked down offering their silent witness to the great and blessed influence which had followed from that small beginning.

Returning to the plateau we tried to secure a good photograph of Omed; but his infirmity made it a difficult

[1] An early convert who has been a faithful worker for over forty years. He still lives, in 1914, and still preaches.

task. In one picture he is seen standing before his house, supported by Mr. Mason; in another, an older picture, we see a strong, bearded face, with high forehead, in a frame of soft hair. Unfortunately there is no earlier likeness extant.

Omed's physical weakness began in 1872. In February Mr. Stoddard wrote:

> Omed is in poor health, and unable to travel much. He would be much more efficient among the mountain Garos than any other man. He could do more good in this way than as a pastor. He has not the knowledge or the studious habits to enable him to advance his people. Still, they are much attached to him, and think that everything would go to ruin, if he should leave them. Omed is also held high in respect by the surrounding heathen. He is frequently called upon to settle their quarrels and disputes. Today he has been to a neighboring village at the call of a deputation, to arbitrate an ugly dispute. At such times all the village turns out to hear the matter. The case was soon settled. Then followed the singing of Garo hymns by Omed and his associates, and the preaching of Christ.

This reputation for wisdom and just judgment was Omed's to the end. Until he could no longer go about, his services as arbitrator were in frequent request; nor did he surrender his itinerant commission to "range the hills, preach, and baptize" without a struggle. Then came a long spell of failing health, which kept him in much against his will. Even then, eager to be out among the mountains, he pluckily attempted, at intervals, to prosecute his mission as in former days. After one such effort, Mr. Stoddard writes:

> Omed is getting much revived of late. He baptized nine yesterday. Today he says he will no longer think of or regard his bodily infirmities, but go from village to village and from mountain to mountain till every Garo has heard of God in Christ reconciling the world unto himself.

Omed

There can be little doubt that the strain and exposure of these journeys, in his weakened condition, brought on the stroke of paralysis which laid him aside. For most men it would have meant the end of active work. Not so in Omed's case, however, for in 1888 Mr. Mason writes:

> Omed, who is slowly recovering from paralysis, has of late been able to go about and preach considerably. He met me at this place (Chotcholja) one evening when I was too ill to continue the services. He could not rest until he had come to my bedside and prayed for me. How much we owe to such prayers, God only knows.

It is pathetic to think of this stricken Garo, leaning heavily on his staff, hobbling half a dozen miles over rough hills, to do this Christian act of kindness.

We must bear in mind the proofs of his sincerity and earnestness and also the deadening effect of those paralyzed years on a nature so active, if we would judge rightly of their inglorious end. Thrice was he excluded from the church, and twice restored. The last exclusion was but a month before his death.

The first is mentioned by Mr. Phillips in his annual report for 1883:

> At Rajasimla, the home of Omed, there is much to make us sad, and especially in relation to Omed's own conduct. More than a year ago, the hand of fellowship was withdrawn from him, and I fear he is only drifting farther and farther from his moorings. It is very sad that he who was the first to lead his fellow Garos to Christ should now be using his influence, consciously or unconsciously, to lead them away from him.

It is important to notice the date. Omed had been in failing health for several years. For how long his walk had been unworthy it is impossible to say. But the church would hardly take any hasty action in the case of so prominent a member. The trouble seems to have been a yielding to the old craving for *chu* with its attendant exhilaration, and a gradual growth of a worldly spirit. His position made these faults conspicuous and disastrous. Saddest of all, they were persisted in after repentance and restoration. So it fell that he died under the church's ban, his bright record stained, and his Master, with himself, dishonored.

We must face the facts, but it would be easy to give them undue significance. They neither support the gibe that the first convert was a fraud, nor do they mean of necessity that he became a castaway. He never denied the faith. His two restorations prove that he sought to retrieve his standing, and prized the fellowship of believers. Mourn we must over the lapse from Christian conduct; but a true reading of the facts forbids us to regard it as a fall from grace. "Omed is outside," wrote Mr. Mason to me once, not long before the end; "but he is not a bad man. His first wife was bad, but she died in a Christian family a much better woman, apparently, than she had been."

Among extenuating circumstances must be placed first the physical cause. We do not know all the effects of the paralytic stroke. It may have dulled other sensibilities than those of the flesh. To a man of Omed's temperament, the long-continued, enforced inactivity must have been peculiarly irksome, and the disfigurement and helplessness keenly felt. He was but human, after all, and of savage stock. The habit of drunkenness is inbred among the Garos, and drastic discipline has been needed to purge it from the church. This man, in his weakness and loneliness, allowed himself to be overcome, as many have done since among ourselves, with far less excuse. The very qualities of independence and resource, with which Omed was naturally endowed, and the rank this gave him above his fellows, may have proved a means by which his feet were ensnared, leading him to trust to himself rather than in God. And from this self-trust to self-indulgence is an easy step. Omed's steps tottered to the end; but in some way, beyond our ken, he surely was sought and found of the Divine Compassion, that "Love that will not let us go." Do we minimize his faults? Nay, rather, we magnify the grace of God.

Omed died at the age of seventy, fourteen years after the stroke, on April 17, 1902. The church which he had founded at Rajasimla has a present membership of over three hundred, though more than twice that number have been baptized through the years.

* * * * * * *

Early next morning, while the dew was still on the grass, we started to climb to Dambora, Omed's birthplace and to make acquaintance with other villages of that rocky region, which was the home of so many of the early converts, and of the boys who attended the Garo Government School.

It was a pleasure to find Bago waiting to accompany us. Wonderfully lithe and alive, he stepped briskly along, tackling the steepest slopes and picking his way through the forests or over the boulders of the turbulent streams, with the sure familiarity of the jungle-bred; and all the while chatting freely to us of his life and work. The photograph is a good one, though the features seem a little too harsh and haggard, probably the result of trying to look natural under the camera's stare. A tuft of gray, like the filaments of a bulb, does duty as a beard.

Smooth, thin, and mobile, with a spiritual light in the clear, tender eyes, a skull-cap crowning the open forehead, and soft ringlets flowing out behind, Bago's face is a study. He looks as if he "pleaded with men," and there is no mistaking the "Book in his hand."

We toiled on for two or three hours, walking where the path was too steep to ride, and finding it extremely hot. Some of the clearings had bared a whole hillside to the blistering sun. It was not much cooler in the jungle where the rank vegetation seemed to hold and stifle the air. But once on the clear, cool crest of Dambora, we breathed again, and found infinite relief. Dambora is most picturesquely placed, a typical Garo village perched on the summit of a crag. The building occupying the place of honor is the chapel, for this is a branch of the Rajasimla church, and the people are nearly all Christians, though entirely heathen a year before our visit. The dun-colored roofs of the houses had bright patches over the eaves, where handfuls of scarlet and gold chillis, highly glazed and finely tapered, gleamed in the sun. As I sat in the saddle trying to sketch the scene, a meeting was going on in the chapel, the missionary presiding. It was pleasant to watch the people leaving their work, and some of them coming up from the jungle at the sound of the gong. When I looked in, a half hour later, Mr. Mason was discussing with them means for the further support of the school. The interior of the meeting-house was of the usual type—elastic floor of plaited bamboos, polished with much sitting, walls to match, and a low roof of timber and thatch. The only appointments were a reading-desk or pulpit, consisting of a platform, with a single upright stem fitted in front, supporting a flat board for the desk. But I was pleased to see a glimmering of artistic taste. Red cloth had been tacked to

Thangkan and Family

Tokong and Bago

the board with wooden pegs, and some rude carving decorated the stem.

After service, including a hymn which these converts of a year sang with zest, our ponies with sharpened appetites took the descent to Rajasimla at a reckless pace, made perilous by the tangle of heavy bamboos overhanging the path. We had to be nimble in dodging these, and once I was swept off backward, and left clinging to the obstacle, while the animal continued on his way!

From Rajasimla we continued our march through the hills toward Chotcholja.

XXXII

SONARAM AND CHOTCHOLJA

CHOTCHOLJA, by all accounts, was a filthy and disgusting place. We will call it a human hog-yard and pass on. There are some things better imagined than described!

It lay on the level, a dirty sprawl of houses by a sandy stream, in a long valley, choked with reed and jungle. Facing the village, on one side, is a range of high cliffs which once "beetled o'er their base." But that was before the earthquake. Being six miles from Rajasimla, it was, of course, well known to the early Christians, and probably preached in by some of the evangelists on their rounds. But no impression was made. The people remained idle, drunken, diseased, demon-devotees, in close proximity to "God's village" for more than a decade. The place was rank heathen and bad at that.

And Sonaram? He had been an unsatisfactory student of the normal class. His poor record made the missionaries chary in using him in their growing work, in spite of their need for men. But the root of the matter was in him, and the Chotcholja of today is both a monument to the grace of God, and a witness to that "poor record retrieved."

In 1876 Mr. Mason was asked for the third or fourth time by Sonaram to be allowed to try a school. In view of his apparent sincerity and earnestness, he was told that if he would go to Chotcholja where there were yet no Christians, and do what he could, he would be given three rupees a month. Sonaram moved his family there, and ere long had a large village school, and a number of converts awaiting baptism. The work aroused opposition. One Sunday Sonaram and these inquirers faced an angry mob of sixty or eighty, who, with weapons in their hands, thought to drive them from their home; but they quietly held on and soon outrode the storm.

In November, 1876, Mr. Mason was in camp at Rajasimla and from there rode over to the village under the cliff. He was at once surrounded by one hundred and fifty or more Garos. Then began the examination of applicants, and twenty-one were accepted.

The next day the same program was repeated, and after accepting ten more they were about to go to the water to baptize when an elderly woman, who had been refused because she seemed unable to answer the questions, called out, " But I wish to be baptized." She was reexamined and accepted. When thirty-two had been baptized and they were about to dismiss the multitude, four more made application, and were examined at the water's edge. Three were received and baptized, so that, where seven months before there was not a Christian and scarcely any knowledge of Christianity, there was now, including the teacher and his wife, a band of thirty-seven Christians, composed of men and women of all ages. This meeting might well be called a two-days' revival—not the revival of a sleeping church but that of dead heathen; for, although some, having weighed the matter well, had decided for the Lord some weeks before, about half were previously undecided. The words of one young married woman, about fifteen years of age, were touching: " She had thought much and believed in Christ, and wished to do his will, but hesitated lest she be found following an ignorant impulse."

"On the way back to camp that night," says Mr. Mason,

> as I was at the turn of the road which bridges a brook in the deep, leafy forest, I could dimly discern in the distance an old man leaning on his staff and beckoning to me. I turned my pony and cantered up to him. He was old, white-headed, and feeble, and with a quivering voice he said, "Teacher, can God forgive the sins of an old man like me?"

It was a cry for help out of a deeper darkness than that of the closing twilight—that from the shadow of sin and the gathering gloom of death. It won an instant and tender response. "Indeed, he not only can, but is waiting, anxious to forgive." "I would go to the ends of the earth to answer such a question," is the comment made as the scene is recalled, and never is the story told without a quiver of the lips.

On returning to Goalpara, Mr. Mason heard that several others at Chotcholja had decided to put on Christ, and sent two of the leading pastors to visit them. They soon reported that they had accepted and baptized twenty-one more. The following January the missionary himself went again, and found all the converts faithful, though suffering persecution. Thirteen more were baptized, and Sonaram said, "There are but two families left unconverted now."

We leap over a decade to January, 1888. Sonaram is dead. Mr. Mason thus describes the contrast:

> Just eleven years ago I made my first visit to Chotcholja. It was a most wild, uncultivated valley. Where was then wild jungle are now thrifty rice-fields. I seldom find a village more filthy and diseased than that was. Now there are few more cleanly. There is a very nice bamboo meeting-house, and last May they organized a church and are giving one-tenth of their

rice harvest, which is nearly their whole income, for the support of a pastor. They are asking that he may be ordained, and to me their request seems wise.

The church, including seven recently baptized, numbers seventy-two. They seem united, earnest, and devoted. Their crops are raised with difficulty, on account of the wild animals. While there one night, I was kept awake most of the night by a herd of wild elephants feeding near their fields. Some one called out, "Elephants are here!" And away went the people in a body, shouting to drive the elephants away. Scarcely had the noise died down, when the call came from another direction, "Elephants are here!" And so it went on much of the night. The next night near there a whole village turned out with torches, men and women, boys and girls, shouting and calling to each other, "*Chandenggrim! Chandenggrim!* (Stand together!) *Dakat! Dakat!* (Don't run!)" Thus, as I stood among them, they, though shaking with fear, drove the herd away. Another night an elephant came in and tore down a house, in spite of the shouts of those near. And as I was going to look at the ruins, a leopard crossed my path; and the next night I was in a village where a tiger had just carried off two hogs!

With their crops and property thus precariously held, the support of a pastor seemed an elephantine undertaking, concerning which they consulted the missionary. Mr. Mason says that he does not recall another instance where he made suggestions to a village church regarding the method of raising funds, believing that if the spirit was willing they would invent a method. In this case something like the following dialogue occurred:

"Sahib, don't you think we ought to have a pastor?"

"Yes, I do. I think it would be well if you could have a pastor."

"Could the mission help us support a pastor?"

"Why should the mission help? Can you not support one yourselves?"

"We have no money; we cannot sell our produce. How can we pay him?"

"If one among you became ill or crippled, could not ten others care for him?"

"Yes."

"If ten of you should wish to undertake some work, do you not think you could feed one man while he was doing that work?"

"Probably."

"Now if a man should become your pastor, could you not, when you harvest your rice, put, say nine measures of that rice into your own granary and one measure into a church granary for that pastor?"

"Yes, we could do that, but that would not be enough to feed the pastor?"

Tokong was the man they were wanting for pastor, and Tokong was present. He came forward and said that he would take what such tenth would come to for his salary, however small it might be, and that if it amounted to more than the estimated need, which was three dollars per month, he would turn the balance back to the church.

And so it was arranged. He was chosen to be their pastor. And the tenth was found to be more than enough for his support. The plan adopted has been kept up ever since. When the paddy is cut, brought in and threshed, each man puts nine parts into his own bin and one part into the church bin. Some of the women, when preparing their daily meal, give in addition, hand-grips of rice as a thank-offering for their food. For this purpose a dish is kept in the floor of the chapel, and often as much as two maunds[1] a week is brought and poured in. There is another dish for money.

The membership in 1889 was one hundred and two. These gave Tokong one hundred and twenty rupees a year. In 1899, the membership had more than doubled,

[1] A maund is about eighty-two pounds.

and the church was supporting a traveling evangelist as well as a pastor. Today (1913) the church totals four hundred ninety-one members. It stands numerically fourth on the list of the churches of the Garo hills. Spiritually it has usually kept a high level, and is still doing very much good. Tokong was pastor to the close of 1891. At that time the Rajasimla church was in a weak and discouraged condition. They thought they could not support a pastor, and were expecting to get on without one. Brother Tokong saw the need and the disheartened condition. He therefore announced to the church that he was coming to be their pastor, whether they called him or not and whether they supported him or not! He came and blessing followed. They sanctioned his coming and gave him support.

Chotcholja looked very pretty and attractive when I saw it in 1898. The people knew we were coming, and had decorated the chapel with greenery and flowers. An avenue of plantain trees led to the door, and above the roof, at the bent tips of two tall bamboos, fluttered tiny flags. These bits of vermilion looked like a pair of gorgeous butterflies basking in the sun. Their rich color lit up the whole landscape, the embowered village, the slaty shale of the great cliffs across the stream, the white sand at their base, and the clear lustrous blue of the vault above. I have seen the same effect produced by a scarlet leaf on an ivy-colored wall in Devon, a red handkerchief on a lad's neck in Italy, a tiny kite floating over the Dacca Bazaar.

Beside the chapel was a snug tentlike house of sweet-smelling grass which they had prepared for us to sleep in. Unhappily we could only stay a few hours. The disappointment was mutual. Tokong with a crowd of lads took me to the nearest cliff. It looked quite close but was really a good distance off and tedious to climb. The whole face of it had come away and crashed down that terrible afternoon of the earthquake. This had caused great masses of rock to be split up, detached, and flung out in the direction of the village to a distance of five or six hundred yards. They dropped evenly, in almost a straight line, one behind the other, as if some giant gunner had been trying to "get the range." Any one of them was big enough to blot out half the village if it had struck home. The force behind must have been terrific. Shot from the toppling cliff, like Vulcanic bolts from an angry sky, and sent far hurtling through the air, the noise and shock of the impact on the swaying earth must have resounded for miles. Gathering momentum as they fell, they bit into the ground, and so blocked the stream that a great wash of sand swirled up, burying them deeper still. But the protruding portions, like the Sphinx at Gizeh, were sufficiently bulky to be astonishing. Enormous gaps separated some of the rocks. One boulder stood, roughly, twelve feet above the sand, and measured a hundred and twenty feet round. Another was larger, with a great tree rooted in it, rising erect from the summit, like a flag-staff on a hill.

While I was examining these relics of a spent force, disintegrating only to destroy, Mr. Mason was sampling the products of a power equally strong to break down and divide, but spiritual and eternal. He was holding service with the Garo Christians in the bamboo church among the trees. We could hear them singing as we stood listening. And above the trees gleamed softly the tiny flags—the blood-red symbols of the Grace that saves. I knew as I looked and listened that this was the power which had changed Chotcholja and given it a name in the book of the kingdom of heaven.

XXXIII

THE FORSAKEN FLOCK AT ADOKGIRI

THIS is the story of a handful of converts suddenly discovered, soon baptized, and then, by a strange mischance, left to their fate and forgotten for nearly five years. They all slipped back into the darkness out of which they came? Ah, well they might! But let us see.

To find them we must cross that curious range in the eastern corner of the northern edge of the hills. It is one of the most rugged and fantastic bits of cliff formation in the district. It looks like a crocodile slowly crawling south. Its body thus bent is almost entirely surrounded by a little river, the Ildek, which takes its rise near the snout, winds past the sprawling feet, turns sharp in the angle, and flows clear around the high ridge of the tail in a long parallel loop. To get to Adokgiri, from any point in the hills, you must cross this river and then negotiate those scaly heights. Every one who has done this writes of the difficulties of the way. It was partly this, no doubt, which accounted for the long neglect of the first disciples there.

But who were they, and how came they by a knowledge of the Truth? The story opens with a trip made in the early days by two Garo evangelists, probably Chakin and Bago. They penetrated to all the hidden villages on the hills around Rajasimla, and came at last to this, the roughest region of all. Little did they expect to find a people prepared of the Lord in such a place. But so it was. News spread even through the thickest jungle, and in some form or other, that news which is preeminently "good" had reached their ears. Perhaps they had seen some of the first Christians on the market-days at Rongjuli; they may even have stood among the crowd of wild Garos who watched the first baptisms at Rajasimla. Who can tell? Certain it is that they had some glimmering of the gospel and were eager to be taught more fully with a view to embracing the faith. The evangelist spent some time with them, and then hastened back to tell Mr. Stoddard, who was then in camp at Rongjuli, February or March, 1872. "Two days' journey from this point," writes the missionary,

> there are several asking for baptism. Two preachers have just come down and report a most interesting state of things. It is a day's march farther into the hills than a missionary has yet been. My plans were laid for going up there; but the state of my health now does not justify the step. Omed and others will soon go and preach and baptize. They have been very cautious about taking any advance steps without the presence of the missionary—a failing on the right side, perhaps—but I encourage Omed to baptize all who believe.

In October he continues the narrative:

> When I wrote you last I spoke of a place not yet visited by a missionary where several were asking for baptism. Omed soon after visited the place, Adokgiri, and baptized eight, on May 17, 1872. Many others in that same village have since left the worship of devils for that of the living God, and asked to be joined to the Lord's people.

Now falls the curtain of oblivion, like descending mists on the moors. Omed was ill. Mr. Stoddard left Assam. His successor, Mr. Keith, was either not told of these people, or was too absorbed in other work to pay them a visit. They passed out of view, and at length out of mind. It was a singular happening.

Five years went by. Then as if by chance, the veil was lifted. From December, 1877, to February, 1878, for six weeks, Mr. Mason was out in camp. He visited all the twenty stations, eight of which had not before seen a missionary. One of the eight was Atiabari, some six miles east of Rajasimla. Here a school had been opened the previous June, and work started. "I intended," he says,

> to make but a passing visit; but at their earnest request spent a day and a night with them. My tent was scarcely pitched when I was surprised to receive the names of nine applicants for baptism, and doubly surprised to find after examination that we could accept not only these but one other!

Ramke and Rangku, who accompanied Mr. Mason, assisted at the examination. Concerning one of the candidates there was hesitancy. This man on the ground that he wanted to be a Christian had cast off his wife, and sent her back to her parents. It seemed a strange reason to give for so wrong-headed an act. The examiners were puzzled. They remonstrated, argued, explained, but all in vain. Nothing could convince him that he had done what was not quite right. At last, thinking there might be something he did not wish to make public, the missionary took him aside, and, walking a little into the jungle, inquired privately into the cause of the action. Judge of his amusement when the recalcitrant husband, apparently so doggedly determined on deserting his lawful spouse, stretched out his hand and remarked, "She's only that high," showing her to be a child about four years of age! So it was the examiners who yielded the point, and the whole ten were baptized!

That evening, around the camp-fire, something was said which revived the memory of the Christians at

Adokgiri, and the missionary was alert. Discussion and inquiry elicited the facts. He resolved to pay them a visit. But the preachers discouraged the idea. "It's impossible," said Rangku, "to get over there and back from here. The distance is too great and the road too rough."

"It's unsafe," said another. "The wild beasts are very thick there."

But the missionary was not to be easily dissuaded. He is one of those who love to bring things to pass.

"I'm not going after the beasts," said he. "If I let them alone they will probably leave me alone. I'll start in the morning. And if I do not reach the place by noon, I'll turn back."

"But the people will not be at home," they urged. "All will be away to market today."

So many reasons made him feel that some were probably weak. And the tough mountain pony was saddled at dawn for the attempt. The journey proved as rough as its reputation. And the wild beasts were certainly "thick." Says Mr. Mason:

> With that mountain pony I rode up and down tracks incredibly steep, clambering over rocks, crawling under bushes. At one place the path was so steep that the natives had cut holes in the path as steps or footholds for their bare feet. I ascended by clinging to my pony's tail as he vigorously climbed. At the top was a clearing, where the houses had been pushed aslant and broken by wild elephants; and then came a descent, down which the pony slid. At the bottom was a little stream, along the sandy bed of which we wriggled our way under the tall elephant-grass that locked densely above our heads. After a bit I heard voices. I knew by the sound that there were Garos lying in wait. Leaning well down to my saddle and looking through the long funnel of the grass, I could see about twenty Garos peering down the ravine waiting for me; each with a spear in hand. I confess that for a moment I was a bit uneasy, for I then recalled that I had been warned against entering that section, as the people were in a

hostile attitude, but having had no purpose of going there I had forgotten it. But riding on, not knowing what might be my reception, I came to the opening where two paths crossed. The wild men were drawn up on either side with spears in hand. I stopped, looked them over, when to my astonishment two men stepped forward and extended their hands. The meaning of the Christian hand-shake I then felt as never before. It was an unmistakable sign of Christian fellowship, and these were two of the very men baptized by Omed five years before. I found that they had been on their way to market, and that when I was in that clearing with my white umbrella, they had from a neighboring hilltop seen me coming, and had returned to see what I was after. And they welcomed me and led me back to their village.

I found that the converts, though so long left to themselves had nevertheless not returned to their demon worship, and but a few of them had returned to drink. Some were even able to spell out and understand Garo sentences, and, in accordance with their desire, I left what Garo Scriptures I had.

Returning to Goalpara, Mr. Mason made up for previous neglect by sending a school-teacher at once to Adokgiri to instruct the discovered disciples. The lad chosen was Philsing. In less than one month he had gathered nineteen scholars, including men and women. Because of the interesting circumstances, the privilege of providing funds for his support was given to the church and Sunday School at Strykersville, New York, Mr. Mason's early home.

At the end of the year he was able to report:

Philsing is doing a good work. Already we are permitted to gather fruit. Six converts have been baptized, and the whole village seems ready to listen.

After two years Mr. Phillips visited the place and baptized six. In 1886 he went again and baptized twenty-six more.

The little church grew steadily and in 1897-1898 a hundred new members were added by baptism. One of their pastors was Chakin, to whose preaching, probably, the earliest interest was due. Altogether more than three hundred persons have been gathered to the little church in that rugged corner. The " forsaken flock " was worth going after. Its history proves that the Good Shepherd himself cared for it when it had no outside help.

XXXIV

A CHURCH AT DEREK

AFTER Messrs. Mason and Phillips had been a few months at Goalpara acquiring a Garo vocabulary and, without text-books or proper teachers, trying to understand the Garos' speech, curiosity to see the Garos in their homes led them to mount their ponies and ride away some ten or twelve miles in the direction of the Garo hills. Having gone over rice-fields, through jungle paths and grassy swales they espied a village where among the houses and beneath the broad-spreading, huge-limbed peepul [1] trees, the busy people were at their work.

To this village the young missionaries made their way. But upon their arrival not a person was to be seen. Having tied and fed their ponies, they sat down upon a log and began to eat their pocket lunch, watching in various directions to see if no one would appear. After a little some lads were seen to run from behind one bush to another and by looking more closely others were discovered thus hiding from view, and some indeed were stretched upon the large limbs of the trees, like squirrels peeking to see what danger was below. Finally a young man was observed behind a bush not far away, who seeing that he was discovered came out trembling and saying, "Wh-wha-what do you want? Why are you here?" The missionaries tried to explain, and as a good number of others gathered about tried to do some preaching. But some years later they were told that at that time they

[1] Spelled also *pipal, pippul;* a sacred fig tree (*Ficus religiosa*).

"put the last words first and the first words last, and the words between were all mixed up." This village was called Derek, and later it was occasionally visited by the missionaries, but the people were not inclined to listen long. When a group had gathered to listen, some leader would say, "Come, we must be at our work."

After the transfer of the school and the station from Goalpara to Tura, among the schoolboys was one who appeared too stupid or too thick-headed to make it seem wise to spend time and money upon him while brighter boys could be found. So he was urged by the missionary to return to his own village and live a good Christian life and thus let his light shine there. Mr. Mason says that he recalls the words of this boy on a former occasion when after a school vacation, speaking in a prayer-meeting, he said that he felt he had been growing in grace because he had but one fight during the vacation. And as Mr. Mason learned more of this village and of the boy's family, he thought that the boy might have really thus grown in grace; and had he known or realized the situation, he might have been loath to give the advice he did. However, instead of going to his own village he returned after a day's journey and asked if he might not be sent to teach a school in a village that was asking for a teacher. Upon inquiry it was found to be Derek that was asking for a school. What could be done? If Derek wanted a school some one should go. Who was there to send? No one could be thought of. Could we send this boy? What kind of teacher would he make? He could read and write. He might teach the pupils to do that much. Finally he was told that if he wished, and would go to Derek and do what he could for those people, he would be allowed three rupees (one dollar) a month for his support. He went, and from reports seemed to be doing well. In fact, after a few months he wrote the missionary, saying that he had had a vision, and in the vision a voice spake to him, saying, "You are here in this village, the people's only light, do for them your very best." Whatever may be thought of the vision, it is certain that God spoke to him that day. Not long afterward he seemed to be winning some of the older schoolboys to himself and to Christ. The older people began to be aroused and alarmed lest there be a break in their village and a division in their ranks. What could be done? They held a council during which one man had a bright thought and said:

> This boy says that he is not afraid of the demons, that there are no demons. Now, there is that demon tree where the vultures roost, which is a great inconvenience to us. Let us ask this boy to go and cut down that tree. If he will do that the demons will kill him and we will be rid of both the tree and the teacher.

To this they agreed and deputed a committee to urge him to cut the tree. He was bright enough to see their purpose, so he consulted with the four or five boys who had joined him, and with them went and cut down that tree. Then all waited for him to die, but to this day he still lives. And as he continued to labor there, first the young men, then the young women, then the middle-aged men and middle-aged women, then the old men, and last of all the old women confessed Christ. A most interesting visit was that when these aged ones told their experiences, some of them referring back to the day of the missionaries' first visit to Derek.

Upon a later visit after a preaching service they had a Sunday School session, and nearly three hundred were present. They asked the missionary to teach a class, but he preferred to see what kind of work was being done, and so walked about from class to class, although there were but few that were able to teach. Among the teachers were two men who were heads of families, too busy to attend school, but who had purchased the little primers and kept these with them so that when they met one able to read, and there was an opportunity, they would ask, "What is this, and what is that?" until they had learned to read, and then they had bought what little Scripture had been translated and printed in their language. And now these two men were acting as teachers, and "As I listened," says Mr. Mason,

> to the expounding of the Word by these two men, my heart was thrilled by the assurance that the Holy Spirit was with them and leading them to know the truth. The history, the geography, the philosophy of the book they did not know, but the meaning of Christ's words they could tell.

At another time, on a visit to the place, it was found that the church was divided into groups for preaching to their heathen neighbors; every member, man or woman, young or old, had some share in this work; some could read, some could talk, some could sing; and if some could do none of these they could go along and increase the company. Thus the church grew, and in 1913 they reported a membership of eight hundred and eighteen, and half as many more belonging to the Christian community. And one of those first boys who helped to cut the tree has for some time been pastor. Not a bright man, but gifted as a preacher, full of fitting illustrations, and filled with the spirit of endurance and perseverance.

Such is the early history of some of the churches. Each church and many of the smaller Christian communities have similarly interesting histories. In places like Rajasimla and Nisangram Christian communities were formed quite separate from their heathen neighbors, but as a rule converts remain in their own villages and in their own homes, letting their light shine where it would be most effective; but even there they have a tendency to draw into groups.

From the first, it has been the belief of the missionaries that the kingdom could be well established among such a people only by the people being led to feel an independence of the missionary Society, and a conviction of their own responsibility, and a spirit of aggressive fellowship with Christ in his redeeming work.

Mr. Mason writes under date of October 9, 1876, concerning a class of workers:

> My first purpose was to show the nature of Christian cooperation, and to explain the Scripture methods of organized effort. I have aimed also to show the magnitude and importance of their work in the kingdom,

first for those "in their immediate vicinity" and then for the "four vast empires of idolaters" by which they are surrounded.

Mr. Phillips writes, "We have ever striven to stand before the churches as their helpers, and I believe that they are more and more realizing that the work is theirs." In their ignorance and feebleness the churches often felt like the little child who wishes to cling to its mother's finger when first learning to walk, but as they grasp the idea of progress and development they bear more readily responsibilities and enlarge their work. In 1889 Mr. Mason writes of his satisfaction at seeing the growth of this working spirit while he was attending a council where most of the more educated and leading members within twenty miles of the place were gathered, when he heard them read papers on such subjects as,

"What are the necessary characteristics of a pastor or evangelist?" "How shall we best gather converts from among the heathen?" "How shall we deal with inactive members?" "What shall be done with those who neglect their children?" Although he was welcome to speak on any subject, the meeting was wholly their own.

Thus their efforts to instill democratic principles and a democratic spirit were not in vain, indeed some high British officials have felt that they were too successful in this line, and that more of an authoritative control would have been wiser. However, the missionaries think that the wisdom of such a course can better be judged after the Garos have had some experience and have learned something by their errors, as well as by their successes.

At times special interest pervaded the churches, and such men as Thangkan, Gongman, Parot, Sujan, and others have done good work. It has been a sorrow to the missionaries to see many strong workers called to their heavenly home. Mr. Phillips in speaking of the death of Gongman says:

> He was an efficient pastor and counselor, a tower of strength in the whole Christian community. Meek and humble, yet a man of clear and decided views, and one on whom all leaned.

From the first attention has been given to Sunday School work as strength permitted.

In 1889 they reported 27 schools with 944 pupils.

In 1892 they reported 42 schools with 2,500 pupils.

In 1898 they reported 72 schools with 3,337 pupils.

And Mrs. Crozier who kept the records and looked after the schools in 1912, reports 112 schools with 5,218 pupils, and says of these schools, "They vary in size from 10 to 231. I estimate that over 6,000 people have entered the Sunday Schools, and that over 4,000 have been fairly regular attendants. In 1914 one hundred and ninety-four certificates and five medals were awarded" by the Indian Sunday School Union upon Scripture examinations. "Doctor Mason also prepared and sent questions to all our Sunday Schools and gave prizes for the best answers."

Thangkan once took "next to the highest mark in all India" at one of the I. S. S. U. examinations.

An annual association was first organized in 1875, and this soon began to send out evangelists to the heathen. Since then four other associations have been organized, and each supports evangelical preachers, so that at times the home mission preachers supported by these churches, in addition to the pastors, have averaged more than one such preacher to each church. Furthermore they have sent and supported three missionaries to people of unknown tongues.

One spent years working for a tribe of the Himalayas. Others have been sent to companies of Garos who have migrated to other parts of Assam, and there is scarcely a mission station for any people in the province, where the missionaries of those fields have not had more or less aid from Garo Christian workers. And now there are Garo Christian churches found in each of the districts of the plains. This field first sent workers into the Kamrup district, where the missionaries of Gauhati took supervision, and they report in 1913 a Garo membership of one thousand two hundred and sixty and probably the baptisms have reached about two thousand and three hundred. To the south of the Garo hills in the Mymensing district, a work was early started among the Garos, which was taken over by the Australian missionaries, who have labored faithfully and now have a prosperous, large, and vigorous work among the Garos there.

XXXV

EDUCATIONAL

Village Schools

FOR a people with none educated, with no written language, with no knowledge of expressing thought save by word of mouth, how could a mission be efficient without reducing their language to written form, and teaching at least some of them to read, and putting into their hands the word of God in their own tongue? Hence from Ramke's first school at Damra to the present, school work has received much of the missionaries' attention and has been one of their most efficient agencies for evangelizing souls and for the upbuilding of Christian characters.

Teachers trained in the station school at Tura are sent out as opportunity affords to open schools in villages. These teachers, all of whom are Christians, infuse the spirit and principles of Christianity into the villagers both in and out of school. The missionaries have found that only as some one can go to a village and settle down there as one of the people, and make his preaching " precept upon precept, line upon line, here a little and there a little," are such people brought clearly to the light and knowledge of Jesus Christ.

The aim at the station school is to have every graduate a worthy exemplar and an eager advocate of the world-saving gospel and the world's only Redeemer. The spirit prevalent in the school inspires many of the graduates bravely to meet opposition, endure hardships, and overcome in the strength of their Lord. Two such teachers have been martyred at their work. But as a rule these teachers, holding on, have seen gathered about them the nucleus of a church which often grew into a membership of hundreds from which have gone out other workers. In 1892 Mr. Mason reported,

> It is through these schools, or rather the teachers of these schools, that work is begun and churches planted in the heathen villages. The ingathering of a large number of the converts is, in the main, through the work of these teachers. But the missionaries have ever been taxed to find funds for the support of these schools. While personally Government officials have at times been in sympathy, at times indifferent, and at times hostile to the idea of educating the Garos, the Government, although necessarily neutral as regards religion, has from the first taken an interest in Garo education, and besides sustaining at times a few schools of their own, they have made grants-in-aid to the mission. In 1878, as we have already seen, the Government made a grant to the mission of all their school funds on condition that the mission add a certain amount and render reports. They also gave three or four stipends and later, upon examination tests, a few scholarships, that enabled a few pupils from the village schools to continue their studies in the station school. But the Government grant and the money received from America never being sufficient to push the work, it was the more necessary to appeal for help to the people of the land, as they became able to see the advantages of education and the benefits of doing for themselves.
>
> At first, being wholly ignorant of the meaning of schools and education, and having a strong prejudice against men of other clans coming among them, the Garos made slow progress in education until its advantages began to become apparent to themselves. As the value of schools began to be realized, villages began the more to ask for schools and were the more ready to build houses, both for the school and for the teacher, also to contribute food toward the teacher's support. The schools increased in number and were scattered among the heathen, while the Christian villages, increasing their efforts for themselves, tried to raise the grade of some of their schools, and also to

relieve the mission of some of its cares. In 1892 one such was started at Nisangram, and now there are some eight or ten schools of this class, taking pupils through a six-year course, supported and managed mainly by the native Christians themselves. In a few cases, aid for these schools is now granted by the Government directly to the villages. At times the mission managed from one hundred to one hundred and twenty village schools. Many other localities begging for teachers, had to be refused, because there were no funds for the support of teachers, and sometimes, no teachers for the schools. Those villages situated in the most promising locations, who could supply the most aid and send the largest number of pupils, were those to be first favored.

In former days Mr. Phillips supervised the schools of the southern half of the hills and Mr. Mason those of the northern half. But they were in constant consultation, and problems and perplexities were discussed, and decisions reached were always unanimous, else no definite new action was attempted. In the more recent years the village schools have been supervised mainly by Mr. Dring and Mr. Harding, each of whom has followed as they were able the same general lines of procedure.

At the end of 1912 Mr. Harding reports that "In 1911-1912 the villages increased their own contributions to the school eighty-one per cent over 1910-1911, and in this year they have increased their contributions over that of the latter year at least one hundred per cent"; also that the Garos, besides spending over seven hundred rupees in support of independent schools of their own, gave forty-seven per cent of the whole cost of the mission schools.

In writing of the Government census of 1901, Rev. P. H. Moore of the Assam Mission speaks concerning the Garo Hills thus:

The educational work is in the hands of our missionaries. Our mission work there has been vigorously pushed and greatly blessed and is a source of constant joy to all our hearts. The Christians have increased from one thousand one hundred and eighty-four in 1891 to three thousand six hundred and forty-seven in 1901.

Station School

As in the beginning the people were all very poor, living only from hand to mouth, no pupils could be obtained for the training-school, unless they could in some way be supported. For some years, therefore, these pupils were required to spend some hours per day in labor for the mission out of school hours, and stipends of money or food to cover cost of living were supplied. But as the interest in school increased and some of the Christians were becoming able to aid their children, the stipends were withdrawn and to those more needy wages were given for definite work, such as the creating of a cotton-ginning establishment and the taking of Government contracts in jungle-clearing and road-repairing. In 1904 stipends were wholly withdrawn, but the number of pupils increased.

The two missionaries, burdened with other work, such as the erection of buildings, preparation of books, care of the churches and village schools scattered over a territory of about four thousand square miles, most of which is a mountainous jungle without roads, were never able to give the training-school the attention it needed, and native teachers could be obtained only as they were here taught. Several attempts were made at using as teachers educated men from Bengal and Assam, but with poor satisfaction. Several efforts were made to get some of the brighter boys further educated in the mission schools of Burma and South India, but to do so, in each case they would have been required to learn and to use as a mother tongue some language for which they would have no use. Hence, except at intervals, up to 1890 Mr. Phillips, though burdened with many other cares, acted as superintendent and much of the time as head master in the schoolroom.

Rev. Charles E. Burdette, Rev. S. A. D. Boggs, Rev. I. E. Munger, and Rev. Walter C. Mason were each appointed with this school work mainly in view. After learning the language they were each able to give some attention to it, but under disadvantages, and each of the first three very soon were called elsewhere. In 1899 Mr. Mason reports: "This school has suffered severely from the frequent changes. During 1896 it was under the care of Mr. Boggs, during 1897 under that of Mr. Phillips, during 1898 under that of Mr. Munger," and from 1899 to 1905 the school was under the supervision of M. C. Mason. From this time the school was classed by the Government as a Middle English School. In 1902 Mr. Mason reports:

For the past few years we have been passing through what appears to be critically pivotal years in the development of our work. The condition of our churches and the needs of our whole mission work forced upon us very important problems in connection with our station school. We felt that by some means: (1) The number of workmen annually turned out from this school must be greatly increased; (2) The quality of the education of those turned out must be considerably improved; (3) The independent manhood of our workers should be largely strengthened; (4) Teachers fitted to teach in our higher schools must be prepared; (5) And the expense of this school should be further removed from the shoulders of the mission to those of the natives. As a help toward solving these problems, with the Chief Commissioner's approval and aid of Rs. 1000, we were led to give ourselves wholly to two radical changes: (1) To the substitution of the Roman or English character for the Bengali which had been thus far used in all our literature: and (2) To

Christian Garo Schoolboys

Mission Schoolgirls. Miss E. C. Bond in Center

the substitution of English for Bengali text-books in subjects for which there were no Garo text-books. In our efforts to solve problems 2, 3, 4, and 5, we have given an additional year's instruction to the brighter boys who wished to take the course, and would do so without aid from the mission. The so-called Post Graduate class being thus self-supporting, prevents the expectation that the mission will give all a higher education. By doing manual labor to support themselves these boys have a healthful influence over the lower classes, in helping them to be less dependent.

While such radical changes had to meet many hindrances, the school continued to prosper. The missionaries, most of the single ladies, and most of the missionaries' wives have taught more or less in this school. Miss Ella C. Bond and Miss L. M. Holbrook, with almost no interruptions, have given daily instruction during their service. A glance at the curriculum in 1898, reported by Mr. I. E. Munger, indicates the general scope of the work of the school, and gives a fair sample of other years.

There are four classes representing four years' work, with monthly examinations, besides a primary department covering four years, somewhat in advance of the village schools. Upon the completion of both primary and normal courses the pupils have had eight years of Garo—reading, writing, spelling, arithmetic, and Scripture; seven years of Bengali—reading, writing, and grammar; and three years of English—reading, writing, and grammar. From the lowest grade the Scriptures are taught daily in every class. There is also a class in school government. Seniors in the normal department are sent weekly to the market camping-ground to exercise their gifts in preaching, besides conducting a weekly service in the station chapel and teaching in the Sunday School. The closing period of each Friday afternoon is set apart for prayer; and the last Friday afternoon of each month, in a debating and literary society, these sons of oldtime warriors are trained in speaking, debating, parliamentary rules, and presiding. Vocal music is successfully taught, and one has only to hear the Garos sing to realize the wonderful hold upon the hearts of these simple people of this form of praise.

Daily military drill and physical training are included in the curriculum, the latter of special importance owing to the free, unrestrained life of these "boys of the Lair" before their entrance upon student life.

In 1882, at the expense of Mr. Phillips and Mr. Mason, a Garo lad, Thangkan Sangma, was brought to America, where he made remarkable use of his time in school until 1884, when he returned with Mr. Mason and took the head teacher's place for two years. He then left the work that he might preach the gospel, taking less than one-half his former salary.

In 1891 Mr. Phillips took another boy, Modhunath G. Momin, to America, where he studied until 1894, since which time he has steadily taught in this station school. In 1910 Walter C. Mason brought Bosin G. Momin, who studied at Granville, Ohio, until 1914, when he returned to Tura expecting to teach in this school. Jobang D. Marak came to America at his own expense in 1905 and studied in Denison University until 1911. He is now employed by the Government as subinspector of schools.

In 1906 the Government began giving to the village school-teachers a capitation fee for each pupil promoted from one class to another by the school officials. And in 1908 through the kindness of a few contributors the mission began to give scholarships to needy and seemingly worthy boys and girls, conditioning them and grading them upon the standing in their studies. These scholarships, writes Mr. Mason, which through the kindness of one interested person have been continued,

have enabled a large number of pupils to attend school who could not otherwise have done so; others have been able to give more time to study. This aid has also inspired a habit of study, and led many to get a better idea of the advantages of giving attention to their work, and thus through them, a new and quite general interest in education has been awakened among the Garos.

In 1910 the Government further began to give scholarships to boys of this Middle English School who passed the required examination, that they might take a high-school education in some other school. This gave a new and strong encouragement to Garo boys to work for a further education. And other boys have joined these, and some are studying in Calcutta, some in Serampore, some at Shillong, some at Gauhati, some at Goalpara, and some in the Dibrugarh medical school. One of these, having finished the high school and passed a scholarship test, has now a Government scholarship for his college course. Others of the high-school students are teachers in this school at Tura. So that the outlook for advance education in this mission school, which is the only school for Garos of so high a grade, is improving, and a high school for the Garos themselves, supported or largely aided by the Government, is strongly hoped for.

Education for Girls

In all India the education of girls is a task beset with difficulty. Even among the Garos, where the women have liberty and superior personal rights, it is not easy to prove to their satisfaction the advantages of education for girls. From the first, however, the girls have been urged to study in the village schools with the boys, and girls are found in most of these schools. Evidences of the girls' susceptibility to "cultivating influences" are abundant. But the need of the girls' help in home work, and the lack of interest on the part of the parents regarding the education of their daughters make progress in this line more slow. In 1874 Mrs. Keith, with "ten promising pupils," all from the Christian village of Rajasimla, some thirty-five miles away, conducted a girls' boarding-school at Goalpara, which in spite of her illness continued with intervals little more than a year.

In answer to appeals for a special teacher for girls, Miss Miriam Russell arrived in Tura in 1879, and in 1881 was ready for teaching a girls' school, but no girls presented themselves for admittance. However, the young missionary was not to be daunted, and soon with a camp outfit she was touring the mountains, far from any but natives, surrounded by filth and disease, smiling at hardships, and finally returning triumphant, followed by ten lusty girls. The next cold season only three girls came, but what of that? "If the mountain will not come to Mohammed, Mohammed must go to the mountain." She went to Nisangram, an influential center, where the Christians quickly built for her a good bamboo house which she used both for residence and for school. Soon this redoubtable New England woman was surrounded by mountains of opportunity in the bright girls about her—her school "a decided success," which the next year with a larger attendance was victoriously "landed at Tura." The first year's fruitage was "deep interest, several able to read the Scriptures, six of whom were buried with Christ in baptism." In 1884 Miss Russell became Mrs. Burdette, and in 1885 from a tour with her husband she returned with twenty-one recruits with which to continue her school. This was a happy year. The faithful "mother" of these once wild Garo girls found many of them improving and some ready to lead in the religious meetings.

Upon the transfer of the Burdettes in October of the

same year to Gauhati, this girls' school was left uncared for until in 1887 when, after a year's tussle with the "crooked idioms of the language," Misses Ella C. Bond, niece of Mrs. Phillips and Mrs. Mason, and Stella H. Mason, sister of Mr. Mason, scoured the villages, and their search was rewarded by twelve girls for the opening once more of the school at Tura. From 1890 to 1898 Miss Mason, followed by Miss Alice J. Rood, was in charge. In 1898 the girls' and the boys' schools were united, which plan has since continued with increasing success. Concerning the girls in this mixed school, Miss Bond, who has charge of the girls' boarding-department says:

> Formerly a large number of the girls came to school either to be supported or to find a husband, and it was difficult to keep them in school more than two or three years. Now they look forward to finishing the course of the school. . . Formerly marriage was their all-engrossing thought. Now a feeling of comradeship exists between boys and girls in school relations, and a healthy interest in school pursuits.

Not infrequently the girls are among the very brightest of their class. Dobaki, niece of Ramke, availing herself of all the school privileges provided in those days, became an assistant teacher until her marriage, when she and her husband, Bakal, kept house in as nearly European style as possible, not to be above their station or go beyond their means. They had bathroom, bedstead with comfortable bedding, a fair supply of dishes, numerous books on shelves, boxes for clothing, and all in good order. Left a widow, Dobaki settled up her husband's business, and by teaching a large girls' school supported her family. In 1902 she became matron of the girls' boarding-department at Tura, and occasionally writes excellent articles for the *Achikni Repeng* and associational gatherings. Her four children—two boys and two girls—are well trained, and are being well educated. Her elder daughter, Alice, studied in the high school of another mission, and is now the noble wife of Jobang Marak, subinspector of schools. Mr. Mason says of her:

> She was to me a marvel in ability to manage and teach a school. When boys were never supposed to yield to the control of a woman she taught a large primary school, mostly boys, many of whom were older than herself, and yet I never knew of a single case of insubordination or even of showing her disrespect.

These women, though perhaps unusual characters, typify the possibilities of Garo women when given the advantages of uplifting environments.

XXXVI

LANGUAGE AND LITERATURE

THE Garo language belongs to the Bodo branch of the Tibeto-Burman family of languages, and is allied to the eastern Asiatic tongues. Alas! says the novice:

> What rough and perky sounds! What grammatical arrangement of sentences! What an accumulation of significant particles! How unlike anything Occidental!

Originally monosyllabic, as linguists claim, the glutinousness of these short syllables confronts the learner with such expressive and pleasing words as *namnikbatsranggenchimkon*. But as one becomes well acquainted with this language, he discovers a richness, a mobility, a capacity, a classification of objects that compels admiration. Its grammatical construction is simple but adequate; its system of case endings and verbal contractions seems quite philosophical. Its vocabulary, however, is for Occidental use very limited. Besides not having terms for objects foreign to them, its dearth of general terms is marked. For example, it has no term for brother, for sister, or for animal. For substitutes one must particularize and use a term meaning older or younger brother or sister, a word designating the kind or class of animal. Such limitations add much to the difficulties of translating Scriptures, as well as of talking of matters of civilized lands.

Again there are among the Garos thirteen different dialects, generally differing so from one another that a person unaccustomed to differences of speech, passing from one to another dialect, will not understand, largely because his attention is given to words not understood, whereas one experienced using what he knows gets their meaning. For these differences consist very largely of different ways of contracting and combining terms. A missionary says that once within a short distance he found in six different villages six different words used for elephant, in speaking of a herd about which the people were much excited. Thus illustrating that, where intercourse is cut off or limited, many differences easily spring up. But the missionaries believe that the hand of the Lord led them first to the most important dialect, since by using this as a base in giving the language a written form they find very little difficulty in their school work in bringing all the divisions to use this one dialect.

In reducing the language to writing, Messrs. Bronson and Keith quite naturally used the Bengali or Assamese characters, and all Garo literature up to 1892 was printed in that form. In that year the missionaries began to test the change of character from Bengali to Roman, and the advantages were found to be so many and so great that from 1902 all Garo literature has been printed in the Roman character. "While this entailed a great amount of labor in transliterating, settling necessary questions, preparing the manuscripts, corresponding with printers, and proof-reading and so forth," the advantages in the work of after-years have proved the saving of an immeasurable amount of labor. Pupils learn its use in a fraction of the time the other required, and the use of typewriters enables the missionaries to prepare the manuscript and do proof-reading with a fraction of the labor before required. Besides much cost of printing was thereby saved, and they were able to get printing done at any press. At times they were able to keep four presses at work, in Assam, Bengal, and Madras. Scriptures and hymns have also been printed in California and New York.

In the printing of books the lack of funds has been a great trial and tax to the missionaries and has often limited the editions so as greatly to multiply their labors. Some of the earlier editions were from five hundred to one thousand copies each. But of late, more people being able to read, large editions are usually issued. In 1909 twelve different books were put through the press, seven of which were from one thousand to twenty thousand copies each. The others were for filling out incomplete Scriptures in the Bengali character, that were especially for the use of the older people. Since 1902 the mission has received no regular appropriations from America in aid of printing books of any sort. In 1910 Mrs. Mary Bartlett Kellogg gave four hundred dollars to help with the printing of Scriptures.

Some years ago the Government aided by purchasing one hundred copies of a Bengali-Garo dictionary of eight hundred and eighty-four octavo pages, and later they printed a Garo-English pronouncing dictionary which defined about ten thousand words besides giving many derivatives. Again one thousand rupees was given to help print primers for use in village schools when beginning the use of the Roman character. The greatest need, however, has been for funds with which to furnish the Scriptures to the Garos at a reasonable price. Much of the time a New Testament would cost a Garo three or four days' work. And yet the superintendent of the Baptist Mission Press in Calcutta said that there were no other people in India who took Scriptures as did the Garos.

In 1900 Rev. I. E. Munger paid for printing five thousand copies of a hymn-book containing over two hundred hymns, as a memorial to Mrs. Munger who had died at Tura.

In 1904 the mission was favored with help from the Queen Victoria Memorial Fund given by Lord Radstock, which enabled them to make free distribution of two hundred copies of Bengali and English Scriptures, one hundred copies of Garo New Testaments, and about one thousand and four hundred copies of the four Gospels in Garo. Again, for 1912 we find this report:

> In an effort to raise money for the reduction of the price of the Garo Scriptures, there was correspondence with our own and other Societies extending over two years. But the effort was at last rewarded by a donation for this purpose of 5250 rupees from the Bible Translation Society of London. And now our Garo Scriptures are sold at the mere cost of binding, and many copies are being taken.

The Christian Literature Society for India has of late published for them a Garo Grammar, a Garo Arithmetic, the story of Queen Victoria, and seems ready to add further such help.

Concerning the translation of Scripture Mr. Phillips says:

> The first translation of the Gospels was made by native helpers under the supervision of Rev. T. J. Keith, and was published in 1876. These translations were later revised and the remainder of the New Testament translated and published by Revs. M. C. Mason and E. G. Phillips, each taking different portions,

and completing it in 1894.

Mrs. Walter C. Mason, who with her husband joined the mission in 1903, says in her interesting pamphlet, "The Victory of the Cross in the Jungles of Assam," "The work of translation has been steadily pressed as

Hospital

Lucy Smith Memorial Library

the workers have had opportunity, with a multitude of other duties always clamoring for attention."

For a list of the books prepared and printed see Appendix II.

In 1906 the mission received a gift from Dr. Stephen Smith of New York for the erection, in honor of his wife, of a Lucy Smith Memorial Library building for the use of this literature department, which contains a reading-room, a show and salesroom, a stock-room and a storeroom. The handling, storing, selling, and shipping of these books requires time and attention, the sales reaching several thousands of rupees per year. The stock reported in hand at the end of 1909 when the building was dedicated was about 14,000 rupees.

XXXVII

THE MINISTRY OF HEALING

VICTIMS of dirt, ignorance, and superstition, the Garos are constant sufferers from such diseases as these vices breed. Fevers and other ailments caused or aggravated by malaria, bowel troubles, and skin diseases are among the more prevalent ailments. A disease called *kala-azar* or black fever not long since prevailed extensively in the Garo hills, as well as in most of the valley districts. In one section of Goalpara, where the greater part of the Garo Christians were living, a census report showed that during ten years there was, due mainly to this disease, a decrease of fifty-one per cent of the population. Although this disease has annually carried away thousands of the valley population, even Government experts have not been able to reach a unitedly satisfactory understanding of it. Leprosy is found in places. Indeed, in occasional places, especially in the Goalpara district, it is prevalent. Mr. Mason once visiting one such place, made a special investigation and entered every house in the place, and found only here and there a person that was seemingly free of this disease in some stage of its progress, or that was not scarred by remedies that had been applied.

Venereal diseases, so prevalent among the peoples of the plains, are less common among the Garos, due to their worship of no sensual gods, their usual practice of monogamy and general faithfulness to marriage vows, together with the severe penalties for adultery which customarily obtained before the English took possession of the hills.

From time immemorial native "doctors" and priests, with practically no knowledge of anatomy or of the diseases they treat, have bought or inherited secrets concerning the preparation of certain remedies for specific maladies. Some of these preparations seem to be quite effective. By such remedies, "According to several reliable witnesses," says Doctor Crozier, "one village that had much leprosy has become quite free of it." But undoubtedly damage and probably death is sometimes caused by these drastic remedies. The more common treatment, however, if treatment it may be called, is the offering of gifts and sacrifices to the demon who is believed to be "biting" the afflicted. Sometimes whole villages spend even days in sacrificing to avert some scourge or pestilence.

For nearly twenty-five years the early missionaries, without medical education, but supplied with some experience and a fund of common sense, continually did what they could to relieve those suffering bodily pain. On every mission tour they took with them a supply of safe and useful medicines for such use and for sale to those who wished to buy in quantities. Mr. Mason says that he has often been amazed at the benefits arising from these treatments, and can but believe that these were often due to special divine blessing in answer to prayer. The confidence of the people in their treatments and power to cure seemed marvelous. Refusing to go to the Government dispensary, they would come and beg of the missionaries medicines and advice. Mr. Mason tells of one man who came to him to get him to bring to life his dog that had just died.

Naturally one of the first and best remedies for such

a people as a whole was soap. From the early days to the present soap has been imported in large quantities by the missionaries. Mr. Mason, telling of an interesting case of soap treatment, says:

> In one village I noticed a lad in his early teens sitting abjectly by himself in the corner of the young men's house. I went to him and inquired concerning his condition, when the people said: "He is dying; he cannot live long. For a long, long time he has been getting weaker and weaker so that now he can not stand." The boy was scaly with dirt. I could see that he first of all needed a washing, but he might not be able to endure so drastic a remedy. So I gave particular directions that water be warmed and brought, and that soap be well applied, and that his hands and his feet be washed at once up to his elbows and knees, and that he be covered to keep him warm. The next day they were to wash the rest of his limbs, and the day following a part of his body, and the fourth day he should be wholly bathed, and fed with appetizing food. A year later I was there again, and I made inquiry about the boy, "Is he dead?" "Dead! No. Look at him. There he stands." I turned and saw indeed a strong and hearty young man.

The missionaries had as well to look after their own ailments very largely, although there were usually civil surgeons to be had in severe cases, of which there were not a few. Some of these surgeons were capable men, some were less so; some were very kind, helpful, and attentive, others were shy; some would take no fees, others would charge sixteen rupees for answering a single question, even about a Garo if connected with the mission. But as a rule the surgeons and other officers, of whom there were from three to five in the district, were kind and social.

About the first of 1900 Dr. Galen Greenfield Crozier, of the University of Michigan, arrived to give his attention to the medical work of the mission. During his first year in the Garo hills he, aside from the task of learning the language, "treated about nine thousand and five hundred patients, performed ninety-two operations, and responded to one hundred and twenty calls for consultation with the Government physician." From the first Doctor Crozier adopted the policy of making the medical work of the mission financially self-supporting, so far as the natives were concerned, and of extending the same by means of medico-evangelistic tours throughout the hills. The second year the sale of medicines was in excess of the cost. And later the salaries of assistants as well as touring expenses were covered.

He began to train Garo young men that they might treat common ailments and perform simple operations, and young women to act as nurses. Some of these have gone on in these studies and are now pursuing a full course in the Berry White Medical School, a Government college at Dibrugarh.

Through Doctor Crozier's energetic labors a good hospital valued at 12,000 rupees was built at the station, and very well equipped, largely with funds contributed by his friends. With the aid of some small grants from the Government he was able to establish three or four dispensaries in different parts of the district, which he placed under the supervision of the natives he had trained. In places these quasi-doctors also taught schools from which have grown Christian communities.

The crowds that visit the station dispensary hear the gospel message from some of the assistants, and thus the gospel light goes along with the medicines. Classes of students in the station school were taught by Doctor Crozier and Miss Robb in physiology, hygienic principles, and sanitary laws. They were also instructed how to treat some of the more common ills they would find when teaching in the villages.

One pastor thus taught cured a patient with three or four doses of medicine where already three bulls had been sacrificed and a fourth was soon to be offered. Fifteen chickens and a hog had been the oblation for the inflamed eyes of a patient, who presenting himself at the mission dispensary, departed with sufficient medicine, secured for the price of one chicken, to cure himself and several others.

During the cold season Doctor Crozier with Mrs. Crozier and native assistants may be found camping from a few days to a month or more in various centers where the churches need quickening spiritually and opportunities for medical work seem greatest. From such a tour Doctor Crozier writes:

Up before sunrise, hard at it all day, the last patient at sunset—except two in the evening after church—and now it is after eleven o'clock—the past days the same—the future no different in prospect—no time when I could rest five minutes in succession till now, except when hurrying through my meals to get back to the work, and a half hour visiting with the people on the veranda, and just now, after coming in, answering a few questions about Samuel suggested by the sermon of the evening. When did I prepare for the evening sermon? All through the past years at the half-hour "morning watch," and the Holy Spirit moved me. Hearts were touched and lives were quickened, so it seemed, and I have faith to believe.

XXXVIII

INDUSTRIAL WORK

MR. MASON, who saw such wonders wrought in the lives of those sturdy wild men, was full of visions for the future. In order to improve their condition he early secured from America a number of agricultural tools and an expensive set of rice-hulling and cleaning machinery, which was worked with success until upon moving to Tura, away from rice-growing lands, he sold it to others. He and Mr. Phillips secured and planted fruit trees and seeds, until we now find upon their compound mangoes, guavas, pomeloes, pomegranates, tamarinds, peaches, plums, litches, papayas, pineapples, bananas, mulberries, raspberries, and a supply of garden vegetables. And from seeds of some of these, in hundreds of Garo villages, may be found peach and other fruit trees. And although orange trees failed to thrive in Tura, large quantities of oranges are now annually sold at the markets, raised largely from seeds which they distributed. They secured coffee seeds from Burma, Manila hemp from the Philippine Islands, cottonseed and sweet potatoes from America, pineapples from Ceylon. While some of these, from lack of proper soil or attention, did not prove successful, others of them have thriven quite satisfactorily. Printing-presses were also obtained from America, natives taught to set type, make printing-rollers, and print leaflets, a periodical, and some books.

With the hope, however, of bringing the Garo people to a higher Christian standard, Mr. Mason, when home on furlough in the early eighties, poured forth his heart in eloquent terms regarding the importance of establishing among the Garos industries and industrial training, whereby they could not only lift themselves up and away from their present narrow interests into new and larger fields adequate for their new-found life, but by which they might become coworkers with Christ and Christendom in financing and furthering the work of salvation, especially in those regions where they seemed particularly fitted to labor. An industrial department seemed to him the sanest method for the development of self-governing, self-supporting, and, so to speak, self-propagating churches. When thousands of able-bodied, strong, sinewy, fearless braves, trained to exert all their powers, physical, moral, intellectual, should have come to themselves along these lines, he saw that type of Christian manhood and womanhood especially needed among Asiatic peoples. He had visions of these boys and girls becoming evangelists to other tribes and nations, and of their exemplifying what India, as well as all lands, should recognize as the only worthy ideal of Christian development for sons of God the Father, his own Son, the world's Saviour, who was carpenter as well as preacher and teacher.

He argued that the command of our Lord to "teach them to observe all things whatsoever I have commanded you" included the duty of working, doing business, making money for the Lord, and of using it for the furtherance of Christ's kingdom, believing that the united work of the laity was the chief agency for the work of the church. He pointed out that while the Garos were an energetic, hard-working, agricultural people, they lived but from hand to mouth, in poverty and destitution, not infrequently reduced to starvation and sometimes to death, because of their ignorance and lack of providence, not for lack of energy or from any general famine conditions of the land at large, which we learn almost never exist. The Garos, he said, occupy a well-wooded, well-watered hill-country from which flow many rivers which furnish an abundance of water-power for the running of mills and factories, especially sawmills and shops for putting into useful shape the timber of their land which is in such demand in the cities and towns of Bengal and Assam. Mills for extracting oil from the castor-bean, mustard and other seeds grown along the foot of their hills, cotton-mills, rice-mills, canning factories, etc., etc., could be established on these streams where the Garo Christians were largely located, and which form natural highways out to the plains.

Mr. Mason appealed for the appointment of a missionary fitted for such work, who would give his time to organizing companies of Garo stockholders for these different undertakings, to teach and lead them in the development of such enterprises. When asked by a member of the Board if he was not afraid of putting a premium on Christianity he replied, No! that he would be well pleased if he could bring Christianity anywhere near up to its par value. He was told that the missionary Society was not intended for that kind of work.

Nevertheless some listened to his appeal, and the attempt was finally approved, and a seemingly well-qualified young man was found and designated to inaugurate the enterprise. He was expected to sail the year following Mr. Mason's return. Mr. Mason took with him several hundred dollars' worth of tools and machines, carpenter's tools, blacksmith's tools, saws and sawing machines, lathes for wood and iron, a forge and anvil, a cotton-gin, etc. While not able to give this work much of his attention, he erected a good-sized building, built a dam, laid out and dug a water course, and constructed a large wooden overshot water-wheel for running the machinery of a small plant at the station.

For various reasons the young man appointed did not go. Another was found and appointed; but before sailing he was vigorously besought and persuaded to go into Western China. Again another man was in view, but he heard the strong calls for China. A fourth, Rev. William Dring, was appointed and reached Tura about the beginning of 1891, nearly eight years after the first appointment for this work. By this time the demands of the mission for school and the more directly evangelical work, toward which Mr. Dring was strongly inclined, had so increased; the calls for a mission house-builder, not only at Tura, but from other missions in Assam, were so strong; and since the missionaries had to be their own architects and their own managers of unskilled workmen, the supervision of such work demanded so much attention that Mr. Dring's time and strength have been too largely absorbed to give direct attention to the original project. Mr. Dring has spent much time in house-building for other missions, both at their stations and as member, and often as chairman, of the property committee for all Assam. And at Tura the missionaries have had to construct over twenty good permanent buildings, a dozen cottages, and scores of the cheaper bamboo buildings that have to be frequently renewed. These necessary labors have combined to prevent the full achievement of Mr. Mason's project of establishing mills and factories.

However, industrial work has by no means been abandoned. Thousands of rupees' worth of tools and machines have been bought and the tools mostly sold to Garos. A cotton-ginning plant was established, mainly

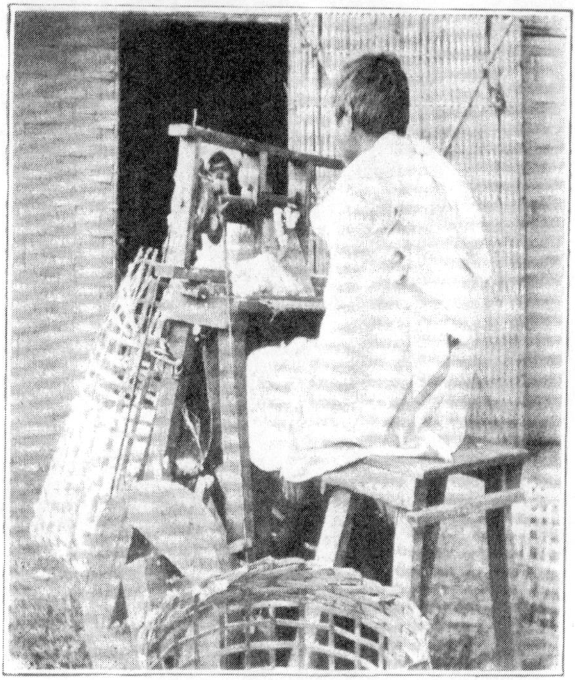

Cotton Gin

Cotton Ginning House

for the supply of work for the support of boys in school. A cheap cotton-gin was invented, many scores of them manufactured and quite extensively used. Three different cotton-gins from America have been purchased. A Pelton water-wheel was substituted for the overshot wheel, but even before the water reservoir was completed the great earthquake of 1897 ruined the tubing, since which a gasoline engine has been secured. It is well to add that the expense of most of this machinery and much of the cost of buildings has had to be secured from individual friends, rather than from funds of the Society.

A score or more of carpenters have been at least partially trained, so that most of the work of the buildings, even to the making of window-sash and panel doors has been done by the Garos thus trained. Scholarships and positions for several young men have been secured from government and other missions for instruction in industrial schools.

In the villages some Christian localities have seemed to settle down into a sleepy, unambitious, more or less self-pitying life; others have used their new energy more in speculation than in production. Such have been more or less damaged by the temptations surrounding such a life, especially since they have to meet on either side heathen and wicked dealers who believe that deceit and lying are essential, legitimate, and proper methods of speculation. Others have been led into litigation. In fact, large numbers led mainly by shrewd unprincipled men, have turned attention from the needs of the Lord's kingdom to efforts for more worldly prosperity by means of legal contentions with landowners whose ancestors had evidently trespassed more or less upon the claims of the Garos. In this way in company with others they have both uselessly sunken hundreds of thousands of rupees and weakened their Christian life. However, not all have been led away, and there is still an interest in Christian work. Many take pride in enlarging their cultivations and in improving their conditions and surroundings, so that in fact a Christian village is quickly noticed as more thrifty and more improved than those of the non-Christian people. They have fences, gardens, and generally better buildings. An educated Hindu acting as a landowner's agent was once heard to say to a large crowd of Hindu ryots whom he was addressing, "What village is that over there?" as he pointed to a Garo Christian village. "That is a Garo village," was the reply. "A Garo village?" "A Christian Garo village," was the further reply. "Well! Do you see the difference between that and the other Garo villages? Why do you not become Christians?" Thus illustrating the fact that when the lower strata of society are uplifted by Christianity, the attention of other strata are not only attracted to them but they also are with them borne upward.

Mr. Mason still believes that had his project of sending one or two devout Christian engineers and organizers to give themselves to this evangelistic industrial leadership, the Garo Christians would not only have largely avoided the evils above mentioned, but would more rapidly have augmented their numbers, and accomplished more in supporting Christian workers, and in sending even more of their own missionaries to the tribes and people beyond. He further believes that the opportunity for such mission work is still as great, and the project as feasible as ever. Such effort would regain the distracted attention of many, and would now find more men with means ready and willing to invest in industrial enterprises. Although the Garos are still comparatively poor, some of them are well-to-do, and individually have supported several Christian workers, and since "many a mickle makes a muckle" a little from many would be even more beneficial. Concerning this project Dr. Samuel W. Duncan, secretary of the American Baptist Foreign Mission Society, wrote:

> Let these hill people once be taught how to utilize their mountain streams, which now idly lash themselves into foam in their plunge from rocky precipices, and the establishment among our native Christians of intelligent, industrious, self-supporting Christian communities would not be a remote possibility. The beginnings in this direction that have been made at Gauhati and Tura have met with such encouragement as to give assurance that this is no wild prophecy. Nothing but financial limitations have interfered with enlargement in this direction.

We understand that the present body of Garo missionaries are unanimously of the opinion that industrial training is at present one of the first needs of the Garo churches. Wise direction of newly vitalized energy into useful labors is a positive force for strengthening Christian life and upbuilding the kingdom, and will produce a people with less affection claiming sympathy and fewer sick that require relief. Building up a people in self-reliance is far better than coddling them, though sometimes even in mission work the latter method seems the more popular.

XXXIX

RETROSPECT AND PROSPECT

FROM this recital of work among the Garos, two things are clear: Much has been done, God helping; and much more awaits our labor, God still accompanying and confirming the effort. It was, at the outset, perhaps as frowning a task as ever confronted a missionary. It had baffled and discouraged the superb administrators of the British Empire. All their policies had failed on the Garos, and they had been forced to the conviction that the most drastic measure of all must be resorted to. Extermination of the Garos had to be considered if surrounding peoples were to be rescued from their cruelty and saved from their wild excesses. The coming of missionaries held out a hope that such desperate measure might be avoided. That hope was strengthened when the two outstanding missionaries to the hill tribes first appeared—Mason and Phillips. With them came the promise of all that true missionary effort had already taught the world to expect. Eagerly did the wise British officials meet the missionaries with confidence and cooperation. Think of the contrast: The officials with the mighty forces of the Empire behind them, yet baffled; and the missionaries armed with nothing but their Christian purpose and the gospel, yet greeted by the Empire as the possible conquerors!

The graphic story of the gospel among the Garos bears out the Government's confidence. The wonderful transformation that was to tame and change the hill tribes soon began. The picture that was presented is not a new one in the history of missions. Constantly is it before the world to reawaken its flagging missionary zeal. On the one side, evil and ignorance long entrenched; on the other, the herald of Christ who must at first confront his colossal task without either voice or language. Then when he finds his tongue and can utter his message in the native dialect, and the prospect of gracious work opens invitingly before him, there enters an unexpected providence into his experience—*meager home support*. It comes largely from the inability of the far-away brethren to see the great opportunity through the missionary's eyes. This must be a providence, else we should not have it with us so continuously. Certainly it has providential effect upon the missionary. It stimulates his strength and ingenuity, increasing the resourcefulness with which he successfully grapples with difficulties. He becomes more and more a marvel to the heathen, who are getting the chief benefit of his development and pertinacity. If he does not exactly make bricks without straw, he does many wholesome and difficult things simply because they must be done, in spite of the slender equipment afforded him. Language is only the first difficulty. Others are sure to follow with pelting haste. Altogether they seem like a desperate disadvantage, with but one chance of overcoming. Doubtless the missionaries themselves are surprised that they are so joyously willing to take the chance, and venture everything for the possible victory. It is a noble type of romantic adventure that only missions affords.

Bronson and Stoddard broke a path to the intricate mountain lair where the Garos were hidden. They gave courage and hope to the real pathfinders who had come to make the venture. Mason and Phillips came with sturdy faith, yet with comparatively faint anticipation of obstacles. That combination seems necessary for the undertaking of heroic labors. Faith was sure to increase with the terrific tests put upon it, and obstacles soon became as real as the steep acclivities that had to be climbed before the wild tribes could be found and blessed.

Still well remembered is the summer day in 1874, when in the old Baptist church in Hamilton, New York, Marcus Mason and Elnathan Phillips, with the modest, refined, consecrated Howes sisters stood before the pulpit to be married. It was a " bridal day " in more senses than one. To the many sympathetic witnesses it was known that a greater devotion than the ordinary bond of marriage was to be tested; for they were all committed to the Garos for life, and at once the real proving of affection and faithfulness was to begin. The bridal hour then begun has continued forty years. Mrs. Mason, apparently the more robust of the sisters, went down, alas, under the strain in eight years! But her devotion still lives in her noble missionary son, Walter. Mrs. Phillips, apparently the more fragile of the sisters, survives, her refined and gentle girl face easily recognizable, though deeply transfigured by all that God has put into the long sacrament of holy toil. It seems almost like a fairy tale to follow on from the earlier day down to the present hour of ripened spirit and physical wear and trembling. But all the way along did stern realities put the " fairies " to rout, and prove how affection and faithfulness to one could grow into lifelong consecration to many. Of this, thousands of Garos happily bound to Jesus Christ today are grateful and loving witnesses. The present Mrs. Mason, for the past twenty-six years standing steadily and strongly at her husband's side, has fitted beautifully into this group and given of her strength to stay the

From "A Beautiful Life," Mrs. Stoddard in 1904.

sinking of others under the inevitable strain of such a life. Fortunate were the wild mountain Garos to fall into such hands. These two missionaries, alike only in their complete self-committal to their Lord, together made a strong team for plowing and cultivating a stony field. They had a persistent Christian practicality that provoked response from a race that was found to possess a fundamental character of its own. They soon discovered in this wild people a basis for their gospel appeal. Hard-headed, yet tender-hearted, the two missionaries eschewed mere religious sentimentalism, and reached into the lives of the people after the gospel fruits of sanity and righteousness. Saved souls were headed toward saved lives. Lives were saved by occupations that were saving, and by ways of conserving time, strength, and material that raised the standards of every-day living. This brought a growing hope of permanent Christian strength, and of power to minister that strength to their fellows.

The Garos were found by the missionaries to be a distinctive tribe both in what they were and in what they promised to be. They are a part of that great Mongolian population occupying eastern and northern Asia. In strong contrast to the people of the surrounding plains, they are virile, active, energetic, and hardworking. The great curse of India is caste. They are entirely free from it. A sister evil is the secluded degradation of women. They know nothing of that. The appalling scourge of Asia, consuming millions of its people, is opium. Mercifully has the Lord kept them untainted by that subtle degeneracy. In the plan of God, therefore, they seem to be a preserved and unexhausted race awaiting the Christian missionary and the training he brings, that they may carry the gospel message to the darkened millions beyond them. They are equipped not only by their mountain segregation from the wasting curses of the plains, but also by many customs followed in common with other Mongolians, which help to make them winsome and effective missionaries.

There has come to be a rubric to be followed in missionary enterprises. They must be evangelical, educational, and medical. Early in the development of this mission, Mason and Phillips saw the need and advantage of industrial education as the accompaniment of earnest evangelism, founding of schools, and the beginnings of a Garo literature. Medical missions, crude of course at first, are but the moving of the true missionary's compassion. Instinctively does it find expression long before the medical missionary comes, or the mission hospital is built. It is an article in his Christian equipment of common sense and helpfulness. Even when the missionary rubric is strictly followed, the guaranty of its success, or the cause of its failure, will be found in the men that work it. There is no failure to be explained in this mission. Yet no one, least of all the missionary heroes themselves, would claim more than a beginning of success after these forty years of exhausting labor. They have a dream of ultimate larger things that checks any present ecstasy of self-congratulation. We, not those modest, heroic men, must insist that such a beginning as theirs is a great achievement.

Is not the progressing social and industrial transformation—the many churches and schools, the Garo Scriptures and literature, the pushing forth of trained and consecrated native leaders—a great achievement? Yet in the dream of the missionaries it is only a beginning. They see a people that win affection and promise development, kept from surrounding evils, and capable of being saved from their own; housed there by God in his almost inaccessible mountains. For what purpose, except it is to become his voice to awaken to righteousness like races? Really to share this dream is to hasten its realization. That prospect and that duty are alike before us.

APPENDICES

I

GLOSSARY

Alda, travelers' rest- or lodging-houses.

Atte, a chopper.

Babu, Indian gentleman.

Borang, a house built in a treetop or on very high posts.

Budgerow, a Bengali boat.

Chota hazri, a light early breakfast, usually tea and toast.

Company's zemindar, a native landlord of the East Indies Company.

Chu, a home-brewed beer.

Chaprassi, office attendant.

Chur, an island or water-deposited land.

Cutchery, public office, court-house.

Daroga, native police officer.

Dao, Bengali name for atte.

Dawks, relays of horses or carriages for a journey.

Dwar, hill valley opening into the plains.

Gando, man's garment, loincloth.

Gosain, a Hindu religious mendicant.

Gumla, a large earthen jug or cask, urn.

Hat, weekly market.

Havildar, native sergeant.

Keddah, an elephant-catching equipment.

Kimas, memorial carved posts to commemorate the dead. See illustration.

Lines, barracks or dormitories for natives.

Lingam, the symbol of Siva, male organ.

Luskar, a territorial Garo officer appointed by Government.

Maund, about 82 lbs.

Machang, an under-cover platform or floor usually two or three feet from the ground upon which to sit, sleep, or place one's belongings.

Mantras, Hindu formulas.

Mauzadar, revenue collecter.

Morah, a light stool made of woven bamboo.

Myna, or *Mina,* probably the hill myna or mina bird (Genus, gracula musica), a bird highly prized because of its most remarkable ability to talk and mimic sounds, often called Garo Hills mina, or Goalpara mina because the Garos marketed them there.

Pong, gourd, calabash.

Raja, a native landholder in India.

Sambasi, bamboo shrine.

Shikari, hunter, sportsman.

Selu, a spear.

Saljong, the god of fertility.

Susumi, the goddess of wealth.

Sinka, a woman's belt embroidered with wampum beads.

Terai, low, wet land along the foot of the mountains.

Tulsi, a plant held sacred by the Hindus.

Turban, an Oriental headdress.

II

GARO BOOKS PUBLISHED BY THE MISSION

RELIGIOUS BOOKS

(* Both characters. † Roman character only. ‡ Bengali character only.)

* New Testament, complete. 12mo, 841 and 464 pp. (Much of this two or three times revised.)

* Genesis, with Explanatory Notes. 12mo, 254 and 113 pp. By M. C. Mason. (Third edition.)

* Garo Hymn-book. (Eleven editions.) 16mo, 296 pp. (295 hymns.) Editors, last edition, Walter C. Mason and G. G. Crozier.

‡ First Catechism. (Many editions.) 16mo, 10 pp.

‡ Religious Catechism, I. 16mo.

‡ Religious Catechism, II. 16mo, 47 pp.

‡ Catechism on the Life of Christ. 12mo. Thangkan Sangma, translator.

‡ Catechism of Bible Teaching. 12mo, 36 pp. (By J. A. Broadus.) E. G. Phillips, translator.

‡ Sunday School Lessons on the Life of Christ. 12mo, 129 pp. E. G. Phillips, translator.

‡ Mission Kamna (a Plea for Garos to Do Mission Work for Other Tribes). 19 pp. By Thangkon Sangma.

‡ Commentary on Matthew in the Form of Sunday School Lessons (incomplete). 8vo, 260 pp. By M. C. Mason.

‡ Pastor's Handbook. 16mo, 24 pp. Bangalsing and Rikman.

* Peep of Day (third edition 10,000). 16mo, 110 pp. Stella H. Mason, translator.

* A Ripe Mango Tract. 32mo, 16 pp. M. C. Mason, translator.

* Nobin Moni Tract. 32mo, 16 pp. M. C. Mason, translator.

† The Life of Christ (Blakesly's Intermediate Grade of Sunday School Lessons). 12mo, 197 pp. E. G. Phillips, translator.

† The Life of Christ (a Skeleton Harmony of the Gospels). 8vo, 15 pp. By M. C. Mason. (Second edition.)

† A Mission Tune-book (Tonic Sol-Fa. 163 tunes). Editor, S. A. D. Boggs.

† A Commentary on the Books of Acts. 12mo, 250 pp. (In the Form of Sunday School Lessons. Embracing Bible Dictionary of 240 Proper Names, and Index of 54 Leading Subjects.) By M. C. Mason.

† A Chart of Old Testament History. By M. C. Mason.

† A Chart of Distances Between Places in Palestine. M. C. Mason, translator.

† The Mirror of the Heart. 12mo, 38 pp. Modhunath Momin, translator.

† Christ the Lord. 64mo. E. G. Phillips, translator.

† Our Work (Notes for a Week of Bible Study). By E. G. Phillips.

† Fellowship with Christ (Notes for a Week of Bible Study). By G. G. Crozier.

TEXT-BOOKS

* First Primer (seventh edition). 12mo, 28 pp. (10,000 copies.)

* Second Primer (third edition). 12mo, 39 pp.

* Primer, Part III. 12mo, 89 pp. (10,000 copies.)

† Skichengani (a New Progressive Garo Primer, 20,000 copies). 12mo. By Miss E. C. Bond.

† Translation of First Primer into English. 16mo, 12 pp. Mrs. C. E. Burdette, translator.

† English Royal School Primer, with Additional Exercises. 16mo, 18 pp. M. C. Mason, translator.

† An English-Garo Vocabulary for the English Royal Primer. 16mo. By Mrs. M. C. Mason. (4,000 copies.)

‡ Phrases in English and Garo. 16mo, 40 pp. By M. Bronson.

† A Garo Grammar (in Garo). 12mo, 36 pp. By E. G. Phillips.

† An Inductive Grammar (in Garo). 12mo, 89 pp. By E. G. Phillips.

Outline Garo Grammar (in English). 8vo, 75 pp. By T. J. Keith.

An Outline Grammar of the Garo Language (in English). 8vo, 31 pp. By E. G. Phillips.

‡ Primary Arithmetic. 12mo, 100 pp. By E. G. Phillips.

* Practical Arithmetic, Part I (revised). 221 pp. By E. G. Phillips.

† Practical Arithmetic, Part II (revised). By E. G. Phillips.

† Answers to above Parts I and II. By Mrs. M. C. Mason and Mrs. E. G. Phillips.

* Mental Arithmetic, Part I (revised). 90 pp. By Mrs. E. G. Phillips.

* Mental Arithmetic, Part II (revised). 221 pp. By Mrs. E. G. Phillips.

Garo and Bengali-English Dictionary. 8vo, 183 pp. By T. J. Keith.

Bengali-Garo Dictionary. 8vo, 884 pp. By Ramke. Edited by M. C. M. and E. G. P.

‡ Introduction to Bengali. 12mo, 36 pp. By Rupsing Sangma.

‡ Way to Health. 12mo, 78 pp. Bakal.

† Introduction to English. 8vo, 44 pp. By M. C. Mason.

† English-Garo Dictionary. 8vo, 191 pp. By Modhunath G. Momin, M. C. Mason, and E. C. Bond.

† Garo-English Dictionary. 12mo, 27 pp. By A. MacDonald and Modhunath G. Momin.

† Geography of the Garo Hills. 12mo, 35 pp. By A. MacDonald.

† Life of Queen Victoria. 12mo, 54 pp. By Toding Marak and M. C. Mason.

† Cigarette Smoking. 24mo, 16 pp. By G. G. Crozier.

* Achikni Ripeng (The Garos' Friend). A monthly periodical in its thirty-fifth year without an interruption.

† Phringphrang (The Morning Star). A monthly periodical edited and managed by native brethren, in its second year.

III

LISTS OF CHURCHES AND SCHOOLS

(These are attached to map opposite page 280.)

1. RAJASIMLA. C. S.

Sodikona. C.
Rangsa. C. S.
Arengdo. C. S.
Dambora. C. S.
Bijagrim. S.

2. NISANGRAM. C. S.

Pangsanggiri. S.
Niapoli. C. S.
Hatibandha. C.
Mondolgram. S.
Bakrapur. C. S.
Siluk. C. S.
Tengasot. C. S.
Damit Aga. C. S.
Damit Apal. C. S.
Bonggare. C. S.
Dalbot. C. S.
Bangsi. C. S.
Dagal. C. S.
Depa. C. S.
Chituk. C. S.

3. DEREK. C. S.

Rangsapara. C. S.
Balijana. C. S.
Rajapara. C. S.
Hatigopa. C. S.
Thakurbila. C. S.
Bolsong. C. S.
Torika. C.
Nibari. C.S.
Kasikagra. C. S.
Narongkol. C. S.
Moamari. C.
Chotipara. C. S.
Kongkera. C.
Dalek. C. S.
Sialu. C. S.
Manikpur. S.
Bhimajuli. S.

4. RONGJULI. C. S.

Kasibari. C. S.
Bodalong. C.
Patpara. S.

5. KONGKAL. C. S.

Kaldang. C. S.
Rongsrek. C.

6. RESU. C. S.

Mendipatal. C.
Gengnang. C. S.
Dilma. C. S.
Soinang. C. S.
Belpara. C. S.
Kantolguri. C.
Tapa. C. S.
Rongrong. C.
Daram. C. S.

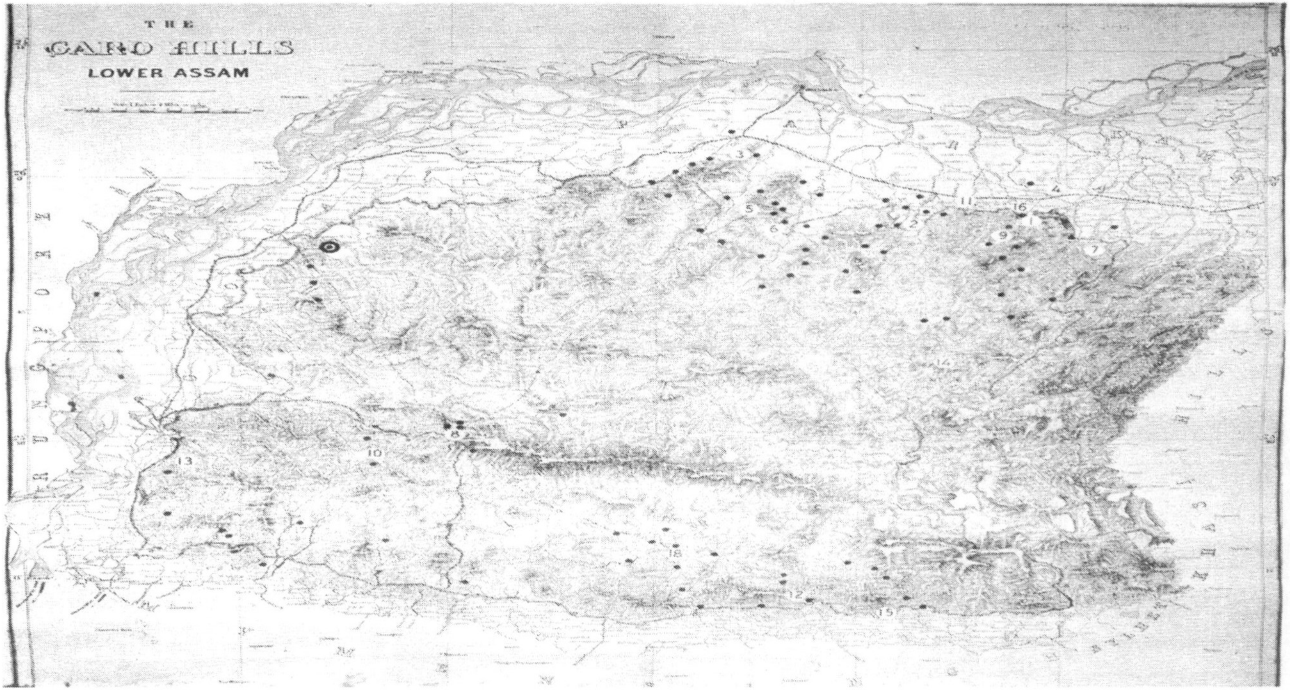

Map of Churches

The numbered discs represent churches. The branch churches and schools are indicated by black dots.

7. Adokgiri. C. S.

Badaka. C. S.
Amguri. C. S.

8. Tura. C. S.

Shamnagar. C. S.
Machangpani. C.
Gimigiri. C. S.
Sekapara. S.
Menggopara. S.
Rongmatchok. S.
Waramgiri. S.
Anogiri. S.
Selbalgiri. S. 2
Rengsanggiri. C. S.
Cheran. C.
Wadanang. C.
Sangsanggiri. S.
Darengiri. C. S.
Amindagiri. C. S.
Darakgiri. C. S.
Chenggapara. C. S.
Baranggapara. C. S.

9. Chotcholja. C. S.

Chibongga. C. S.
Kalkuta. C. S.
Makre Adap. C. S.
Watregiri. C. S.
Wakkram. S.
Daranggiri Petchong. C. S.
Daranggiri Sang. C. S.
Wari. C.

10. Okapara. C. S.

Bongpara. C.
Rangsakona. C. S.
Mukhdangra. C. S.
Dengnakpara. C. S.
Rongkongiri. C.
Dopgiri. C.
Churabudugiri. C. S.
Amakgiri. C. S.
Kinpara. C. S.
Akinpara. C.
Churabudugiri (2). C.
Kerupara. C.
Okapara Songsarik. C.

11. Amjonga. C. S.

Nidangaung. C. S.

12. Bagmara. C. S.

Adinggiri. C.
Chambilgiri. C. S.
Bamongiri. C. S.
Dabitgiri. C. S.
Gitinggiri. C. S.
Rongrengpal. C.
Rengdim. C. S.
Asim Rongru. C.
Wagesik. C. S.

13. Boldamgiri. C. S.

Boldamgiri Wa. C. S.
Kalaipara. C.
Dibajani. C.

14. Rongjeng. C. S.

Barengiri. S.
Mejolgiri (1). C. S.
Mejolgiri (2). C. S.
Gabil. C.
Nongbak Rongma. C.
Mangsang. C.
Gabil Rongdu. C.

15. Dambuk. C. S.

Wagekona. C.
Ampanggiri. C.

Halwa. C. S.
Dambuk Ading. C. S.
Rongara. C. S.
Chenggni. C.
Bonbera. C. S.
Mahadeo. C. S.

16. SANTIPUR. C. S.

Salpara. C. S.
Atiabari. C. S.

17. BABELAPARA

Gobinathkila. C. S.
Babelakona. C. S.
Baljuri. C.
Santangpara. C.
Ampatigiri. C. S.

18. SILKIGIRI.

Silkigiri. C. S.
Sembu. C. S.
Ringkap. C.
Balwat. C. S.
Dasinggiri. C.
Asim Rompha. C.
Chokpotgiri. C.
Kenigiri. C.
Bonigiri. C.

Chart, Showing Service of Missionaries, Baptisms, and Church-Membership

Year	Baptized to Date	Membership
1867	40	40
1868	115	
1869	177	172
1870	202	
1871	215	213
1872	286	286
1873	424	
1874	433	400
1875	466	391
1876	547	488
1877	701	610
1878	808	724
1879	884	704
1880	1,009	786
1881	1,086	821
1882	1,160	827
1883	1,235	828
1884	1,252	869
1885	1,387	870
1886	1,473	870
1887	1,617	986
1888	1,746	1,117
1889	1,965	1,180
1890	2,115	1,230
1891	2,320	1,336
1892	3,041	2,018
1893	3,330	2,257
1894	3,569	2,378
1895	3,746	2,410
1896	3,953	2,451
1897	4,855	3,329
1898	5,245	3,600
1899	5,444	3,606
1900	5,682	3,631
1901	6,068	3,807
1902	6,299	3,834
1903	6,582	3,887
1904	6,967	4,120
1905	7,332	4,340
1906	7,637	4,532
1907	7,882	4,576
1908	8,326	4,739
1909	8,684	4,887
1910	9,126	5,123
1911	9,517	5,314
1912	9,853	5,348
1913	10,310	5,777
1914		

Rev. and Mrs. I. J. Stoddard — *h*
Rev. and Mrs. T. J. Keith — *h*
Rev. and Mrs. Marcus C. Mason — *F*
Rev. and Mrs. E. G. Phillips — *E*
Miss Miriam Russell — *m*
Rev. and Mrs. Charles E. Burdette — *t*
Miss Ella C. Bond — *F*
Miss Stella H. Mason — *h*
Rev. and Mrs. William Dring
Rev. and Mrs. S. A. D. Boggs — *t*
Miss Alice Rood — *h*
Rev. and Mrs. I. E. Munger — *h*
Miss Henrietta Morgan *t*—*t*
Miss Isabella Wilson *t*—*t*
Rev. and Mrs. G. G. Crozier, M. D.
Rev. and Mrs. Walter C. Mason
Miss Linnie Holbrook — *F*
Rev and Mrs. Fred W. Harding — *F*
Miss Agnes Robb — *h*
Rev. and Mrs. Asher K. Mather
Miss Omie Carter

Meaning of Initials:

h, home.
F, furlough.
E, expiration of service on field.
m, married.
t, transferred.